PATTERNS FOR WORSHIP

PATTERNS FOR WORSHIP

CHURCH HOUSE PUBLISHING
Church House, Great Smith Street, London SW1P 3NZ

Published by Church House Publishing,
Church House, Great Smith Street,
London SW1P 3NZ.

Text © The Central Board of Finance
of the Church of England 1989, 1995
Illustrations by Taffy © The Central Board
of Finance of the Church of England 1995

Commended edition first published 1995

ISBN 0 7151 3750 6

The Central Board of Finance is indebted to the
churches, societies, publishers and individuals
whose copyright texts have been included in
Patterns for Worship, either in original or in adapted
form. For details see Acknowledgements, page 330,
and Sources, page 333.

Cover design by Julian Smith
Editorial and page design by AD Publishing Services
Printed in England by Cambridge University Press

CONTENTS

Preface   vii
Commendation   x

1   **Introduction**
     Why a new book?   1
     Urban priority areas   2
     Family services   3
     Family   4
     Common prayer?   5
     Reading the Bible   6
     Service structure   10
     Assumptions about structure   11
     Dry bones?   12

2   **The Basic Outline**
     A Service of the Word: the authorized text   13
     A Service of the Word: instructions and guidelines   20
     The Eucharist: instructions and guidelines   27

3   **Resource Sections**
     Note on numbering   32
     Index of themes and seasons   32
     A   Introductions   33
     B-D   Confessions
     B   – invitations to confession   37
     C   – confessions   40
     D   – absolutions   50

     E   The Ministry of the Word   53

     F   Affirmations of faith   57

     G-J   Prayers
     G   – responses, endings, introductions to the
           Lord's Prayer   63
     H   – responsive intercessions and litanies   66
     J   – prayers after communion or endings for
           A Service of the Word   92

K-Q Praise

K	– short acclamations and responses	104
L	– acclamations and responses	106
M	– longer acclamations and responsive scriptures	115
N	– proper prefaces	126
P	– thanksgivings	131
Q	– scriptural songs	150

R-S Action

R	– introductory words to the Peace	171
S	– words for dedication	176
T	**Blessings and endings**	177

4	**The Commentary**	191
5	**Sample Services**	243
	Index of Bible References	328
	Copyright Information	330

PREFACE

This is one of a series of books produced by the Liturgical Commission and its individual members since 1984 – *Lent, Holy Week, Easter, The Promise of His Glory, Enriching the Christian Year* and *Celebrating Common Prayer* – which act as a kind of hinge between *The Alternative Service Book 1980* and its successor in the year 2000.

These books share some characteristics which distinguish them from the ASB. They all contain large sections of resource material – as the introduction to *Lent, Holy Week, Easter* says, 'We are providing a directory from which choices may be made. We think of this book as a manual to be used with selectivity, sensitivity and imagination.' The element of choice, present in the rubrics in the ASB, is exploited to the full, but with a proper sense of that peculiarly Anglican feel both for restrained language and for proper structure which holds our Church together. Another characteristic of these books follows from that. If there is to be choice, then the choice must be an informed one, and so there are what the *Lent, Holy Week, Easter* introduction calls 'Hints to facilitate presentation'. All these volumes have not only notes which give hints about presentation, but also introductions discussing both the background and the use of the texts provided. Another common characteristic is a real desire to produce texts which can be used by the whole Church, born of the Commission's hard work on our doctrinal unity.

Patterns for Worship began life in the 1985 report by the General Synod Standing Committee *The Worship of the Church* which had suggested:

> a 'directory' with a wealth of resource material including supplementary material for each of the many points in the service where there is room for the individual's own words. The directory would need to set boundaries to the proposed freedom, and points which might be theologically divisive would have to be watched.

In 1986 the House of Bishops agreed that the Commission should proceed to prepare a handbook(s) which aimed:

- to provide some indication of different ways of doing liturgy, taking into account sociological, architectural and churchmanship differences

- to indicate where advantage might be taken of notes and rubrics in the ASB to develop and enrich the liturgy

- to provide outline structures and mandatory sections for some main services, which, if authorized alongside the ASB, would provide greater freedom for those who wish either to enrich or shorten the services (including family services and worship in urban priority areas).

In preparing *Patterns for Worship*, the Commission consulted widely, not only with the regular meetings of the Diocesan Liturgical Committee Chairmen and Secretaries, and with bodies such as the Board of Education and the Committee for Black Anglican Concerns, but with those who live in inner urban areas. In the summer of 1988, Commission members undertook a series of liturgical consultations and workshops in urban priority area parishes, with the assistance of the local diocesan liturgical committees. All these helped to shape the resulting report.

The Synod report edition of *Patterns for Worship* was published in 1989, being seen by the House of Bishops largely as a document for consultation. The House of Bishops, though recognizing the 'various and urgently expressed calls for liturgical proposals – and the widely based consultations which the Commission has undertaken –' was 'mindful of those who want a period of stability in the liturgical life of the Church, and who might be anxious lest the Commission's proposals extend the bounds of choice and variety of liturgical provision more widely than has been customary in the Church of England'. Clearly, there was much in *Patterns for Worship* that could be used without any authorization, but the first of the parts which required such authorization did not reach the Synod until 1992, when *A Service of the Word*, including Alternative Confessions and Absolutions, and *Affirmations of Faith* were authorized by Synod from November 1993. All of the material, including the introduction, that was authorized at that time is reproduced in this volume. But none of the eucharistic material which was contained in the first edition of *Patterns for Worship* has been included, as it has not been authorized.

The fact that *Patterns for Worship* contains both authorized and commended material, the way in which the resource sections are organized, the provision of sample services together with illustrations, and the general presentation of this kind of liturgical material, is different from many of the other books the Commission has produced. The Commission hopes that this will contribute to the debate about the shape and range of what the Commission provides for our Church's worship in the period after 2000. But more than that, we hope and pray that it will be a significant and much-used resource for the worship of the Church as it goes through into the next millennium.

+David Sarum
Chairman of The Liturgical Commission
The Conversion of St Paul 1995

PATTERNS FOR WORSHIP

The liturgical texts in this publication are either authorized by the General Synod under Canon B 1 or commended by the House of Bishops of the General Synod. They are published with the agreement of the House.

Under Canon B 4 it is open to each Bishop to authorize forms of service to be used within his diocese and he may specify that the services should be those commended by the House. If the Bishop gives no direction in this matter a priest remains free, subject to the terms of Canon B 5, to make use of the services as commended by the House.

On behalf of the House of Bishops
GEORGE CANTUAR: Chairman

1

INTRODUCTION

Why a new book?

The coming of *The Alternative Service Book* in 1980 marked a new stage in the development of Anglican worship. In one sense the ASB looked back 400 years to the principle established by Cranmer of having all the texts for worship available in one book: the ASB gathered and distilled the best of all the experiments of the years since 1965, summing up and, some hoped, ending that period of experimentation.

But in another sense the ASB looked forward to a new era of flexibility in Church of England worship. At many points the text provided alternative options or open-ended phrases such as 'using these or other appropriate words', 'these or other suitable words', and 'or other suitable prayers'. In Rite A such phrases govern the opening welcome, introduction to confession, the form of the intercessions, the Peace, extra words of distribution, and the prayer after communion. This principle of allowing considerable freedom in some areas of the liturgy, where there is no danger of harm or division if people do different things, was extended in the services in the 1985 book *Lent, Holy Week, Easter*, where the provision for the *Agape* is basically a list of instructions about how to do it.

The Commission's aim in producing *Patterns for Worship* is to meet some of the current needs of the Church's worship, reflected most acutely in urban priority areas and in services (often called 'Family Services') at which all age groups, including children, are present. We have used the already established principle of flexibility to provide forms of worship which can still be seen as part of the Anglican family, while encompassing the enormous variety that exists within the Church at present.

Patterns includes three main items:

● Clear outline structures for main services, indicating what must be used and what is entirely flexible.
   The basic form of A Service of the Word, as a 'third service', alternative to Morning or Evening Prayer, was authorized by the

General Synod in November 1993, and is reproduced here in Chapter 2. The 'Instructions' for the use of this service provide useful information, both on the basic principles and structures of worship and also guidelines on the construction of services. These will help those who are providing 'family' and other services which are not alternative to Morning or Evening Prayer, and enable those responsible for planning more mainstream services to have a clear grasp of the structures embodied in them. The sample services in the report edition have been revised, so that everything provided in them is currently authorized. These are set out with bold type and illustrations, and may be copied from the page by parishes which wish to do so. Some of these sample services are also published separately as service cards.

● Sections of resource material grouped under various headings, roughly in the order in which they might come in a service.
An introductory paragraph to each section gives guidance on how to use it, and on how to take advantage of the notes and rubrics in *The Alternative Service Book* to enrich the liturgy.

● A commentary, to show how the structures and resource sections might be used, and how worship relates to differences in architecture, churchmanship and cultural background.
This is offered particularly as an aid to assist in the training of parish worship planning groups.

Urban priority areas

The flexibility of the *Patterns* approach will help churches to do what the *Faith in the City* report suggests, in moving away from a 1300-page book for the congregation, and providing for liturgy to 'emerge out of and reflect local cultures'. That report asked for 'short, functional service booklets or cards', and we have provided these. The report also asked for liturgy that promoted 'a greater involvement of the congregation' and was 'more concrete and tangible than abstract and theoretical'. The new writing we have done is designed to meet those needs, as may be seen from our writing criteria on page 218. But the needs of the UPA parish for worship reflecting local culture, language and concrete expression are not best met by a group of experts at the centre laying down all the words of liturgy. They are better met by creating the framework and the environment which will enable a new generation of leaders of worship to create genuinely local liturgy which is still obviously part of the liturgy of the whole Church.

Family services

Many of the same things could be said about family services: clear simple structures, concrete language, and responsiveness to local culture and gifts are all necessary. The family service in the Church of England varies enormously from place to place. In some places it is but a pale and timid reflection of the standard fare: the Chelmsford report on non-statutory worship, *For the Family*, uses words like 'inhibited and awkward', 'stilted, uncreative and frankly boring' about some services, 'led in a very conservative and staid fashion'. Some of the criticisms of the family service voiced in the Church today are:

- Worship is 'childish' and the focus is on children to such an extent that adults are forced to deny their adulthood by joining in.
- It focuses so strongly on the nuclear family that it makes those in other styles of household – the single, bereaved, divorced and elderly – feel less a part of the church family.
- Both structure and content are so free and variable that people see no links with traditional Anglican worship.
- It fails to act as a 'bridge' to more mainline worship: some worshippers never move on from a monthly family service.
- Its worship is banal, superficial, dominated by a 'compere' or a strong teaching aim, providing little God-centred worship.
- Worship depends on the whim of the worship leader because so much is new; and because it is not a 'statutory' service, there is sometimes little or no consultation with the PCC.

But in other places the family service is the main sign of hope for the Church, reflecting an enormous amount of creative energy and the kind of God-centred worship that is resulting in a considerable growth of new Christians. Many of the points listed above might be countered by a positive list:

- The family service provides a place where those unfamiliar with formal worship can begin to feel at home.
- One reason for this is that it can be a bridge, in reflecting local culture more easily than the rest of the Church's worship.
- Another reason is that people sometimes welcome the excuse to accompany their children, and then find they understand teaching which is simple and visual, and sometimes at a more 'introductory' level.
- It is a place where genuine inter-generational activity takes place, with adults and children learning from each other in worship.
- It can help regular church attenders to discover new dimensions in worship.

- It provides an opportunity for people to grow and use their gifts by sharing in planning, leading and contributing to worship.
- It provides a way of introducing new elements into worship (in a congregation likely to be less critical of them?) – drama, dance, audiovisuals, new hymns or methods of teaching.

Family

All this begs the question of what we mean by 'family'. Who is the family service for? Family Service (or 'Family Communion') is often used as a more folksy title for the Eucharist or Holy Communion, to emphasize that it is for the whole church family every week, or that provision is made for children as well as adults. 'All-age worship' is another title for this, to stress that people of all ages can worship together. But 'Family Service' has also replaced 'Children's Church' as a title, to mean a random collection of adults and children, or a large number of children, while Junior Church teachers have a monthly break.

We would want to interpret 'family' in its widest sense. All are daughters or sons; some are sisters, brothers, parents, cousins, grandparents. Some are part of a nuclear family of parents and children, or a single-parent family, or a kinship family including grandparents or aunts, or a reconstituted family where parents bring children from previous relationships. Others, with no marriage or blood relationship, are part of an intentional family or household, deliberately committed to one another for caring and mutual support, and sometimes for a specific purpose such as being a mission house for the local church. And some families may be mixtures of these different types.

The Church needs to acknowledge and value all of these, and to embrace also those who live alone, or without such immediate family relationships. The Church at worship should acknowledge the presence and gifts of children, and be open to inter-generational learning and experience of worship: it should not be focused exclusively on the needs of the traditional English middle-class nuclear family. And, as the *Children in the Way* report argues, 'family' is not the only model for the Church, and can sometimes damage people by appearing to exclude them. For this reason we do not think the title 'Family Service' should be adopted formally by the Church of England, and we look for a more satisfactory alternative to emerge. The 'pilgrim church' model provides some exciting educational (and processional?) possibilities, but we doubt whether 'Pilgrim Service' would convey the required image!

Much more could be said about the family service, such as the need for clear aims for the planning group, and for a regular review of where this service fits in relation to the rest of the local church's worship. We hope that the *Patterns for Worship* proposals and guidelines will encourage change away from the unhelpful aspects of the 'Family Service', while ensuring that its creative, vibrant life is not locked up in non-statutory, non-eucharistic and mini-family centred worship. It must be part of the living, contemporary tradition of the whole Church's worship.

Common prayer?

Inevitably, a directory approach such as that in *Patterns for Worship* raises questions about the concept of 'common prayer', and about whether or how doctrinal conformity can be secured. 'Common prayer' does not in fact exist, in the sense of being able to walk into any church in the land and find exactly the same words to follow. Nor should we pretend that it would be either good or right to return to a position – well over a century ago – when that might have been the case. Rather, 'common prayer' exists in the Church of England in the sense of recognizing, as one does when visiting other members of the same family, some common features, some shared experiences, language, patterns or traditions. To accept a variety of forms, dictated by local culture, is part of our Anglican heritage, spelt out by Archbishop Thomas Cranmer in his 1549 *Preface*: 'it often chanceth diversely in diverse countries'.

What are the marks of Anglican worship that we might expect to find (or have a right to find?) in any service? We believe that some of the marks which should be safeguarded for those who wish to stand in any recognizable continuity with historic Anglican tradition are:

- a clear structure for worship
- an emphasis on reading the word of God and on using psalms
- liturgical words repeated by the congregation, some of which, like the creed, would be known by heart
- using a collect, the Lord's Prayer, and some responsive forms in prayer
- a recognition of the centrality of the Eucharist
- a concern for form, dignity, and economy of words.

Another mark of Anglican worship is a willingness to use forms and prayers which can be used across a broad spectrum of Christian belief. This may sometimes mean that, for the sake of the unity of the Church, we refrain from using some words which reflect one of the traditional 'party' positions. Most debates about doctrinal conformity are really about 'how to stop the other person doing something you don't like because you think it is on the verge of being heretical'. We think the provisions of the Canons sufficiently safeguard this. Canon A 5 states that the doctrine of the Church of England 'is to be found in the Thirty-nine Articles of Religion, the Book of Common Prayer, and the Ordinal'. In other words, these texts represent a doctrinal norm, and nothing in new services, whether approved by the General Synod (Canon B 2), or approved by the Convocations, Archbishops or Ordinary (Canon B 4), or considered suitable or varied (insubstantially) by the minister (Canon B 5) may be 'contrary to, nor indicative of any departure from the doctrine of the Church of England in any essential matter'. Forms of service also have to be reverent and seemly.

Our suggestion in the report edition of *Patterns* was that one way of securing doctrinal orthodoxy and avoiding the divisions caused by 'party' texts would be to have some parts of the service with a limited number of options: for example, the creed, confession and absolution, specific prayer about the departed, and the eucharistic prayer. This led to a discussion about whether it is possible to identify a 'core' of Anglican worship, which is further pursued in the Commission's book of essays *The Renewal of Common Prayer* (SPCK/Church House Publishing 1993). The concept, and the identity of the 'core', has also been tested to some extent in the Synod in the authorization process for *A Service of the Word*. There will be some who will think that even such a minimum amount of regulation as this goes counter to what we have said about local creativity, and infringes local control of worship. To them we would point out the traditional function of 'catholic' faith and worship in providing a critique or alternative viewpoint for looking at local (or national) culture.

Reading the Bible

While the Bible-reading part of our worship may sometimes be done well, there is always scope for improvement. People tell us some of the reasons why reading the word of God fails to have the effect it ought to have:

● The readings are treated as if they are boring. This may sometimes be due to the version used, the length of the reading, or the way in which it is read, as if it were a duty to be done and not part of the worship.

● Partial or unhelpful meanings are imposed on the readings, for example by bad introductions. The readings should be introduced in such a way as to help people to listen together, to reflect on their particular situation in the light of the Word. For this reason, we do not think books of 'standard' introductions should be produced.

● Many churches do not use the lectionary provision. They omit readings and change them to fit the service theme: sometimes only a few verses are read, to be used as the sermon text. This results in a narrower overall diet of scripture, sometimes determined by the particular interests of the minister.

● There is a general devaluing of the practice of listening to scripture being read, and of reading it well. Readers need training. Even in family services it is wrong to have children reading who cannot be heard, or who read without understanding: the same should be true for adults.

● There is a reluctance to use the Old Testament, even in the Advent to Christmas period when it is the controlling reading.

● Few people have thought about the reasons for reading the Bible in worship.

● Congregations suffer from a presentation that is often unimaginative and expects little response.

● Current lectionary provision is comparatively poor.

We offer three possible solutions:

1 The Church should rediscover the excitement of reading the scriptures in worship, as something that makes the people of God what they are.
This means helping everyone to understand why we read scripture in worship. We read scripture not just to teach and instruct, but in order to link us firmly with the tradition, to ensure that we listen to the whole counsel of God, to deliver us from the personal whim or interest of the preacher or worship leader, to allow one part of scripture to throw kaleidoscopic light on another, to identify ourselves again as the people to whom God is speaking. The

Doctrine Commission's report *Believing in the Church* makes the point strongly that by publicly rehearsing its corporate story the community is proclaiming its identity as the people of God. Shared stories bind people together.

If scripture is there just for teaching purposes, some in the congregation (and ministers as well) easily respond, 'I can think of something better – perhaps not in the Bible – on that theme!' But the readings are not there just to illustrate a theme, or help people think about some piece of teaching. They are there because they are normative to and determinative of Christian faith and experience: they both set the boundaries and have an active, stimulating, energizing effect – releasing energy like a hammer breaking rock in pieces. We should encourage congregations to respond to the recitation of the great acts of God (allow more pauses for meditation, more responses, short prayers or a verse of a psalm after the reading. See the Commentary section on The Ministry of the Word, page 210).

2 Each church should improve its approach to, and presentation of, the readings to encourage the congregation to 'own' them.
Some churches encourage the congregation to use the Sunday readings for personal meditation during the preceding or following week, or have them discussed in home groups. Changes in presentation might mean the actual involvement of the congregation, in interjections and responses (or stamping feet as in the synagogue when the story of Haman is read!). The congregation can be involved in both drama and dialogue readings. It might mean changing the visual presentation, removing distractions by putting out all lights apart from a spotlight on the reader, or using more deliberate storytelling techniques and different parts of the building to focus the reading. Some of this depends on architecture, space and numbers, and little can be indicated in the lectionary. It is more a matter of using the imagination, though it is possible to give an indication where a long story reading might be broken up, for example by songs, or to show how a dialogue (or other types of scripture) might be read in parts, as in *The Dramatised Bible*.

3 The Church of England should make further and more imaginative lectionary provision.
The lectionary is currently the subject of considerable international

discussion, with two different basic approaches. One follows the principle of continuous sequential reading of scripture (Cranmer's pattern). The other is the thematic approach found in the lectionary drafted by the Joint Liturgical Group which was used in *The Alternative Service Book 1980*. The Joint Liturgical Group produced a four-year version of the thematic lectionary in 1991. The continuous sequential approach is to be found in the Roman Catholic three-year lectionary, a revised ecumenical version of which (*The Revised Common Lectionary*) is gaining ground among the North American churches. The Commission's *Lent, Holy Week, Easter* and *The Promise of His Glory* have a slightly different pattern of three-year lectionary. So the scene is set for further debate on the Commission's proposals.

Two further contributions to this debate were offered in the report edition of *Patterns*. First, there was a proposal, illustrated in *Patterns* and worked out more fully in *Promise*, for two different levels of adherence to the lectionary: a 'closed season' around the main seasons of the Church's year, when a restricted seasonal lectionary would be mandatory, and an 'open season' for the rest of the year with several different options, one of which could clearly be a series of 'storyline' sets of readings suitable for family services.

Second, the importance of 'story' should be allowed to have an effect on the way the lectionary is constructed. The reasons for this come not only from those working in inner urban areas and with children, but from the needs of the whole church. Narrative is comforting and satisfying, challenging because it involves the hearers, emotionally irreplaceable – a more natural part of our life communication than didactic speech. There would be value in including more story provision in our lectionary:

● it is easy to listen to, identify with, remember and retell
● it links the community clearly with the tradition of God's saving action
● in worship, it can more easily be used to stimulate praise, as we hear what God has done, rather than receive instruction
● it is important for children: action stories keep things moving, add a sense of excitement and humanity.

When we examine the ASB Sunday lectionary for stories, we find glaring omissions. We have the call of Abraham (twice) but nothing of Lot, Hagar, Ishmael or Isaac. There is nothing from the Joseph saga. Moses in the bulrushes, the plagues, the spies in Canaan, the fall of

Jericho, Achan, Deborah, Barak – all excellent story material, easily memorable and good listening even if some are long – are all missing. None of the Samson stories are there. In the New Testament, while we have Peter's declaration, the transfiguration and the raising of Lazarus every year, the only feeding miracle is John 6, and the only part of John 4 is theological dialogue rather than the narrative. Omissions include Mary and Martha, the man born blind, Jesus calming the storm, Legion, the pool of Bethesda, the story of the rich fool.

Service structure

A glance at history shows us the pedigree of the different strands of non-eucharistic worship which we find today in the family service, Morning and Evening Prayer, and the first half of Holy Communion. There are three strands in antiquity: the Word Service (first part of Holy Communion), Daily Prayer (Morning and Evening Prayer), and the Teaching or Instruction. (The evidence here is from the writings of Justin Martyr and the *Apostolic Tradition* of Hippolytus, but it is also to be found in many other places.)

The Word Service in Justin consists of readings from the prophets or memoirs of the apostles, read for as long as time allowed. This is followed by a discourse, and common prayer. This core of material is still recognizable in all major traditions, even though other elements were added in the intervening centuries. Usually there is an approach, with prayer and praise, and possibly penitence; then the readings, the last of which is a Gospel reading; followed in turn by a sermon, the creed and intercessions. What sort of 'shape' does this give us? It would be possible to see the climax of such a service either in the reading of the Gospel (even though it is a later addition), or in the intercessions, as the response of faith: the living sacrifice of the Church responding to the Word proclaimed and preached.

The content of daily prayer in Hippolytus' *Apostolic Tradition* is less precise. The emphasis is on the *times* of daily prayer – prayer in the heart, with a few people, or many. The later evidence of East and West suggests that the main times were morning and evening, and the service consisted of praise in fixed psalms, hymns and songs, together with intercession. Later developments saw many introductory prayers, the continuous recitation of the Psalter, and readings from scripture of ever-increasing length, with other Christian writings. The earlier heart of daily prayer, praise to God at certain times of the day, came to be lost by the lengthier psalm-singing and readings, and so its structure was distorted.

The 'Teaching' type of service centring on instruction in the word of God is referred to in the *Apostolic Tradition* and may be a direct offspring of the corresponding synagogue service, a Bible study with no particular liturgical shape.

As history proceeds, these three types of service, which major respectively on reading the word of God, on prayer and praise, and on teaching, do not remain distinct. By the time Cranmer at the Reformation reduced the seven medieval 'hours' into Morning and Evening Prayer, prayer and praise were combined with an emphasis on reading and teaching the Word.

Before we draw some conclusions from this, a further glance at history suggests that Christians in the early Church were not divided up according to *age*, but rather according to *stage*, so that catechumens (those preparing for baptism, however old they were) were excluded from the Eucharist. Their formal departure at the end of the Word Service would have been a dramatic feature of the liturgy in a large building, probably involving some upheaval in the congregation as a whole. Perhaps we might make similar structural provision today. As they did in the early Church, we are again providing (for instance in the ASB provision for family baptism) not only for individuals but for whole families to move from a non-Christian to a Christian lifestyle. We should no longer be organizing our church life and worship on the assumption that people grow from being less Christian to more Christian in parallel with their age (and so older people but not children are admitted to communion).

Assumptions about structure

In *Patterns for Worship* we work on the basis of some conclusions from this.

First, a clear structure is essential. Its main components should stand out so that worshippers can see the shape, development and climax of the service – so that they 'know where they are going'. It is helpful if this is reflected in the way the service is laid out for printing.

Second, as we see the three different types of service come together in history, and as it is fairly unlikely that a parish would have three different types of Word Service each Sunday, we need a balance in any one service between prayer and praise, word and teaching. This means we should not have a service which is nothing but teaching, without praise and prayer; nor a service which is nothing but praise, without some word and teaching.

Third, we would want to argue that Word Services of different structures should be regarded as an interchangeable first part of Holy Communion.

Fourth, in making the distinction between the Service of the Word and the Breaking of Bread, between the first and second parts of the Eucharist, we should allow for a pattern to develop where there is a sufficient break between the two parts (perhaps with an extended Peace, with or without refreshments) for those enquiring about the Christian faith and baptism to go without embarrassment, at the end of the Service of the Word.

The authorization by General Synod in November 1993 of *A Service of the Word* has provided the Church with a clear one-page service structure in line with these principles. The notes show how many of the resources used in the service can be varied to meet local need, while describing clearly those things which will ensure an element of common prayer. And the note amending page 71 of the ASB shows how a fairly flexible Word Service may be put together with the Breaking of Bread following the principles described above.

Dry bones?

The three parts of *Patterns for Worship* – service outlines, resource sections, and commentary – might be thought of as skeletons, or the bare bones and outlines of services, flesh to clothe them with, in terms of the resource material, and the working instructions or hints on how to make it all work. But like Ezekiel's army in the valley of dry bones, the skeletons need not only flesh and instructions, but the breath of the Lord himself, to bring them to life. So we offer to the Church dry bones, flesh and words, knowing that our brothers and sisters who lead the Church's worship will pray with us for the breath of God's Spirit to fill his people as they find a door open in heaven.

2
THE BASIC OUTLINE

A Service of the Word: the authorized text___

Authorization

A Service of the Word and *Affirmations of Faith* are authorized pursuant to Canon B 2 of the Canons of the Church of England for use from 10 November 1993 to 31 December 2000.

Decisions as to which of the authorized services are to be used (other than occasional offices) shall be taken jointly by the incumbent and the parochial church council.

Introduction

A Service of the Word is unusual for an authorized Church of England service. It consists almost entirely of notes and directions and allows for considerable local variation and choice within a common structure. It is important that those who prepare for and take part in *A Service of the Word* should have a clear understanding of the nature of worship and of how the component parts of this service work together. Leading people in worship is leading people into mystery, into the unknown and yet the familiar. This spiritual activity is much more than getting the words or the sections in the right order. The primary object in the careful planning and leading of the service is the spiritual direction which enables the whole congregation to come into the presence of God to give him glory. Choices must be made responsibly by leaders of this service or by groups planning worship with them, whether the service is an occasional one, or a regular one which might use a service card. The notes and the text of *A Service of the Word* should be read together as they interpret one another.

The Ministry of the Word

At the heart of the service is *The Ministry of the Word*. This must not be so lightly treated as to appear insignificant compared with other parts of the service. The Readings from Holy Scripture are central to this part, and, together with the season, may determine the theme of the rest of the worship. At certain times of the year, as Note 5 says, the readings come from an authorized lectionary, so that the whole Church is together proclaiming the major events in the Christian story. Telling that story and expounding it in the 'sermon' can be done in many different and adventurous ways. Some are suggested in Notes 5 and 7, but there are many others. The word 'sermon' is used in the service and explained in the note, precisely because it would be too limiting to use words like 'address', 'talk', 'instruction', 'meditation'. The items in sections 5 to 8 may come in any order, and more than once. So the sermon may be in parts, and there may be more than one psalm or song, and of course hymns may be inserted as well. But on most occasions it will be appropriate for this part of the service to have a creed or affirmation of faith as its climax.

Preparation

With the Ministry of the Word becoming clear it will be easier to see how *The Preparation* for it, and the response to it in *The Prayers* fit in. People need to know when the service has started (Note 1). What happens at the beginning can create an atmosphere for worship and set the tone and mood for what follows. The gathering of the congregation and the call to worship are to be marked by a liturgical greeting between minister and people. Leaders should have worked out exactly where this comes among the singing, scripture sentence, introduction (perhaps to the theme), and opening prayer. All these should draw the members of the congregation together and focus their attention on almighty God.

This part of the service will usually include the Prayers of Penitence, though these may come later if, for instance, the theme of the Ministry of the Word appropriately leads to penitence. Authorized Prayers of Penitence include all those confessions and absolutions in the *Book of Common Prayer* and *The Alternative Service Book 1980*, together with several other seasonal and thematic forms, mostly for occasional use, which are set out in Resource Sections C and D (pages 40-52). The climax of this part of the service is either the collect or, if that is included in the prayers, one of the items of praise in section 3. The collect does not have to be that of the day; it may be a thematic one based on the readings (in which case it should be at section 4, or be used to sum up the prayers (in section 9).

Prayers

Part of the response to the Word is the creed, but the response should be developed in *The Prayers* which follow. There are many different options for this part of the service. These range from a series of collect-type prayers to congregational involvement in prayer groups, visual and processional prayers, with responsive forms and a number of people sharing the leading of intercessions in between. But, whatever the form, it is essential that *The Prayers* also includes thanksgiving. A section of thanksgiving, which may include the spoken word, music and hymns, may be the proper climax to this part of the service.

Conclusion

Many different words have been used for *The Conclusion*, each of which has something to contribute to our understanding of how the service ends: dismissal, farewell, goodbye, departure, valediction, commission, blessing, ending, going out. . . What is essential, as with the way the service starts, is that it should have a clear liturgical ending: options are listed in Note 9.

Once the service is planned, leaders will want to check through to ensure there is the right balance between the elements of word, prayer and praise, and between congregational activity and congregational passivity. Does the music come in the right places? Is there sufficient silence (Note 4)? This is something leaders can be afraid of, or fail to introduce properly. And is there a clear overall direction to the service: is it achieving the purpose of bringing the congregation together to give glory to God?

A Service of the Word

In this form of service, the material is described as 'authorized' or 'suitable', which expressions shall have the following meanings:

- 'authorized' means approved by General Synod in accordance with the provisions of Canon B 2
- 'suitable' means a form used at the discretion of the minister conducting the form of service on any occasion, but such that the material so used shall be neither contrary to, nor indicative of any departure from, the doctrine of the Church of England in any essential matter.

This service is authorized as an alternative to Morning Prayer and Evening Prayer. It is not intended for daily prayer, but to provide a structure for Sunday services and weekday services of an occasional nature.

Notes

1 **Liturgical Greeting** (section 1)
The service shall have a *clear beginning*. The liturgical greeting may follow some introductory singing, or a hymn or a sentence of scripture, and may be followed by a brief introduction or an opening prayer.

2 **Penitence** (section 2)
Authorized Prayers of Penitence includes those forms of confession and absolution in Resource Sections C and D. The minister introduces the confession with suitable words.

3 **Hymns, Canticles, Acclamations, and the Peace** (section 3)
Points are indicated for some of these, but if occasion requires they may occur elsewhere.

4 **Silence**
Periods of silence may be kept at different points of the service. It may be particularly appropriate in sections 1, 2, 5 and 9.

5 **Readings** (section 5)
There should preferably be at least *two readings from Holy Scripture*, but it is recognized that if occasion demands there may only be one reading. They may be dramatized, sung or read responsively. The readings shall come from an authorized lectionary during the periods from Advent 3 to Epiphany 1 and

from Palm Sunday to Trinity Sunday and whenever the service is combined with the Eucharist.

6 **Psalms** (section 6)
The service shall normally include a *psalm or psalms*. These might be said or sung in the traditional way, but it is also possible to use a metrical version, a responsive form or a paraphrase such as can be found in many current hymnbooks. The psalm may occasionally be replaced by a song or canticle the words of which are taken directly from scripture, a 'scriptural song'.

7 **Sermon** (section 7)
The term *sermon* may include less formal exposition, the use of drama, interviews, discussion and audio-visuals. Hymns or other sections of the service may be inserted between parts of the sermon. The sermon may come after one of the readings, or before or after the prayers.

8 **Sermon and Creed** (sections 7 and 8)
The *sermon* and a *creed* or authorized *affirmation of faith* may be omitted except on *Sundays and Principal Holy Days*.

9 **Conclusion** (section 11)
The service shall have a *clear ending*. This shall include one or more of the following forms: the Peace, the Grace, or a suitable ascription or blessing. If a responsive conclusion (such as the Dismissal at section 55 in ASB Rite A) is used, it shall come last.

A Service of the Word

The preparation

1 The minister welcomes the people with a **liturgical greeting**.

2 **Authorized Prayers of Penitence** are used here or in **The prayers**.

3 *Venite, Kyries, Gloria*, a hymn, song, or a set of responses may be used.

4 The **Collect** is said either here or at section 9.

The ministry of the Word

This includes

5 **Readings (or a Reading) from Holy Scripture**

6 **A psalm**, or, if occasion demands, a scriptural song

7 **A sermon**

8 **An authorized creed**, or, if occasion demands, an authorized **affirmation of faith**

The prayers

These include

9 **Intercessions and thanksgivings**

10 **The Lord's Prayer**

The conclusion

11 The service concludes with a **liturgical ending**.

Page 71 of *The Alternative Service Book 1980* is amended as follows to include *A Service of the Word*.

**Morning Prayer or Evening Prayer
or A Service of the Word
with Holy Communion Rite A**

47

	MP	**EP**
Penitence	1-7 optional	24-30
Versicles	8	31
Psalms	9, 10	32, 33
1st Reading	11	34
Canticle	12 optional	35 optional
2nd Reading	13	36
Canticle	15	38
Apostles' Creed	16	39 optional
Collect of the day	20	43
Daily Collect(s)	21 optional, 22	44 optional, 45

A Service of the Word

Greeting	1
Penitence	2 optional
Canticles, etc.	3 optional
Collect	4
Reading(s)	5
Psalm	6
Gospel	5
Sermon	7
Creed	8

	HC
General Intercession	
or	
Prayer for the Church and World	20, 21, 81
Penitence (if not used above)	23-29, 80
The Peace	30-31
The Preparation of the Gifts	32-35
The Eucharistic Prayer	36-41
The Communion	42-49, 66, 85
After Communion	50-56, 77, 86

The Shorter Form of Evening Prayer is not suitable for combination with Holy Communion.

References to Morning Prayer and Evening Prayer on pages 239, 251, and 260 of the ASB shall also be taken as referring to *A Service of the Word*.

A Service of the Word: instructions and guidelines

The authorized text of *A Service of the Word* shows that it is designed to be a service on its own, an alternative to Morning or Evening Prayer on Sundays and for occasional weekday services. It is also possible to combine it with Holy Communion Rite A (see pages 27-29). In the service there should be a balance between four main ingredients:

Word
Prayer
Praise
Action

Structure

The basic structure is provided in *A Service of the Word*. On occasions when the service is not an alternative to Morning or Evening Prayer, it is possible to vary the structure, and to put these main items into any order. It is possible to have word, prayer and praise as major blocks of material within the service. So, for instance, using the authorized outline, the service begins with a liturgical greeting, followed by Bible reading, sermon and creed with a scriptural song to lead into prayer, including penitence, the collect and the Lord's Prayer; the service could then end with praise and thanksgiving. But more often, word, prayer and praise will come more than once in the service, as in example 2 on page 24. Care should be taken to ensure that some logical progression, or development in the congregation's relationship to God, is reflected in the structure of the service.

How it works

It is important to have a clear structure, such as that in *A Service of the Word*, even though the detail may vary from week to week. The emphasis on different parts of the structure may be varied according to the theme, which may in turn be determined by the lectionary or the content of the 'Ministry of the Word' section. The 'skeleton' will then need 'flesh' in terms of items from the resource sections of this book, *The Alternative Service Book 1980,* the seasonal books produced by the Liturgical Commission, other resource books, or items produced through the work of a parish worship preparation group. It is often best to begin with the Ministry of the Word.

Word

First read the section 'Ministry of the Word' in the introduction to *A Service of the Word*, together with Notes 5-8.

● Decide about the readings from Holy Scripture (Note 5): follow the lectionary – or select one of the alternative routes. If occasion demands, there need only be one reading. If this service is the first part of the Holy Communion, there should be two readings, and one of them should be the Gospel. How are they to be presented?

● Decide about the psalms, scripture song or canticle (Note 6).

● Decide about the sermon, which need not take a traditional form (Note 7). There may be more than one person taking part, the congregation may divide into groups for all or part of the time, or the sermon may come in a number of parts at different points in the service. There should normally be some time for silent reflection after the readings or sermon.

Prayer

Next read the section 'Prayers' in the introduction to *A Service of the Word*, together with Note 4 and Sections 2, 9 and 10 in the service.

Decide which form of prayer to have:

● an outline form filled in by the minister
● an outline form with extempore prayer or biddings from the congregation, or from a group
● a litany
● a series of set prayers.

It is best not to mix the forms too much, though a set prayer may be a good way to end or sum up one of the other forms. The Lord's Prayer and the collect should be used at every Sunday service.

Praise

Praise may be said or sung. Select hymns, songs or items from the Praise pages of the Resource Sections of *Patterns* or elsewhere. A set of versicles and responses may be used at Section 3.

Action

This is not of the same order as the other three, and may be done at the same time as one of them. For example, dramatic action might interpret the Word, or a procession or dance might help to express praise. Other actions might be:

- a movement by the congregation, such as standing or joining hands
- movement with an object, e.g. candle or Bible
- a change in lighting or visual presentation.

The action may be the climax towards which the service moves, or an action that begins the worship and sets the theme for it.

Beginning and ending

Next, read the sections 'Preparation and Conclusion' in the introduction to *A Service of the Word*, together with Notes 1, 2 and 9.

- Decide how the service is to begin and end: each should be clear.

- Decide what is to go into 'The Preparation', and what other material you want to add. Prayers of penitence, with an authorized form of confession and absolution, may come at Section 2 or Section 9, in 'The Prayers'. The collect may also come later, in Section 9. All the forms of confession and absolution in Resource Sections C and D in this book are authorized.

- Decide whether and where to add creed, affirmation of faith, notices, collection, invitations or biddings, explanation, silence.

- Decide how these ingredients relate to the aim and structure of the rest of the service. For example, prayers of penitence might be part of the preparation, at the beginning, to clear away any barrier to hearing God, or could be the climax towards which the service moves (as in an Ash Wednesday service). The full structure might then look like one of the following samples:

*(NOTE: In these examples a blue bullet ● indicates material that must be used. An asterisk * indicates that only a limited number of texts is authorized.)*

EXAMPLE 1
A block structure

Items you must include *(though individual items and order will vary)*		Additional items *you may want to add*
Preparation ● Greeting	← 1 →	Scripture sentence
	2 →	Hymn
	3 →	Opening prayer
	4 →	Invitation
	5 →	* Confession
	6 →	* Forgiveness
Word		
	7 →	Introduction
● Old Testament	← 8	
● Psalm or paraphrase	← 9	
● New Testament	← 10	
	11 →	Song or hymn
● Talk	← 12	
	13 →	Hymn
Prayer * Collect	← 14	
● Form of intercession	← 15	
Praise ● Versicles and responses	← 16	
	17 →	Hymn
Action All stand while the candle is carried out	← 18	
● Blessing or ending	← 19	

EXAMPLE 2
The conversation structure

Word – Prayer – Praise – Action may come many times within the same service. Imagine a conversation between God and the congregation. The **Word** items present what God is saying, and the other three items may be used as the response or reply to God. The service may be built from a series of **Presentation** and **Response** units, like building blocks. This example is from Morning Prayer:

PRESENTATION		RESPONSE
Word Scripture sentence	← 1	
	2 →	**Praise** Hymn of adoration
Word Invitation	← 3	
	4 →	**Prayer** ● Confession
Prayer * Declaration of forgiveness	← 5	
	6 →	● **Praise** Open our lips. . . Glory be. . .
	7 →	Song
Word ● Psalm ● Old Testament	← 8 ← 9	
	10 →	**Praise** Song
Word ● New Testament	← 11	
	12 →	**Praise** Song
	13 →	* Creed
	14 →	* Lord's Prayer
	15 →	* Collect
Word ● Sermon	← 16	
	17 →	Hymn

Themes

A theme may determine the pattern of the worship. The traditional Morning and Evening Prayer pattern allows the word and praise to throw light on each other. A thematic approach means very often that the worship leader decides the way the word is to be heard, and the response that needs to be made. Care must be taken to make sure that the whole service does not become a sermon, with explanations and exhortations introducing every item.

Some examples of a thematic approach
1 *Maundy Thursday foot-washing*
2 *Baptism service*
3 *Wisdom lays her table* (Proverbs 9: see Commentary page 205)

Guidelines

When you have completed the service outline, consider this checklist. Parts of this are amplified in the descriptive commentary in Chapter 4.

1   Is there a balance between word, prayer, praise and action? For instance, the Word section may be top heavy with long readings and long introductions, or too many short readings.   ❑

2   Is the worship directed to God, addressing him rather than the people?   ❑

3   Is the Service of the Word moving towards Holy Communion? If so, it must include an authorized form of penitence, a Gospel reading and (on Sundays) a creed or affirmation of faith.   ❑

4   What space is there for reflection or silence in the service?   ❑

5   How much of the service might be classed as 'entertainment'? Is this justified? Is there a balance between receiving (listening, watching, contemplating) and responding? Check on posture: is there too much sitting down or standing up at one time? Is there enough action?   ❑

6   Is the structure and direction of the service clear enough for people to know where it is going? Does the service have an overall coherence, or is it just one entertainment item after another?   ❑

7 Is the music used in such a way as to further and develop the main thrust of the service? Is there too much musical praise, with too many choir items, or too long a section of choruses from the band, or hymns too close to one another? ☐

8 Does the service enable the gifts of a variety of people in the church to be used in both planning and taking part? ☐

9 Compare this service with other services in the month. An occasional completely new form of worship may stimulate people to discover new dimensions to their ordinary worship, but a new pattern each week may be confusing and unsettling, particularly to children. If people are familiar with both structure and content of the service, they feel more secure and can take part more easily. For a family service, for instance, it may be better to have a standard structure, with 'windows' or 'slots' which can be changed from week to week. ☐

10 Especially if you are planning family worship, check that the contents are not divisive, and can be used by children, single people, the bereaved, members of broken families. It is hurtful and not constructive to require a mixed congregation to join in prayers thanking God for our homes and families and all the happiness that parents and children share. ☐

The Eucharist:
instructions and guidelines_____

The Holy Communion service is made up of two parts, the Word and the Sacrament.

The Word part consists of:

- the first part of the Eucharist *OR*
- Morning or Evening Prayer (see Section 47, reproduced above on page 19) *OR*
- A Service of the Word (as in Section 47 above).

The Sacrament part consists of:

- penitence (if it does not come in the Word part).
- the Peace
- preparation of the gifts
- eucharistic prayer
- breaking of the bread
- communion
- conclusion.

These features are not all of equal weight.

How it works _____

First, decide the structure. This will involve decisions about:

- which of the three options above should be used for the Word part
- where to place those ingredients which are normal but may vary in position, for example, where penitence is to come, and where the Peace is shared.

Second, add to this structure:

- other elements which are compulsory, but may vary in form. When *A Service of the Word* is combined with the Eucharist, the readings must come from an authorized lectionary. But the creed could be the Apostles' Creed or an authorized Affirmation of Faith from Resource Section F.
- those ingredients in the service which are not compulsory, e.g. the collect for purity, the *Gloria in excelsis*, the prayer of humble access, the choice of post-communion prayers.
- those parts of the service where 'ad lib' or unofficial material may be used, or where there is provision made in the Resource Sections,

e.g. the opening greeting, the introduction to the Peace, prayers at the preparation of the gifts, seasonal prayers after Holy Communion, responsive prayers.

The Peace
Most modern rites place the Peace between the prayers and the preparation of the gifts. Note the scope for placing it elsewhere, for example at the end of the service, as well as the option to introduce it with other words, which may be composed for the occasion or the locality.

Preparation of the Gifts
Customs vary on the solemnity with which this is done. In some places, variable prayers may be used. These should be *preparatory*, as the title for this part implies, and not dramatically overshadow the eucharistic prayer.

Eucharistic Prayer
One of the authorized forms must always be used. A eucharistic prayer, whether it takes the form of extended monologue with acclamations, or a dialogue between president and congregation, normally includes the following:

- thanksgiving for creation, redemption and the work of the Spirit
- the memorial prayer for the Church to receive and grow in the life of Christ
- doxology, offering praise to God the Holy Trinity.

These are the 'deep structures' of the prayer and they need to be clear in the shape of the ideas expressed within them – including the tone of voice(s) used as it is proclaimed.

The pattern of the prayer is normally:

- an opening dialogue
- an introduction to praise
- an extended act of thanksgiving
- the narrative of the institution
- the memorial prayer
- the prayer for the blessing of the Spirit
- the concluding doxology.

But variations are permitted within this framework as follows:

- the proper preface: any of the prefaces in *The Alternative Service Book* may be used, or others may be specially selected or composed, provided that they balance with the style and overall length of the rest of the prayer.
- acclamations: the customary 'Christ has died' may be replaced by a number of alternatives, printed in *Lent, Holy Week, Easter*.
- chorus or metrical versions of the *Sanctus* and Doxology may be used, instead of those printed.

The eucharistic prayer leads into the Lord's Prayer.

Breaking of the Bread
This symbolic action prepares for the sharing of the bread and wine. It may be done in silence or one of the forms in the ASB may be used.

Invitation to communion
There are forms for this at Sections 45 and 85 of Holy Communion Rite A, and these are reflected in the sample services.

Communion
Local customs vary. However the bread and wine are shared, it should be done decently and in order. Bread and wine not required for communion are reverently consumed at the end of the distribution or after the service. This is not a significant liturgical act and need not be done at the holy table or by the president.

After communion
Variable prayers after communion, or responsive prayers, may be used at this point. Other alternative prayers and dismissals are provided in Resource Sections J and T.

3
RESOURCE SECTIONS

Note on numbering   32

Index of themes and seasons   32

A   **Introductions**   33

B-D   **Confessions**
B   – invitations to confession   37
C   – confessions   40
D   – absolutions   50

E   **The Ministry of the Word**   53

F   **Affirmations of faith**   57

G-J   **Prayers**
G   – responses, endings, introductions to
          the Lord's Prayer   63
H   – responsive intercessions and litanies   66
J   – prayers after communion or endings for
          A Service of the Word   92

K-Q   **Praise**
K   – short acclamations and responses   104
L   – acclamations and responses   106
M   – longer acclamations and responsive scriptures   115
N   – proper prefaces   126
P   – thanksgivings   131
Q   – scriptural songs   150

R-S   **Action**
R   – introductory words to the Peace   171
S   – words for dedication   176

T   **Blessings and endings**   177

Note on numbering

In the Resource Sections of *Patterns for Worship*, a three-part system of numbering is used, e.g. 7J24.

● The **first number** indicates the theme or season, e.g. 7 for Ascension, Kingship. Items for a particular theme or season can be found by looking for the appropriate number using the 'Index of themes and seasons' below.

● The **letter** identifies the section of the service, from the Contents list on page 31. Thus J = prayers after communion or endings for A Service of the Word.

● The **last number** is a continuous numbering within each section.

Only the letter and the last number appear in the 'Index of Bible References' on page 328.

Index of themes and seasons

1	Advent
2	Incarnation, Christmas, Annunciation, Mary
3	Epiphany, Light
4	Lent, Penitence
5	Cross
6	Resurrection, Heaven, Glory, Transfiguration, Death, Funerals
7	Ascension, Kingship
8	Spirit, Pentecost, Gifts, Healing, Baptism and Confirmation
9	Trinity
10	Creation, Harvest, Bread, Vine, Eucharist
11	Word
12	Church, Mission and Ministry, Unity
13	City, World and Society
14	Family
15	Saints (see also Resurrection)
16	Kingdom, Freedom, Reconciliation
17	Love, Peace, Joy
0	General

A INTRODUCTIONS

The way a service begins can sometimes set the tone for all that
follows, so it is important to prepare. Well-prepared notices, including
some announcement of the day's theme, can serve to unite a
congregation as a family with many concerns coming together for
worship. The Peace may be used as an introduction. ASB Rite A
provides for a sentence of scripture, a hymn, canticle or psalm (which
might be an introit by choir alone, or a solo invitation to worship),
and a greeting which the president may vary. Some ways of varying
this greeting are indicated below. A prayer of preparation for worship
might be used, similar in intention to that in Section 3 of Rite A:
some examples of this are given below, but must replace rather than
be used alongside Section 3. A spoken verse of a hymn might be used.
'**Alleluia!**' may be added at appropriate seasons to many of these
introductions.

Greetings and other introductions

In the name of Christ   6A1
(who died and was raised by the glory of the Father)
we welcome you:
grace, mercy and peace be with you all.
And also with you.

The grace and mercy of our Lord Jesus Christ be with you.   0A2
And also with you.

Grace, mercy and peace from God our Father   0A3
and the Lord Jesus Christ be with you.
And also with you.
1 Timothy 1.2

May the light and peace of Jesus Christ our Lord be with you.   0A4
The Lord bless you.

Grace and peace to you from God.   0A5
May he fill you with truth and joy.

This is the day which the Lord has made.
Let us rejoice and be glad in it.
Psalm 118.24

0A6

Christ has brought us out of darkness:
to live in his marvellous light.
1 Peter 2.9

0A7

The Lord of glory be with you.
The Lord bless you.
*(This greeting may be used before or after other introductions. 'The
Lord of glory' may be replaced by other similar phrases, for example
'The risen Lord', 'The Lord of mercy', 'The Lord of all creation'.)*

0A8

Responsive introductions

We are hard pressed on every side, but not crushed;
perplexed, but not in despair;
persecuted, but not abandoned;
struck down, but not destroyed.
We always carry around in our body the death of Jesus:
so that the death of Jesus may be revealed.
We fix our eyes not on what is seen:
but on what is unseen and eternal.
2 Corinthians 4.8-10

5A9

We have come to the city of the living God,
to the heavenly Jerusalem,
with thousands of angels in joyful assembly.
Alleluia!
We have come to God the judge of all,
to Jesus the mediator of the new covenant.
Alleluia!
Hebrews 12.22-24,28

6A10

Jesus suffered outside the city
to make us holy through his blood.
Let us come to him,
looking for the city which is to come.
Through him we offer our sacrifice of praise to God.
Lord, open our lips:
and our mouth shall proclaim your praise.
Hebrews 13.12,15

13A11

We stand before the throne of God
with countless crowds
from every nation and race, tribe and language.
Salvation belongs to our God!
(Alleluia!)

Revelation 7.9

15A12

O Lord, open thou our lips:
and our mouth shall show forth thy praise.
O God, make speed to save us:
O Lord, make haste to help us.
Glory be to the Father and to the Son, and to the Holy Spirit:
as it was in the beginning, is now and ever shall be,
world without end. Amen.
Praise ye the Lord:
the Lord's name be praised.

Psalm 51.15; 70.1

0A13

O Lord, we call to you: come to us quickly.
Hear us when we cry to you.

Let our prayer be set forth in your sight as incense:
the lifting up of our hands as the evening sacrifice.

Glory to the Father, and to the Son,
and to the Holy Spirit:
as it was in the beginning, is now,
and shall be for ever. Amen.
(Alleluia!)

Psalm 141.1,2

0A14

Praise our God, all you his servants:
those who fear him, both small and great.

Revelation 19.5

0A15

Praise God! For the Lord, our almighty God, is King!
Happy are those who have been invited
to the wedding-feast of the Lamb.
(Alleluia!)

Revelation 19.6,9

0A16

Great is the Lord and worthy of all praise.
Amen! Praise and glory and wisdom,
thanksgiving and honour, power and might,

0A17

be to our God for ever and ever! Amen.
(Alleluia!)

Revelation 5.13

We will praise the name of the Lord;   0A18
ascribe greatness to our God.
Lord, open our lips:
**and our mouth shall proclaim your praise.
(Alleluia!)**

Deuteronomy 32.3; Psalm 51.15

The Lord our God, the Almighty, reigns.   0A19
Let us rejoice and shout for joy,
and give God the glory.
**Glory to the Father, and to the Son,
and to the Holy Spirit:
as it was in the beginning, is now,
and shall be for ever. Amen.
(Alleluia!)**

Revelation 19.6

Opening prayers

Lord, direct our thoughts,   0A20
teach us to pray,
lift up our hearts to worship you
in Spirit and in truth,
through Jesus Christ. Amen.

Loving Lord,   0A21
fill us with your life-giving,
joy-giving, peace-giving presence,
that we may praise you now with our lips
and all the day long with our lives,
through Jesus Christ our Lord. Amen.

B-D CONFESSIONS

B Invitations to confession

Section 6 in Holy Communion Rite A allows for other suitable words to be used to introduce the confession. Some suggestions are given here; others may be found in *Enriching the Christian Year* (Michael Perham, SPCK/Alcuin Club 1993) and *In Penitence and Faith* (David Silk, Mowbray 1988). If the confession is early in the service, the words of invitation should be related to the greeting. If it is in the middle of the service, some word from the Gospel would be suitable. There should be a time for silent reflection between the invitation and the confession.

Advent
When the Lord comes, he will bring to light things now hidden in darkness, and will disclose the purposes of the heart. In that light, we confess our sins.

1B1

Christmas
The angel said, you shall call his name Jesus, for he will save his people from their sins. Christ Jesus came into the world to save sinners. We confess our sins in penitence and faith.
Matthew 1.21

2B2

Epiphany
The grace of God has dawned upon the world with healing for all. Though we have grieved him, yet he will heal us if we confess our sins in penitence and faith.
Malachi 4.2

3B3

Ash Wednesday
The sacrifice of God is a broken spirit; a broken and contrite heart he will not despise. Our sin is always before us: we acknowledge our transgressions in penitence and faith.
Psalm 51.17

4B4

Lent

Christ himself bore our sins in his body on the tree, that we might die to sin and live to righteousness. By his wounds we are healed. Let us confess our sins.

1 Peter 2.24

4B5

Cross

God shows his love for us in this: while we were still sinners Christ died for us. Sure of reconciliation through the death of his Son, we confess our sins to God.

Romans 5.8

5B6

Easter

Christ our passover lamb has been offered for us. Let us then rejoice by putting away all malice and evil and confessing our sins with a sincere and true heart.

1 Corinthians 5.7,8

6B7

Ascension

Jesus is our high priest, tempted like us, yet without sin. He lives for ever in heaven to intercede for us. Through him we approach the throne of grace with confidence, and confess our sins.

Hebrews 4.15,16

7B8

Pentecost

The Spirit of truth will convict the world of guilt about sin, righteousness and judgement. We have grieved the Holy Spirit. We confess our sins in penitence and faith.

John 16.8

8B9

Healing

The grace of God has dawned upon the world with healing for all. Let us come to him, in sorrow for our sins, seeking healing and salvation.

Titus 2.11

8B10

Trinity

Holy, holy, holy: when our eyes have seen the Lord of hosts we echo the words of Isaiah, 'Woe is me! I am doomed.' We long for the fire of God's cleansing to touch our unclean lips, for our iniquity to be removed and our sin wiped out. So we meet Father, Son and Holy Spirit with confession on our lips.

Isaiah 6.5,7

9B11

Creation

God's whole creation groans. The land produces thorns and thistles and is ready for burning. Our sin affects all around us. We confess our sin in penitence and faith.

Romans 8.22; Genesis 3.18

10B12

Word

The word of God is living and active. It judges the thoughts and intentions of the heart. All is open and laid bare before the eyes of him to whom we give account. We confess our sins in penitence and faith.

Hebrews 4.12

11B13

City

Jesus saw the city and wept over it, because it did not recognize the time of God's coming. We confess our part in the self-centredness, blindness and sin of the life of our city.

Luke 19.41

13B14

Family

Jesus said, Before you offer your gift, go and be reconciled. As brothers and sisters in God's family, we come together to ask our Father for forgiveness.

Matthew 5.24

14B15

Saints

We run the race set before us, surrounded by a great crowd of witnesses. Therefore let us lay aside every weight, and the sin which clings so closely, bringing them to Jesus in penitence and faith.

Hebrews 12.1

15B16

Kingdom

Jesus says, Repent, for the kingdom of heaven is close at hand. So let us turn away from sin and turn to him, confessing our sins in penitence and faith.

Matthew 4.17

16B17

Eucharist

Ye that do truly and earnestly repent you of your sins, and are in love and charity with your neighbours, and intend to lead a new life, following the commandments of God, and walking from henceforth in his holy ways; Draw near with faith, and take this Holy Sacrament to your comfort; and make your humble confession to Almighty God, meekly kneeling upon your knees.

0B18

C Confessions

The forms of confession in this section are authorized as an appendix to *A Service of the Word* under Canon B 2: see page 13. The forms of confession in the Order of Holy Communion and Morning and Evening Prayer in the *Book of Common Prayer* may be used on any occasion. These or one of the forms in the ASB should normally be used. It may sometimes be helpful to vary the form on particular occasions, in which case a confession and an absolution from this authorized list should be used.

Incarnation, Christmas

Christ the Light of the world has come to dispel the darkness of our hearts. In his light let us examine ourselves and confess our sins.

2C1

Silence is kept

Lord of grace and truth,
we confess our unworthiness
to stand in your presence as your children.
We have sinned:
forgive and heal us.

The Virgin Mary accepted your call
to be the mother of Jesus.
Forgive our disobedience to your will.
We have sinned:
forgive and heal us.

Your Son our Saviour
was born in poverty in a manger.
Forgive our greed and rejection of your ways.
We have sinned:
forgive and heal us.

The shepherds left their flocks
to go to Bethlehem.
Forgive our self-interest and lack of vision.
We have sinned:
forgive and heal us.

The wise men followed the star
to find Jesus the King.
Forgive our reluctance to seek you.
We have sinned:
forgive and heal us.

Lent, Penitence

Let us admit to God the sin which always confronts us. 4C2

Lord God,
we have sinned against you;
we have done evil in your sight.
We are sorry and repent.
Have mercy on us according to your love.
Wash away our wrongdoing and cleanse us from our sin.
Renew a right spirit within us
and restore us to the joy of your salvation,
through Jesus Christ our Lord. Amen.
Psalm 51

Cross, Failure in Discipleship

Lord Jesus Christ, 5C3
we confess we have failed you as did your disciples.
We ask for your mercy and your help.

Our selfishness betrays you:
Lord, forgive.
Christ have mercy.

We fail to share the pain of your suffering:
Lord, forgive.
Christ have mercy.

We run away from those who abuse you:
Lord, forgive.
Christ have mercy.

We are afraid of being known to belong to you:
Lord, forgive.
Christ have mercy.

Resurrection, Heaven, Glory, Transfiguration, Death, Funerals

O Jesus Christ, risen master and triumphant Lord, 6C4
we come to you in sorrow for our sins,
and confess to you our weakness and unbelief.

We have lived by our own strength,
and not by the power of your resurrection.
In your mercy, forgive us.
Lord, hear us and help us.

We have lived by the light of our own eyes,
as faithless and not believing.

In your mercy, forgive us.
Lord, hear us and help us.

We have lived for this world alone,
and doubted our home in heaven.
In your mercy, forgive us.
Lord, hear us and help us.

Trinity, Mission

O King enthroned on high, 9C5
filling the earth with your glory:
holy is your name,
Lord God almighty.
In our sinfulness we cry to you
to take our guilt away,
and to cleanse our lips to speak your word,
through Jesus Christ our Lord. Amen.

Creation, Harvest

We confess our sin, and the sins of our society, 10C6
in the misuse of God's creation.

God our Father, we are sorry
for the times when we have used your gifts carelessly,
and acted ungratefully.
Hear our prayer, and in your mercy:
forgive us and help us.

We enjoy the fruits of the harvest,
but sometimes forget that you have given them to us.
Father, in your mercy:
forgive us and help us.

We belong to a people who are full and satisfied,
but ignore the cry of the hungry.
Father, in your mercy:
forgive us and help us.

We are thoughtless,
and do not care enough for the world you have made.
Father, in your mercy:
forgive us and help us.

We store up goods for ourselves alone,
as if there were no God and no heaven.
Father, in your mercy:
forgive us and help us.

City, World and Society

Lord God, our maker and our redeemer,
this is your world and we are your people:
come among us and save us.

13C7

We have wilfully misused your gifts of creation;
Lord, be merciful:
forgive us our sin.

We have seen the ill-treatment of others
and have not gone to their aid;
Lord, be merciful:
forgive us our sin.

We have condoned evil and dishonesty
and failed to strive for justice;
Lord, be merciful:
forgive us our sin.

We have heard the good news of Christ,
but have failed to share it with others;
Lord, be merciful:
forgive us our sin.

We have not loved you with all our heart,
nor our neighbours as ourselves;
Lord, be merciful:
forgive us our sin.

Reconciliation

Let us return to the Lord our God and say to him:

16C8

Father,
we have sinned against heaven and against you.
We are not worthy to be called your children.
We turn to you again.
Have mercy on us,
bring us back to yourself
as those who once were dead
but now have life through Christ our Lord. Amen.

Luke 15

Love, Peace

17C9

Come, let us return to the Lord and say:

**Lord our God,
in our sin we have avoided your call.
Our love for you is like a morning cloud,
like the dew that goes away early.
Have mercy on us;
deliver us from judgement;
bind up our wounds
and revive us;
in Jesus Christ our Lord. Amen.**

Hosea 6

General

0C10

God our Father,
we come to you in sorrow for
our sins.

For turning away from you,
and ignoring your will for our lives;
Father, forgive us:
save us and help us.

For behaving just as we wish,
without thinking of you;
Father, forgive us:
save us and help us.

For failing you by what we do,
and think and say;
Father, forgive us:
save us and help us.

For letting ourselves be drawn away from you
by temptations in the world about us;
Father, forgive us:
save us and help us.

For living as if we were ashamed
to belong to your Son;
Father, forgive us:
save us and help us.

General

God our Father,
long-suffering, full of grace and truth.
You create us from nothing and give us life.
You redeem us and make us your children in the water of baptism.
You do not turn your face from us,
nor cast us aside.
We confess that we have sinned
against you and our neighbour.
We have wounded your love and marred your image in us.
Restore us for the sake of your Son,
and bring us to heavenly joy,
in Jesus Christ our Lord. Amen.

0C11

General

Almighty and most merciful Father,
we have wandered and strayed from your ways like lost sheep.
We have followed too much the devices and desires of our
    own hearts.
We have offended against your holy laws.
We have left undone those things that we ought to have done;
and we have done those things that we ought not to have done;
and there is no health in us.
But you, O Lord, have mercy upon us in our need.
Spare those who confess their faults.
Restore those who are penitent,
according to your promises declared to mankind in Christ Jesus
    our Lord.
And grant, O most merciful Father, for his sake,
that from this time we may live a disciplined, righteous and
    godly life,
to the glory of your holy name. Amen.

0C12

General

Almighty God, Father of our Lord Jesus Christ,
maker of all things, judge of all people,
we acknowledge and confess
the grievous sins and wickedness
which we have so often committed
by thought, word and deed
against your divine majesty,
provoking most justly your anger
and indignation against us.

0C13

We earnestly repent,
and are deeply sorry for these our wrongdoings;
the memory of them weighs us down,
the burden of them is too great for us to bear.
Have mercy upon us,
have mercy upon us, most merciful Father,
for your Son our Lord Jesus Christ's sake,
forgive us all that is past;
and grant that from this time onwards
we may always serve and please you
in newness of life,
to the honour and glory of your name,
through Jesus Christ our Lord. Amen.

General

Man born of woman has but a short time to live.[1]

0C14

We have our fill of sorrow.
We blossom like a flower and wither away.
We slip away like a shadow and do not stay.

Holy God,
holy and strong,
holy and immortal,
have mercy upon us.

In the midst of life we are in death;
where can we turn for help?
Only to you, Lord,
who are justly angered by our sins.

Holy God,
holy and strong,
holy and immortal,
have mercy upon us.

Shut not your ears to our prayers,
but spare us, O Lord.

Holy God,
holy and strong,
holy and immortal,
have mercy upon us.

You know the secrets of our hearts;
forgive us our sins.

---

[1] *Or:* Those born of woman have but a short time to live.

Holy God,
holy and strong,
holy and immortal,
have mercy upon us.

Eternal and merciful judge,
both in life and when we come to die,
let us not fall away from you.

Holy God,
holy and mighty,
holy and merciful Saviour,
do not abandon us to the bitterness of eternal death.

General
Almighty God,   0C15
long-suffering and of great goodness:
I confess to you,
I confess with my whole heart
my neglect and forgetfulness of your commandments,
my wrong doing, thinking, and speaking;
the hurts I have done to others,
and the good I have left undone.
O God, forgive me, for I have sinned against you;
and raise me to newness of life;
through Jesus Christ our Lord. Amen.

General
My God, for love of you   0C16
I desire to hate and forsake all sins
by which I have ever displeased you;
and I resolve by the help of your grace
to commit them no more;
and to avoid all opportunities of sin.
Help me to do this,
through Jesus Christ our Lord. Amen.

Kyrie Confessions

Notwithstanding any other provision made in the ASB, short sentences may be inserted between the petitions of the Kyrie, suitable for particular seasons or themes. The insertion of such sentences may replace any form of confession, provided that the sentences are of a penitential character, and are followed by an authorized form of absolution. Some examples follow.

Spirit

You raise the dead to life in the Spirit: 8C17
Lord, have mercy.
Lord, have mercy.

You bring pardon and peace to the broken in heart:
Christ, have mercy.
Christ, have mercy.

You make one by your Spirit the torn and divided:
Lord, have mercy.
Lord, have mercy.

Word

May your loving mercy come to me, O Lord,   11C18
and your salvation according to your word:
Lord, have mercy.
Lord, have mercy.

Your word is a lantern to my feet and a light to my path:
Christ, have mercy.
Christ, have mercy.

O let your mercy come to me that I may live,
for your law is my delight:
Lord, have mercy.
Lord, have mercy.

Word

God be gracious to us and bless us,   11C19
and make your face shine upon us:
Lord, have mercy.
Lord, have mercy.

May your ways be known on the earth,
your saving power among the nations:
Christ, have mercy.
Christ, have mercy.

You, Lord, have made known your salvation,
and reveal your justice in the sight of the nations:
Lord, have mercy.
Lord, have mercy.

City

Lord Jesus, you wept over the sins of your city.

13C20

On our city:
Lord, have mercy.
Lord, have mercy.

Lord Jesus, you heal the wounds of sin and division, jealousy
    and bitterness.
On us:
Christ, have mercy.
Christ, have mercy.

Lord Jesus, you bring pardon and peace to the sinner.
Grant us peace:
Lord, have mercy.
Lord, have mercy.

D Absolutions

The forms of absolution in this section are authorized as an appendix to *A Service of the Word* under Canon B 2: see page 13. If possible, an absolution should be chosen which reflects the style, in language and length, of the confession. This is likely to be where the last number of both confession and absolution is the same. 'Us' and 'our' are said by those who are not ordained priest: words in italics indicate the points where changes may be necessary.

May the God of all healing and forgiveness 2D1
draw *us* to himself,
that *we* may behold the glory of his Son,
the Word made flesh,
and be cleansed from all *our* sins
through Jesus Christ our Lord. **Amen.**

May almighty God, 2D2
who sent his Son into the world to save sinners,
bring *you* his pardon and peace, now and for ever. **Amen.**

May the Father of all mercies 5D3
cleanse *us* from *our* sins,
and restore *us* in his service
to the praise and glory of his name,
through Jesus Christ our Lord. **Amen.**

God who is both power and love, 6D4
forgive *you* and free *you* from *your* sins,
heal and strengthen *you* by his Spirit,
and raise *you* to new life in Christ our Lord. **Amen.**

May the Father forgive *us* 9D5
by the death of his Son
and strengthen *us*
to live in the power of the Spirit
all *our* days. **Amen.**

The Lord enrich *you* with his grace, 10D6
and nourish *you* with his blessing;
the Lord defend *you* in trouble and keep *you* from all evil;
the Lord accept *your* prayers,
and absolve *you* from *your* offences,
for the sake of Jesus Christ, our Saviour. **Amen.**

May God who loved the world so much
that he sent his Son to be our Saviour
forgive *us our* sins
and make *us* holy to serve him in the world,
through Jesus Christ our Lord. **Amen.**

13D7

May God our Father forgive *us our* sins,
and bring *us* to the fellowship of his table
with his saints for ever. **Amen.**

16D8

May the God of love
bring *us* back to himself,
forgive *us our* sins,
and assure *us* of his eternal love
in Jesus Christ our Lord. **Amen.**

17D9

The almighty and merciful Lord
grant *you* pardon and forgiveness of all *your* sins,
time for amendment of life,
and the grace and strength of the Holy Spirit. **Amen**.

0D10

Almighty God,
who in Jesus Christ has given us
a kingdom that cannot be destroyed,
forgive *us* our sins,
open *our* eyes to God's truth,
strengthen *us* to do God's will
and give *us* the joy of his kingdom,
through Jesus Christ our Lord. **Amen.**

0D11

May almighty God have mercy on *us*,
forgive *us our* sins,
and bring *us* to everlasting life,
through Jesus Christ our Lord. **Amen.**

0D12

God, the Father of mercies,
has reconciled the world to himself
through the death and resurrection of his Son, Jesus Christ,
not counting our trespasses against us,
but sending his Holy Spirit
to shed abroad his love among us.
By the ministry of reconciliation
entrusted by Christ to his Church,

0D13

receive his pardon and peace
to stand before him in his strength alone,
this day and evermore. **Amen.**

E THE MINISTRY OF THE WORD

Samples of new lectionary material

Around the main festivals, the use of one of the authorized lectionaries will encourage the churches to be telling the same story. The early church used this principle of **thematic reading** for festivals, and we can see this reflected in the traditional readings for Lent and Easter, Advent, Christmas and Epiphany. Outside that time, in 'ordinary time', it can be acknowledged that churches have differing needs, which may be met by different readings.

This sample lectionary is designed to show how provision could be made for the semi-continuous reading of scripture in short units of five or six weeks, which could be substituted for other authorized readings in 'ordinary time'. The principle here is the same as that for Lectionary 2 in *The Promise of His Glory*, where a further selection of similar material may be found. It attempts to provide examples of story material suitable both for family services and for adult worship. There is also a sample of thematic material especially suitable for children.

Note 5 in *A Service of the Word* (see page 16) gives permission for sets of readings such as these to be used outside the periods from Advent 3 to Epiphany 1 and from Palm Sunday to Trinity Sunday, but not when the service is combined with the Eucharist.

NOTES
1 The controlling reading, in bold and usually with a title attached, must always be read in some form.

2 Where necessary these units may be shortened or amended, to fit the period available, and to avoid having the same or similar readings at the point at which the church moves to one of these units from the ASB or another lectionary, or from one unit to another.

3 The standard form of some of the readings is a short one, often with verses omitted so that an extended story can be included within one reading. The chapter and verse numbers in brackets indicate a

longer version which may be the basis for teaching or group study, or may be read if there is sufficient time, or be the subject of dramatic or visual presentation. Long readings may also be broken up by teaching or songs.

4 Many of the collects in the ASB were chosen to illustrate the theme of the readings and will not be suitable for this lectionary. Other collects should be chosen. The purpose of the collect is to draw people together in prayer and to prepare for what is to follow, but not necessarily to reflect a theme.

5 Some introductory sentences are provided with each unit. Other sentences may also be used.

6 Churches may also wish to design their own reading scheme for a limited period of the year in 'ordinary time', on similar principles. Where they do so they should ensure that an adequate amount of scripture is chosen; that justice is done to the balance of the book and to the general teaching of scripture; and that the PCC or an appropriate lay group is involved in the decisions.

Old Testament	New Testament	Gospel	Psalm

1 Jacob

In the womb Jacob grasped his brother's heel; as an adult he wrestled with God.
Hosea 12.3

Blessed is he whose help is the God of Jacob.
Psalm 146.5

	Old Testament	New Testament	Gospel	Psalm
1	**Gen 25.19-34** *(Jacob and Esau 1)*	Rom 9.10-16	Luke 1.26-33	Ps 105.4-11
2	**Gen 27.11-19** (1-45) *(Jacob and Esau 2)*	2 Tim 1.3-7	Mark 3.31-35	Ps 50.16-end
3	**Gen 28.10-22** (27.46 – 28.22) *(Jacob's journey to Bethel)*	Rev 7.9-12	John 1.47-51	Ps 119.17-24
4	**Gen 29.15-30** (29.1-30) *(Jacob marries)*	Eph 5.25-33	Luke 15.11-14	Ps 146.3-9
5	**Gen 32.22-33** (32.3 – 33.16) *(Reconciliation)*	2 Cor 5.16-20	Matt 5.3-9	Ps 34.3-8

Old Testament	New Testament	Gospel	Psalm

2 Joseph

All things work together for good to those who love God, who are called according to his purpose.
Romans 8.28

God sent me before you to preserve life.
Genesis 45.5

	Old Testament	New Testament	Gospel	Psalm
1	**Gen 37.3-13,18-24** (37.1-end) *(An unhappy family)*	Rom 8.28-32	John 7.1-6	Ps 57.1 7
2	**Gen 39.1-15,20-end** (39,40.1-14) *(Joseph in trouble)*	Rom 8.33-end	Matt 5.27-30	Ps 138
3	**Gen 41.15-25, 29-40** (41) *(Joseph, Governor of Egypt)*	Rom 12.6 13	Luke 12.27-31	Ps 105.16-23
4	**Gen 42.6-25,29-30, 35-36** (42,43) *(Joseph meets his brothers)*	Rom 13.1-5	Matt 21.28-32	Ps 103.1-12
5	**Gen 44.1-4,14-18, 24 – 45.9** (44,45) *(Joseph reveals his identity)*	Rom 13.8-11	Matt 5.23-26	Ps 32
6	**Gen 46.1-7,28-30; 47.7-11** (46.1-7,28-34; 47.1-12) *(A reunited family)*	Rom 15.1-6	Matt 6.25-27	Ps 126
7	**Gen 50.1-15** *(The death of Jacob)*	Rom 16.25-27	Luke 10.23-24	Ps 128

3 People Jesus met

Everyone who calls out to the Lord for help will be saved.
Romans 10.13

'Sir, we want to see Jesus.'
John 12.21

	Old Testament	New Testament	Gospel	Psalm
1	1 Kings 13.3-8	Acts 14.8-11	**Luke 6.6-11** *(The man with the paralyzed hand)*	Ps 6
2	2 Kings 5.9-15	Hebrews 11.1-3,6	**Luke 7.1-10** *(The Roman centurion)*	Ps 103.1-8
3	Hosea 2.19-end	James 2.1-4	**Luke 7.36-50** *(Simon the Pharisee)*	Ps 103.6-18

Old Testament	New Testament	Gospel	Psalm
4 Daniel 4.24-27	2 Peter 2.17-end	**Luke 8.26-39** *(Legion)*	Ps 107.10-22
5 Ezekiel 3.1-3	2 Tim 3.14-end	**Luke 10.38-42** *(Martha and Mary)*	Ps 84
6 Amos 8.11-13	Rev 22.1,2	**John 4.5-26** (-34) *(The Samaritan woman)*	Ps 65
7 Jonah 2.2-9	James 5.13-15	**John 5.1-18** *(The man at the pool)*	Ps 41
8 Isaiah 42.6-9	2 Cor 4.1-6	**John 9.1-12** (-end) *(The man born blind)*	Ps 146

4 Time for a feast

Taste and see how good the Lord is!
Psalm34.8

Happy are those who have been invited to the wedding-feast of the Lamb!
Revelation 19.9

1 Isaiah 55.1-2,10-11	Rom 5.6-11	**Luke 5.27-32** (-35) *(Matthew holds a party)*	Ps 49
2 Exodus 16.12-18	2 Cor 9.6-10	**Luke 9.10-17** *(Feeding of the 5000)*	Ps 104.24-end
3 Proverbs 25.6,7	1 Peter 5.5-7	**Luke 14.1-14** *(Dinner at a Pharisee's house)*	Ps 113
4 Proverbs 9.1-6	Phil 3.18-end	**Luke 14.15-24** *(God's great feast)*	Ps 23
5 Genesis 3.2-6	Acts 16.25-34	**Luke 19.1-10** *(Tea and forgiveness)*	Ps 32.1-7
6 Exodus 12.21-28	1 Cor 10.16,17	**Luke 22.7-20** *(The Last Supper)*	Ps 69.13-22

F AFFIRMATIONS OF FAITH

These were authorized by the General Synod in November 1993.

Notwithstanding the provisions in Rites A or B of *The Alternative Service Book* 1980, the Apostles' Creed or the Athanasian Creed in an authorized form may be used in place of the Nicene Creed.

The following adaptations of the historic creeds and other affirmations of faith may only be used in non-statutory services or in an authorized Service of the Word. On any occasion, suitable words of introduction or conclusion (such as those indicated) to the creed or affirmation of faith may be used.

The Nicene Creed may be used responsively as follows:

OF1

We believe in one God,
the Father, the almighty,
maker of heaven and earth,
of all that is,
seen and unseen.

We believe in one Lord, Jesus Christ,
the only Son of God,
eternally begotten of the Father,
God from God, Light from Light,
true God from true God,
begotten, not made,
of one Being with the Father.
Through him all things were made.
For us men and for our salvation
he came down from heaven;
by the power of the Holy Spirit
he became incarnate of the Virgin Mary, and was made man.
For our sake he was crucified under Pontius Pilate;
he suffered death and was buried.
On the third day he rose again
in accordance with the scriptures;
he ascended into heaven

and is seated at the right hand of the Father.
He will come again in glory
to judge the living and the dead,
and his kingdom will have no end.

We believe in the Holy Spirit,
the Lord, the giver of life,
who proceeds from the Father and the Son.
With the Father and the Son he is worshipped and glorified.
He has spoken through the Prophets.

We believe in one holy, catholic and apostolic Church.
We acknowledge one baptism for the forgiveness of sins.
We look for the resurrection of the dead,
and the life of the world to come. Amen.

In addition to the Nicene Creed, the Apostle's Creed and the
Athanasian Creed, the following creeds and affirmations of faith are
also authorized.

Do you believe and trust in God the Father,
who made all things?
We believe and trust in him.

Do you believe and trust in his Son Jesus Christ,
who redeemed the world?
We believe and trust in him.

Do you believe and trust in his Holy Spirit,
who gives life to the people of God?
We believe and trust in him.

This is the faith of the Church.
This is our faith.
We believe and trust in one God,
Father, Son and Holy Spirit. Amen.

Do you believe and trust in God the Father,
who made all things?
I believe in God, the Father almighty,
creator of heaven and earth.

Do you believe and trust in his Son Jesus Christ,
who redeemed the world?
I believe in Jesus Christ, his only Son, our Lord.
He was conceived by the power of the Holy Spirit

and born of the Virgin Mary.
He suffered under Pontius Pilate,
was crucified, died and was buried.
He descended to the dead.
On the third day he rose again.
He ascended into heaven,
and is seated at the right hand of the Father.
He will come again to judge the living and the dead.

Do you believe and trust in the Holy Spirit,
who gives life to the people of God?
I believe in the Holy Spirit,
the holy catholic Church,
the communion of saints,
the forgiveness of sins,
the resurrection of the body,
and the life everlasting.

This is the faith of the Church.
This is our faith.
We believe in one God,
Father, Son and Holy Spirit.

We proclaim the Church's faith in Jesus Christ: 2F4

We believe and declare that our Lord Jesus Christ,
the Son of God, is both divine and human.

God, of the being of the Father,
the only Son from before time began;
human from the being of his mother, born in the world.

Fully God and fully human;
human in both mind and body.

As God he is equal to the Father,
as human he is less than the Father.

Although he is both divine and human
he is not two beings but one Christ.

One, not by turning God into flesh,
but by taking humanity into God.

Truly one, not by mixing humanity with Godhead,
but by being one person.

For as mind and body form one human being
so the one Christ is both divine and human.

The Word became flesh and lived among us;
we have seen his glory,
the glory of the only Son from the Father,
full of grace and truth.

from the Athanasian Creed

0F5

We believe in God the Father,
God almighty, by whose plan
earth and heaven sprang to being,
all created things began.
We believe in Christ the Saviour,
Son of God in human frame,
virgin-born, the child of Mary
upon whom the Spirit came.

Christ, who on the cross forsaken,
like a lamb to slaughter led,
suffered under Pontius Pilate,
he descended to the dead.
We believe in Jesus risen,
heaven's king to rule and reign,
to the Father's side ascended
till as judge he comes again.

We believe in God the Spirit;
in one church, below, above:
saints of God in one communion,
one in holiness and love.
So by faith, our sins forgiven,
Christ our Saviour, Lord and Friend,
we shall rise with him in glory
to the life that knows no end.

(May be sung to any 87 87 or 87 87D tune. Recommended tunes are Lux Eoi (Arthur
Sullivan), Alleluia (SS Wesley), Abbot's Leigh (Cyril Taylor). Churches in membership
of the Christian Copyright Licensing scheme should record use on their return.)

Let us affirm our faith in Jesus Christ the Son of God:

2F6

Though he was divine,
he did not cling to equality with God,
but made himself nothing.
Taking the form of a slave,
he was born in human likeness.
He humbled himself,
and was obedient to death –

even the death of the cross.
**Therefore God has raised him on high,
and given him the name above every name:
that at the name of Jesus
every knee should bow,
and every voice proclaim that Jesus Christ is Lord,
to the glory of God the Father. Amen.**
Philippians 2.9-11

Let us declare our faith   6F7
in the resurrection of our Lord Jesus Christ:

**Christ died for our sins
in accordance with the scriptures;
he was buried;
he was raised to life on the third day
in accordance with the scriptures;
afterwards he appeared to his followers,
and to all the apostles:
this we have received,
and this we believe. Amen.**
1 Corinthians 15.3 7

We say together in faith: 0F8

**Holy, holy, holy
is the Lord God almighty,
who was, and is, and is to come.**

We believe in God the Father,
who created all things:
**for by his will they were created
and have their being.**

We believe in God the Son,
who was slain:
**for with his blood,
he purchased us for God,
from every tribe and language,
from every people and nation.**

We believe in God the Holy Spirit –
**the Spirit and the Bride say, 'Come!'
Even so come, Lord Jesus! Amen.**
Revelation 4.8,11; 5.9; 22.17

Let us declare our faith in God:

We believe in God the Father,
from whom every family
in heaven and on earth is named.

We believe in God the Son,
who lives in our hearts through faith,
and fills us with his love.

We believe in God the Holy Spirit,
who strengthens us
with power from on high.

We believe in one God;
Father, Son and Holy Spirit. Amen.
Ephesians 3

This affirmation of commitment may be used after an authorized
creed or affirmation of faith:

Will you continue in the apostles' teaching and fellowship,
in the breaking of bread, and in the prayers?
With the help of God, I will.

Will you persevere in resisting evil, and,
whenever you fall into sin, repent and return to the Lord?
With the help of God, I will.

Will you proclaim by word and example
the good news of God in Christ?
With the help of God, I will.

Will you seek and serve Christ in all people,
loving your neighbour as yourself?
With the help of God, I will.

Will you acknowledge Christ's authority over human society,
by prayer for the world and its leaders,
by defending the weak, and by seeking peace and justice?
With the help of God, I will.

G-J   **PRAYERS**

The forms of prayer in Section H may replace the intercessions in the Holy Communion, or be used in the prayer section of *A Service of the Word*, or after the third collect in Morning or Evening Prayer.

The forms in Section H are also intended as models for those constructing their own prayers. It may help to note the pattern generally used here, which is designed to help those who do not have the full text of the prayers in front of them. The prayers may be introduced with a form such as, 'We pray to the Lord, saying. . .' (the words of the response). Alternatively there may be a series of short prayers or biddings, followed by silence and one of the standard forms of response from section G.

G Responses, endings, introductions to the Lord's Prayer

Responses

In faith we pray:
we pray to you our God.
    0G1

Lord, have mercy.
Lord, have mercy.
    0G2

Lord, in your mercy:
hear our prayer.
    0G3

Hear us:
hear us, good Lord.
    0G4

Lord, hear us:
Lord, graciously hear us.
    0G5

For. . . let us pray to the Father:
in Christ our Lord.
    0G6

Jesus, Lord of. . . (*a phrase which can be varied*)
in your mercy, hear us.
    0G7

Father, Lord of. . . (*a phrase which can be varied*)   0G8
in your mercy, hear us.

Endings for the intercessions

The congregational ending of the Rite A Holy Communion
intercessions (**'Merciful Father. . .'**), and the endings of the
intercessions that follow, may be replaced by one of these standard
endings:

Lord of the Church: 0G9
hear our prayer,
and make us one in heart and mind
to serve you with joy for ever. Amen.

God of mercy: 0G10
you know us and love us
and hear our prayer:
keep us in the eternal fellowship
of Jesus Christ our Saviour. Amen.

*The last paragraph in Section 21 of the Rite A Holy Communion
intercessions ('Rejoicing. . . love') may be replaced by one of the
following, which give a weightier ending, and look forward to the
communion.*

Bring us all to your heavenly city, to the joyful gathering of thousands   0G11
of angels, to the assembly of your first-born, to the spirits of good
people made perfect, to Jesus the mediator of the new covenant and to
the sprinkled blood that promises peace.
Merciful Father. . .
Hebrews 12.22-24

Hasten, Lord, the day when people will come from east and west,   0G12
from north and south, and sit at table in your kingdom and we shall
see your Son in his glory.
Merciful Father. . .
Luke 13.29

Lord and all-just judge, grant to us and to all those who long for your   0G13
appearing the crown of righteousness on the great day of your
coming.
Merciful Father. . .

Fill our hunger with the good food that lasts, the bread of God which   0G14
comes down from heaven and gives life to the world, with Jesus your
Son.
Merciful Father. . .
John 6.33

Introductions to the Lord's Prayer _____

Let us now pray with confidence to the Father, in the words our   0G15
Saviour taught us.

Let us pray for the coming of God's kingdom in the words our Saviour   0G16
taught us.

We praise the Father, and pray in the words of Christ himself.   0G17

Lord, remember us in your kingdom, as we pray in the words you gave   0G18
us.

Jesus taught us to call God our Father, so we have the courage to say. . .   0G19

(*not at the eucharist*) Gathering our prayers and praises into one, let   0G20
us pray as our Saviour taught us.

H Responsive intercessions and litanies

Advent

In joyful expectation of his coming
we pray to Jesus, saying,
Maranatha.[1]
Come, Lord Jesus.

1H1

Come to your Church as Lord and Judge.
We pray for. . .
Help us to live in the light of your coming
and give us a longing for your rule.
Maranatha.
Come, Lord Jesus.

Come to your world as King of the nations.
We pray for. . .
Before you rulers will stand in silence.
Maranatha.
Come, Lord Jesus.

Come to your people with a message of victory and peace.
We pray for. . .
Give us the victory over death, temptation and evil.
Maranatha.
Come, Lord Jesus.

Come to us as Saviour and Comforter.
We pray for. . .
Break into our failure and distress
and set us free to serve you for ever.
Maranatha.
Come, Lord Jesus.

Come to us from heaven with power and great glory,
to lift us up to meet you,
with all your saints and angels,
and to live with you for ever.
Maranatha.
Come, Lord Jesus.

Christmas

Christ, who was born in a stable,
give courage to all who are homeless;
in your mercy:
hear our prayer.

2H2

[1] This Aramaic word means 'Our Lord, come.'

Christ, who fled into Egypt,
give comfort to all refugees;
in your mercy:
hear our prayer.

Christ, who fasted in the desert,
give relief to all who are starving;
in your mercy:
hear our prayer.

Christ, who hung in agony on the cross,
give strength to all who suffer;
in your mercy:
hear our prayer.

Christ, who died to save us,
give peace to all who seek pardon.
God of mercy:
**you know us and love us
and hear our prayer:
keep us in the eternal fellowship
of Jesus Christ our Saviour. Amen.**

Christmas

To us a child is born, to us a son is given.
Wonderful Counsellor,
give your wisdom to the rulers of the nations.
Lord, in your mercy:
hear our prayer.

Mighty God,
make the whole world know
that the government is on your shoulders.
Lord, in your mercy:
hear our prayer.

Everlasting Father,
establish your reign of justice and righteousness.
Lord, in your mercy:
hear our prayer.

Prince of peace,
bring in the endless kingdom of your peace.
Lord, in your mercy:
hear our prayer.

2H3

Almighty Lord,
hear our prayer,
and fulfil your purposes in us,
as you accomplished your will
in our Lord Jesus Christ. **Amen.**
Isaiah 9.6

Christmas [2]

Father, in this holy night your Son our Saviour was born as a 2H4
human child. Renew your Church as the Body of Christ.
Lord, in your mercy:
hear our prayer.

In this holy night Christians the world over are celebrating his birth.
Open our hearts that he may be born in us today.
Lord, in your mercy:
hear our prayer.

In this holy night there was no room for your Son in the inn.
Protect with your love those who have no home and all who live in
poverty.
Lord, in your mercy:
hear our prayer.

In this holy night Mary in the pain of labour brought your Son
to birth. Hold in your hand (. . . *and*) all who are in any kind of pain or
distress today.
Lord, in your mercy:
hear our prayer.

In this holy night your Christ came as a light shining in the darkness.
Bring comfort to (. . . *and*) all who suffer in the sadness of our world.
Lord, in your mercy:
hear our prayer.

In this holy night shepherds in the fields heard good tidings of joy.
Give us grace to preach the gospel of Christ's redemption.
Lord, in your mercy:
hear our prayer.

In this holy night the angels sang 'Peace to God's people on earth'.
Strengthen those who work for your peace and justice in (. . . *and in*)
all the world.
Lord, in your mercy:
hear our prayer.

---

[2] When used during the day the words 'on this holy day' are substituted for 'in this holy night'. Insertions
into this intercession should be very brief in order not to unbalance the structure of this prayer.

In this holy night strangers found the holy family, and saw the baby
lying in the manger. Bless our homes and all whom we love, and help
us to live as the holy family.
Lord, in your mercy:
hear our prayer.

In this holy night heaven is come down to earth and earth is raised
to heaven. Keep in safety (. . . *and*) all those who have gone through
death in the hope of heaven.
Lord, in your mercy:
hear our prayer.

In this holy night angels and shepherds worshipped at the manger
throne. Receive the worship we offer in fellowship with Blessed Mary
and all the saints.
Merciful Father,
accept these prayers
for the sake of your Son,
our Saviour Jesus Christ. Amen.

Lent

We pray to the Lord for courage to give up distractions and to give
ourselves to him this Lent, saying:

4H5

Lord, meet us in the silence:
give us strength and hear our prayer.
Give your Church the courage to give up her preoccupation with
herself and to give more time to your mission in the world.
(*We pray for N our bishop and . . .*)

May the blood and water flowing from the side of Jesus bring
forgiveness to your people and help us to face the cost of proclaiming
salvation.

Lord, meet us in the silence:
give us strength and hear our prayer.

Give your world the courage to give up war, bitterness and hatred, and
to seek peace.
(*We pray for . . .*)

May the shoulders of the risen Jesus, once scourged by soldiers,
bear the burden of political and military conflict in our world.

Lord, meet us in the silence:
give us strength and hear our prayer.

Give us the courage to give up quarrels, strife and jealousy
in our families, neighbourhoods and communities.
(We pray for. . .)

May the presence of the risen Jesus,
his body once broken and now made whole,
bring peace and direction as we live with one another.

Lord, meet us in the silence:
give us strength and hear our prayer.

Give us the courage to give up our selfishness as we live for others,
and to give time, care and comfort to the sick.
(We pray for. . .)

May the wounded hands of Jesus bring his healing touch,
and the light of his presence fill their rooms.

Lord, meet us in the silence:
give us strength and hear our prayer.

Give us the courage to give up our fear of death
and to rejoice with those who have died in faith.
(Especially we hold. . . in our minds.)

May the feet of the risen Lord Jesus, once nailed to the cross,
walk alongside the dying and bereaved in their agony,
and walk with us and all your Church
through death to the gate of glory.

Lord, meet us in the silence:
give us strength and hear our prayer,
here and in eternity. Amen.

Cross
Father (*in this week of the passion*),
Simon from Cyrene was forced to carry the cross for your Son.
Give us grace willingly to lift heavy loads from those we meet
and to stand with those condemned to die.
Lord, hear us:
Lord, graciously hear us.

Your Son watched the soldiers gamble to share his clothes.
Look with forgiveness
on those whose hearts are hardened by their work,
and those who know not what they do.
Lord, hear us:
Lord, graciously hear us.

The thief looked for the coming of the kingdom,
and heard Christ say 'Today you shall be with me.'
Give pardon and hope, healing and peace
to all who look death in the face.
Lord, hear us:
Lord, graciously hear us.

In Mary and John your Son created a new family at the cross,
Fill us with your love,
and give all your children a secure hope for the future.
Lord, hear us:
Lord, graciously hear us.

The centurion was astonished to recognise your Son in the
    crucified Messiah.
Open the eyes of those who do not know you
to grasp in your Son the meaning of life and death.
Lord, hear us:
Lord, graciously hear us.

Nicodemus came to take your Son's body away.
Give hope and faith to the dying and bereaved,
gentleness to those who minister to them,
and courage to those whose faith is secret.
Lord, hear us:
Lord, graciously hear us.

Simon and Nicodemus, Mary and John
were drawn into the life of your church in Jerusalem.
Bring into your Church today a varied company of people,
to walk with Christ in the way of his passion,
and to find your salvation in the victory of his cross.
Lord of the Church:
hear our prayer,
and make us one in heart and mind
to serve you with joy for ever. Amen.

Resurrection, Heaven, Glory, Transfiguration, Death
(In joy and hope let us pray to the Father saying:
in Christ our Lord.)

6H7

That our risen Saviour may fill us with the joy of his glorious and
life-giving resurrection...
let us pray to the Father:
in Christ our Lord.

That isolated and persecuted churches may find fresh strength in the
good news of Easter. . .
let us pray to the Father:
in Christ our Lord.

That God may grant us humility to be subject to one another in
Christian love. . .
let us pray to the Father:
in Christ our Lord.

That he may provide for those who lack food, work, or shelter. . .
let us pray to the Father:
in Christ our Lord.

That by his power war and famine may cease through all the world. . .
let us pray to the Father:
in Christ our Lord.

That he may reveal the light of his presence to the sick, the weak and
the dying, to comfort and strengthen them. . .
let us pray to the Father:
in Christ our Lord.

That he may send the fire of the Holy Spirit upon his people,
so that we may bear faithful witness to his resurrection,
let us pray to the Father:
in Christ our Lord. Amen.

Resurrection

We pray to Jesus who is present with us to eternity, saying,
Jesus, Lord of life:
in your mercy, hear us.

6H8

Jesus, light of the world,
bring the light and peace of your gospel
to the nations. . .
Jesus, Lord of life:
in your mercy, hear us.

Jesus, bread of life,
give food to the hungry. . .
and nourish us all with your word.
Jesus, Lord of life:
in your mercy, hear us.

Jesus, our way, our truth, our life,
be with us and all who follow you in the way. . .
deepen our appreciation of your truth,

and fill us with your life.
Jesus, Lord of life:
in your mercy, hear us.

Jesus, Good Shepherd who gave your life for the sheep,
recover the straggler, bind up the injured,
strengthen the sick
and lead the healthy and strong to play.
Jesus, Lord of life:
in your mercy, hear us.

Jesus, the resurrection and the life,
we give you thanks
for all who have lived and believed in you. . .
raise us with them to eternal life.
Jesus, Lord of life:
in your mercy, hear us,
accept our prayers, and be with us always. Amen.

Heaven, Death, Funerals and Memorials
(In our grief we pray,
Lord of mercy:
Lord, hear us.)

6H9

Almighty God,
you bring your chosen people together in one communion,
in the body of your Son, Jesus Christ our Lord.
We rejoice in your light and your peace
for your whole Church in heaven and on earth.
Lord of mercy:
Lord, hear us.

* Give to all who mourn a sure confidence in your loving care,
that we may cast all our sorrow on you,
and know the consolation of your love.
Lord of mercy:
Lord, hear us.

Give your faithful people pardon and peace,
that we may be cleansed from all our sins,
and serve you with a quiet mind.
Lord of mercy:
Lord, hear us.

* This paragraph may be omitted

Give us strength to meet the days ahead
in the joyful expectation of eternal life with those you love.
Lord of mercy:
Lord, hear us.

Give to us who are still in our pilgrimage,
and who walk as yet by faith,
your Holy Spirit to lead us
in holiness and righteousness all our days.
Lord of mercy:
Lord, hear us.

Give us grace to entrust *N* to your unfailing love
which sustained *him/her* in this life.
Lord of mercy:
Lord, hear us.

May all who have been made one with Christ
in his death and in his resurrection
die to sin and rise to newness of life.
Lord of mercy:
Lord, hear us.

Ascension
Let us seek the Father's blessing and the gifts of the Spirit,   7H10
praying through Christ our Lord:

Lord Jesus Christ, pray to the Father.
Lord, send us your Spirit.

Jesus Christ, great high priest, ever living to intercede for us,
pray for the Church, your broken body in the world. . .
Lord Jesus Christ, pray to the Father.
Lord, send us your Spirit.

Jesus Christ, king of righteousness, enthroned at the right hand of the
    Majesty on high,
pray for the world, and subject it to your gentle rule. . .
Lord Jesus Christ, pray to the Father.
Lord, send us your Spirit.

Jesus Christ, son of man, drawing humanity into the life of God,
pray for your brothers and sisters in need, distress or sorrow. . .
Lord Jesus Christ, pray to the Father.
Lord, send us your Spirit.

Jesus Christ, pioneer of our salvation, bringing us to glory
through your death and resurrection,
surround with your saints and angels those who have died trusting
   your promises.
Lord Jesus Christ, pray to the Father.
Lord, send us your Spirit.

Jesus Christ, Lord over all things,
ascending far above the heavens and filling the universe,
pray for us who receive the gifts you give for work in your service.
Lord Jesus Christ, pray to the Father.
Lord, send us your Spirit.

Jesus Christ, keep the Church
in the unity of the Spirit and in the bond of your peace,
and bring the whole created order to worship at your feet;
for you are alive and reign with the Father and the Holy Spirit,
one God, now and for ever. **Amen.**

Spirit, Pentecost, Gifts, Healing, Baptism and Confirmation
(We pray to God the Holy Spirit, saying: 8H11
Holy Spirit, come upon us.)

Come, Holy Spirit, creator, and renew the earth:
Holy Spirit, come upon us.

Come, Holy Spirit, counsellor,
and touch our lips that we may proclaim your word:
Holy Spirit, come upon us.

Come, Holy Spirit, power from on high;
make us channels of peace and ministers of healing:
Holy Spirit, come upon us.

Come, Holy Spirit, breath of God,
give life to the dry bones around us,
and make us a living people, holy and free:
Holy Spirit, come upon us.

Come, Holy Spirit, wisdom and truth;
strengthen us to be bold in faith:
Holy Spirit, come upon us.

Spirit, Pentecost, Gifts, Healing, Baptism and Confirmation
(We pray that God's Holy Spirit may direct our lives, saying: 8H12
Come to bless us:
and fill us with your Spirit.)

'The fruit of the Spirit is
love, joy and peace' –
Father, we know that your world needs love and harmony.
Come to bless us:
and fill us with your Spirit.

'The fruit of the Spirit is
patience, kindness and goodness' –
Father, we know that our world is starved of love and care.
Come to bless us:
and fill us with your Spirit.

'The fruit of the Spirit is
faithfulness, gentleness and self-control' –
Father, we know that our world is short of truth and justice.
Come to bless us:
and fill us with your Spirit.

Send us out in his power
to live and work to your praise and glory;
through him to whom we belong,
Jesus Christ our Lord. Amen.
Galatians 5.22,23

Spirit, Pentecost, Gifts, Healing, Baptism and Confirmation
(We pray for God to fill us with his Spirit, saying: 8H13
Lord, come to bless us:
and fill us with your Spirit.)

Generous God, we thank you for the *power* of your Holy Spirit.
We ask that we may be strengthened to serve you better.
Lord, come to bless us:
and fill us with your Spirit.

We thank you for the *wisdom* of your Holy Spirit.
We ask you to help us understand better your will for us.
Lord, come to bless us:
and fill us with your Spirit.

We thank you for the *peace* of your Holy Spirit.
We ask you to keep us confident of your love
wherever you call us.
Lord, come to bless us:
and fill us with your Spirit.

We thank you for the *healing* of your Holy Spirit.
We ask you to bring reconciliation and wholeness

where there is division, sickness and sorrow.
Lord, come to bless us:
and fill us with your Spirit.

We thank you for the *gifts* of your Holy Spirit.
We ask you to equip us for the work which you have given us.
Lord, come to bless us:
and fill us with your Spirit.

We thank you for the *fruit* of your Holy Spirit.
We ask you to reveal in our lives the love of Jesus.
Lord, come to bless us:
and fill us with your Spirit.

We thank you for the *breath* of your Holy Spirit
given by the risen Lord.
We ask you to keep the whole Church, living and departed,
in the joy of eternal life.
Lord, come to bless us:
and fill us with your Spirit.

Generous God, you sent your Holy Spirit
upon your Messiah at the River Jordan,
and upon the disciples in the upper room.
In your mercy fill us with your Spirit:
hear our prayer,
and make us one in heart and mind
to serve you with joy for ever. Amen.

Trinity, Heaven, General

High and holy God,
robed in majesty,
Lord of heaven and earth,
we pray that you will bring
justice, faith and salvation to all peoples.
(Especially we pray. . .)
Lord, hear us:
Lord, graciously hear us.

You chose us in Christ to be your people
and to be the temple of your Holy Spirit;
we pray that you will fill your Church
with vision and hope.
(Especially we pray. . .)
Lord, hear us:
Lord, graciously hear us.

9H14

Your Spirit enables us to cry, 'Abba! Father!',
affirms that we are fellow-heirs with Christ
and pleads for us in our weakness;
we pray for all who are in need or distress.
(Especially we pray. . .)
Lord, hear us:
Lord, graciously hear us.

In the baptism and birth of Jesus,
you have opened heaven to us
and enabled us to share in your glory:
the joy of the Father, Son and Holy Spirit
from before the world was made.
(Especially we remember. . .)
May your whole church, living and departed,
come to a joyful resurrection in your city of light.
Lord, hear us:
Lord, graciously hear us.

[Handwritten annotation: You have made yourself known to us as Father, Son and Holy Spirit, may we rejoice in that truth and the hope you give us for this life & the life to come]

Harvest, Evangelism
(Let us pray to God, the Lord of the Harvest, that he will
bring to fruition all that he desires for his creation, saying:
Father, Lord of creation:
in your mercy, hear us.)

10H15

Lord of the Harvest,
when we lift up our eyes to perceive with Christ's eyes,
we see that the fields of the world are already white for harvest.
We pray for your Church,
that it may be spiritually equipped to reap the harvest of souls.
Father, Lord of creation:
in your mercy, hear us.

Lord of the Harvest,
the harvest is plentiful and the labourers are few,
but you make your Church fruitful with many ministries.
We pray for our parish,
that we may grasp the opportunities of the present time.
Father, Lord of creation:
in your mercy, hear us.

Lord of the Harvest,
you have created the universe by your eternal Word,
and have blessed humankind in making us stewards of the earth.
We pray for your world,
that we may share and conserve its resources,

and live in reverence for the creation and in harmony with
  one another.
Father, Lord of creation:
in your mercy, hear us.

Lord of the Harvest,
whose Son has promised that the Spirit will lead us into all truth,
we pray for the community in which you have set us,
for one another and for ourselves,
that we may bear the harvest of the Spirit
in love and joy and peace.
Father, Lord of creation:
in your mercy, hear us.

Lord of the Harvest,
though you have given the human race a rich land,
a land of streams and springs, wheat and barley,
vines and oil and honey,
we have made by sin a world of suffering and sorrow.
We pray for those who bear the weight of affliction,
that they may come to share the life of wholeness and plenty.
Father, Lord of creation:
in your mercy, hear us.

Lord of the Harvest,
your Christ, the first fruits of the resurrection,
will put in the sickle for the harvest of the dead at the end of time.
We pray that we may rejoice
with all who have died in the faith of Christ,
as he brings safely home all whom you have given him
and gathers us all to share together in the banquet of the age to come.

Merciful Father,
accept these prayers
for the sake of your Son
our Saviour Jesus Christ. Amen.

Word

Gracious God, fountain of all wisdom,
we pray for all Christian people;
for Bishop N,
and for those who teach and guard the faith. . .
May the word of Christ dwell richly in our hearts,
and knit us together in the bond of your love.
Hear us:
hear us, good Lord.

2 We pray for the leaders of the nations,
and for those in authority under them. . .
Give them the gift of your wisdom,
and a right discernment in all things.
Hear us:
hear us, good Lord.

3 We pray for our . . . *(city/town/village/community);*
for those who live and work here,
and for those who visit this place. . .
Speak your word of peace in our midst,
and help us to serve one another as Christ has served us.
Hear us:
hear us, good Lord.

4 We pray for those who do not believe,
and yet who long to know you, the very Word of life. . .
Open their ears to hear your voice,
and open their hearts to the knowledge of your love in Christ.
Hear us:
hear us, good Lord.

5 We pray for those bowed down with grief, fear or sickness,
especially. . .
May your living Word bring comfort and healing
to all those in need.
Hear us:
hear us, good Lord.

We give thanks for all those who have died in the faith of
Christ and we rejoice with (*N and*) all your saints,
trusting in the promise of your word fulfilled.
Lord of the Church:
hear our prayer,
and make us one in heart and mind
to serve you with joy for ever. Amen.
from Psalm 119

Church, Mission and Ministry, Unity
(We pray that Christ may be seen in the life of the Church, saying: 12H17
Jesus, Lord of the Church:
in your mercy, hear us.)

You have called us into the family
of those who are the children of God.
May our love for our brothers and sisters in Christ

be strengthened by your grace.
Jesus, Lord of the Church:
in your mercy, hear us.

You have called us to be a temple
where the Holy Spirit can dwell.
Give us clean hands and pure hearts
so that our lives will reflect your holiness.
Jesus, Lord of the Church:
in your mercy, hear us.

You have called us to be a light to the world
so that those in darkness come to you.
May our lives shine as a witness
to the saving grace you have given for all.
Jesus, Lord of the Church:
in your mercy, hear us.

You have called us to be members of your body,
so that when one suffers, all suffer together.
We ask for your comfort and healing power
to bring hope to those in distress.
Jesus, Lord of the Church:
in your mercy, hear us.

You have called us to be the Bride
where you, Lord, are the Bridegroom.
Prepare us for the wedding feast
where we will be united with you for ever.
Jesus, Lord of the Church:
hear our prayer,
and make us one in heart and mind
to serve you with joy for ever. Amen.

World
(We pray for God's faithfulness to be known in our world, saying: 13H18
faithful God:
glorify your name.)

In a world of change and hope,
of fear and adventure;
faithful God:
glorify your name.

Amidst human sin & failure,

In human rebellion and obedience,
in our seeking and our finding;
faithful God:
glorify your name.

In the common life of our society,
in prosperity and need;
faithful God:
glorify your name.

As your church proclaims your goodness
in words and action;
faithful God:
glorify your name.

Among our friends
and in our homes;
faithful God:
glorify your name.

In our times of joy,
in our days of sorrow;
faithful God:
glorify your name.

In our strengths and triumphs,
in our weakness and at our death;
faithful God:
glorify your name.

In your saints in glory
and on the day of Christ's coming;
faithful God:
glorify your name.

Family
(We pray for the family of the Church, for loving relationships,
and for the life of families around us, saying:
Jesus, Lord of love:
in your mercy, hear us.)

14H19

Jesus, born in poverty and soon *then* a refugee,
be with families today who are poor
and live in hunger and want. . .
Jesus, Lord of love:
in your mercy, hear us.

Jesus, who grew in wisdom and in favour with God and the people
in the family of Joseph the carpenter,
bring wisdom and the presence of God
into the work and growth of families today. . .
Jesus, Lord of love:
in your mercy, hear us.

Jesus, who blessed marriage in the wedding at Cana,
be with those preparing for marriage
and with those who come to the end of their resources. . .
Jesus, Lord of love:
in your mercy, hear us.

Jesus, who healed Peter's mother-in-law,
bring healing to hurt relationships and families today. . .
Jesus, Lord of love:
in your mercy, hear us.

Jesus, who on the cross said,
'Mother, behold your son',
provide today for those who lose their families,
the bereaved and childless, orphans and widows. . .
Jesus, Lord of love:
in your mercy, hear us.

Jesus, who on the seashore provided food for the disciples,
bring the whole Church on earth and in heaven
into your risen presence to eat at the eternal banquet.
Jesus, Lord of love:
in your mercy, hear us,
accept our prayers and be with us always. Amen.

Family
Sovereign Lord, your Son has revealed you as our heavenly Father,   14H20
from whom every family in heaven and on earth is named.
Father of all:
hear your children's prayer.

You have made your Church a spiritual family, a household of faith.
Through baptism we are reborn as the brothers and sisters of Christ.
Deepen our unity and fellowship in him.
Father of all:
hear your children's prayer.

You sent your Son to give his life as a ransom for the whole
    human family.
Give justice, peace and racial harmony to the world he died to save.
Father of all:
hear your children's prayer.

You gave your Son a share in the life of a family in Nazareth.
Help us to value our families, to be thankful for them,
and to live sensitively within them.
Father of all:
hear your children's prayer.

Your Son drew around him a company of friends.
Bring love and joy to all who are alone.
Help us all to find in the brothers and sisters of Christ a loving family.
Father of all:
hear your children's prayer.

You are the God of the dead as well as of the living.
In confidence we remember those of the household of faith who have
    gone before us.
Bring us with them to the joy of your home in heaven.
Father of all:
hear your children's prayer.

Saints
United in the company of all the faithful and looking for the coming   15H21
    of the kingdom,
let us offer our prayers to God, the source of all life and holiness.

Merciful Lord,
strengthen all Christian people by your Holy Spirit
that we may live as a royal priesthood and a holy nation
to the praise of Christ Jesus our Saviour.
Lord, have mercy.

Bless *N* our bishop, and all ministers of your Church,
that by faithful proclamation of your word
we may be built on the foundation of the apostles and prophets
into a holy temple in the Lord.
Lord, have mercy.

Empower us by the gift of your holy and life-giving Spirit
that we may be transformed into the likeness of Christ
from glory to glory.
Lord, have mercy.

Give to the world and its peoples
the peace that comes from above,
that they may find Christ's way of freedom and life.
Lord, have mercy.

Hold in your embrace all who witness to your love
in the service of the poor and needy;
all those who minister to the sick and dying;
and all who bring light to those in darkness.
Lord, have mercy.

Touch and heal all those whose lives are scarred by sin and pain,
that, raised from death to life in Christ,
their sorrow may be turned to eternal joy.
Lord, have mercy.

Remember in your mercy those gone before us
· who have been well-pleasing to you from eternity;
preserve us who live here in your faith,
guide us to your kingdom, and grant us your peace at all times.
Lord, have mercy.

Hasten the day when those who fear you in every nation
will come from east and west, from north and south,
and sit at table in your kingdom.
Lord, have mercy.

And so we give you thanks
for the whole company of your saints in glory,
with whom in fellowship we join our prayers and praises;
by your grace may we like them be made perfect in your love.
**Blessing and glory and wisdom,
thanksgiving and honour and power,
be to our God for ever and ever. Amen.**

Kingdom, Freedom, Reconciliation
(We pray for the coming of God's kingdom, saying: 16H22
Father, by your Spirit:
bring in your kingdom.)

You came in Jesus to bring good news to the poor,
sight to the blind, freedom to the captives,
and salvation to your people:
anoint us with your Spirit;
rouse us to work in his name.
Father, by your Spirit:
bring in your kingdom.

your people
Send us to bring help to the poor
and freedom to the oppressed.
Father, by your Spirit:
bring in your kingdom.

your people
Send us to tell the world
the good news of your healing love.
Father, by your Spirit:
bring in your kingdom.

your people
Send us to those who mourn,
to bring joy and gladness instead of grief.
Father, by your Spirit:
bring in your kingdom.

your people
Send us to proclaim that the time is here
for you to save your people.
Father, by your Spirit:
bring in your kingdom.

Lord of the Church: *Help us all to support your*
hear our prayer, *people in our prayer.*
and make us one in heart and mind
to serve you with joy for ever. Amen.
Isaiah 61.1-3

Evening Litany
(We pray to the Lord, saying: 0H23
in faith we pray:
we pray to you our God.)

That the rest of this day may be holy, peaceful
and full of your presence;
in faith we pray:
we pray to you our God.

That the work we have done and the people we have met today
may bring us closer to you;
in faith we pray:
we pray to you our God.

(That we may be forgiven our sins and failures;
in faith we pray:
we pray to you our God.)

That we may hear and respond to your call to peace and justice;
in faith we pray:
we pray to you our God.

That you will sustain the faith and hope
of those who are lonely, oppressed and anxious;
in faith we pray:
we pray to you our God.

That you will strengthen us in your service,
and fill our hearts with longing for your kingdom;
in faith we pray:
we pray to you our God.

God of mercy:
**you know us and love us
and hear our prayer:
keep us in the eternal fellowship
of Jesus Christ our Saviour. Amen.**

General

(We pray for strength to follow Jesus, saying:
Saviour, we hear your call:
help us to follow.)

Jesus said: 'If one of you wants to be great,
you must be everyone's servant.'
Saviour, we hear your call:
help us to follow.

Jesus said: 'Unless you change
and become humble like little children,
you can never enter the kingdom of heaven.'
Saviour, we hear your call:
help us to follow.

Jesus said: 'Happy are the humble;
they will receive what God has promised.'
Saviour, we hear your call:
help us to follow.

Jesus said: 'Be merciful as your Father is merciful;
love your enemies and do good to them.'
Saviour, we hear your call:
help us to follow.

Jesus said: 'Love one another, as I love you;
there is no greater love than this,
to lay down your life for your friends.'
Saviour, we hear your call:
help us to follow.

OH24

Jesus said: 'Go to people everywhere
and make them my disciples,
and I will be with you always, to the end of time.'
Saviour, we hear your call:
help us to follow.

God of mercy:
**you know us and love us
and hear our prayer:
keep us in the eternal fellowship
of Jesus Christ our Saviour. Amen.**

General

(We pray for God's grace, saying: OH25
Lord, receive our praise:
and hear our prayer.)

Lord God, through your grace we are your people:
through your Son you have redeemed us;
in your Spirit you have made us as your own.

We pray for. . . (*new Christians, the church*)
Make our hearts respond to your love.
Lord, receive our praise:
and hear our prayer.

We pray for. . . (*the world, society, the local community*)
Make our lives bear witness to your glory in the world.
Lord, receive our praise:
and hear our prayer.

We pray for. . . (*people in need, Christian service*)
Make our wills eager to obey, and our hands ready to heal.
Lord, receive our praise:
and hear our prayer.

We give thanks for. . .
Make our voices one with all your people in heaven and on earth.
Lord of the Church:
**hear our prayer,
and make us one in heart and mind
to serve you with joy for ever. Amen.**

General

(Let us pray to the Lord, saying: OH26
Lord, have mercy.)

For the peace that comes from God alone, for the unity of all peoples,
and for the salvation of our souls,
let us pray to the Lord.
Lord, have mercy.

For the Church of Christ, for *N* our Bishop, (*for. . .*),
and for the whole people of God,
let us pray to the Lord.
Lord, have mercy.

For the nations of the world, (*for. . .*),
for Elizabeth our Queen and for all in authority,
let us pray to the Lord.
Lord, have mercy.

For this city (*or town or village or community*), (*for. . .*),
for our neighbours and our friends,
let us pray to the Lord.
Lord, have mercy.

For the good earth which God has given us,
and for the wisdom and will to conserve it,
let us pray to the Lord.
Lord, have mercy.

For the aged and infirm, for the widowed and orphans,
for the sick and suffering, (*for. . .*), and for all in any need,
let us pray to the Lord.
Lord, have mercy.

For the poor and the oppressed, for the unemployed and the destitute,
for prisoners and captives,
and for all who remember and care for them,
let us pray to the Lord.
Lord, have mercy.

(*For. . .*), let us pray to the Lord.
Lord, have mercy.

For the dying, for those who mourn (*the death of . . .*),
for the faithful whom we entrust to the Lord in hope,
as we look forward to the day when we share the fulness of the
    resurrection,
let us pray to the Lord.
Lord, have mercy.

Rejoicing in the communion of (*. . . and of all*) the saints,
let us commend ourselves, and one another, and all our life, to God.

Silence is kept

For yours is the majesty, O Father, Son, and Holy Spirit;
yours is the kingdom and the power and the glory, now and for ever.
Amen.

General
*(Suitable for use in Section 3 of A Service of the Word; some of the
acclamations in Section L may also be suitable at this point.)*

O Lord, shew thy mercy upon us: OH27
and grant us thy salvation.

O Lord, save the Queen:
and mercifully hear us when we call upon thee.

Endue thy ministers with righteousness:
and make thy chosen people joyful.

O Lord, save thy people:
and bless thine inheritance.

Give peace in our time, O Lord:
**because there is none other that ruleth the world,
but only thou, O God.**

O God, make clean our hearts within us:
and take not thy Holy Spirit from us.

General
Make your ways known upon earth, Lord God: OH28
your saving power among all peoples.

Renew your Church in holiness:
and help us to serve you with joy.

Guide the leaders of this and every nation:
that justice may prevail throughout the world.

Let not the needy be forgotten:
nor the hope of the poor be taken away.

Make us instruments of your peace:
and let your glory be over all the earth.

General

In your glory, Lord, protect us by the power of your name: OH29
that we may be one as you are one.

We are in the world but not of it:
protect us from the evil one.

Give us your word and the full measure of your joy:
sanctify us by your truth.

May your Spirit unite us in the love and glory of Father and Son:
may we be one that the world may believe.

As you sent your Son into the world:
so send us, to make your glory known.

John 17.11-18

J Prayers after communion and endings for A Service of the Word

The forms of prayer in this section are provided both as ending prayers for *A Service of the Word* and also as prayers after communion, though sometimes the language will indicate that they can serve only the latter function. The rubric in Section 51 of the ASB Rite A provides for other suitable prayers to be used. Some of these prayers (especially those in bold type) are suitable for the whole congregation to join in, when it is possible to print them in full or to add to the local repertoire of what is known by heart.

Prayer at this point should not be general intercession, but a brief combination of thanksgiving and petition for grace to go out and serve God.

Other prayers suitable for use at this point in the service may be found in Chapter VII of *The Promise of His Glory* and in *Enriching the Christian Year* (or other compilations from the Liturgical Commission), as well as in the ASB services of Morning and Evening Prayer and Prayers for Various Occasions, pages 105-107.

Before Advent

Almighty God, by your gift   1J1
the tree of life was set at the heart of the earthly paradise,
and the bread of life was set at the heart of your Church.
Let this divine nourishment bring us,
not to judgement, but to life eternal,
in Jesus Christ our Lord.

Advent

Generous God,   1J2
you have fed us at your heavenly table.
Kindle us with the fire of your Spirit
that when Christ comes again
we may shine like lights before his face;
who with you and the Spirit lives for ever.

Advent

Loving Father,   1J3
your Son Jesus Christ has come to us
in word and Spirit, in bread and cup.
Make us holy,
bring us to perfection

as we stand before him
when he comes to judge the living and the dead,
Jesus Christ our Lord.

Advent

God our guide,

1J4

you have fed us with bread from heaven
as you fed your people Israel.
May we who have been spiritually nourished
be ready to follow you all our days;
we ask this in the name of Jesus Christ our Lord.

Advent

Gracious Lord,

1J5

in this holy sacrament
you give substance to our hope.
Bring us at the last
to that pure life for which we long;
through Jesus Christ our Lord.

Advent

Almighty God,

1J6

by whose command time runs its course;
forgive our impatience,
perfect our faith,
and, while we wait for the fulfilment
of your promises,
grant us to have a good hope
because of your word;
through Jesus Christ our Lord.

Incarnation, Christmas, Annunciation, Mary

Father of all,

2J7

the child born for us is the Saviour of the world.
May he who has made us your children
welcome us into your kingdom,
where he is alive and reigns with you now and for ever.

Incarnation, Christmas, Annunciation, Mary

We praise and thank you, creator God,

2J8

for you have not left us alone.
Every year we celebrate your birth, Emmanuel.
Every Eucharist celebrates your death,
in the broken bread and the cup we share,

until that day when we shall see you face to face,
in Jesus Christ our Lord.

Incarnation, Christmas, Annunciation, Mary
Son of Mary, Son of God,   2J9
may we who have joined the worship of the angels
never lose that heavenly vision.
May we who like the shepherds,
have seen in your birth a new kind of love,
show that love in our lives,
to your praise and glory for ever.

Epiphany, Light
God of glory,   3J10
you nourish us with your word
which is the bread of life.
Fill us with your Holy Spirit,
that through us the light of your glory
may shine in all the world.
We ask this in the name of Jesus Christ.

Lent, Penitence
God of compassion,   4J11
through your Son Jesus Christ
you have reconciled your people to yourself.
As we follow his example of prayer and fasting,
may we obey you with willing hearts
and serve one another in holy love;
through Jesus Christ our Lord.

Lent, Penitence
Merciful God,   4J12
you have called us to your table
and fed us with the bread of life.
Draw us and all people to your Son,
our Saviour Jesus Christ.

Lent, Penitence
Eternal God,   4J13
comfort of the afflicted and healer of the broken,
you have fed us at the table of life and hope.
Teach us the ways of gentleness and peace,
that all the world may acknowledge
the kingdom of your Son, Jesus Christ our Lord.

Lent, Penitence

Faithful God,
may we who share this banquet
glory in the cross of our Lord Jesus Christ,
our salvation, life and hope,
who reigns as Lord now and for ever.

4J14

Lent, Penitence

God of our pilgrimage,
you have led us to the living water.
Refresh and sustain us
as we go forward on our journey,
in the name of Jesus Christ our Lord.

4J15

Cross

Jesus, Son of God, our true and only Saviour:
you died like a criminal on a cross;
but you are God who forgives.
Once broken, helpless and in pain,
you are God in whom there is hope.
You have shown us a love beyond words:
give us your forgiveness, hope and love.

5J16

Resurrection, Heaven, Glory, Transfiguration, Death, Funerals

God of our salvation,
you have restored us to life,
you have brought us back again into your love
by the triumphant death
and resurrection of Christ.
Continue to heal us,
as we go to live and work
in the power of your Spirit,
to your praise and glory.

6J17

Resurrection, Heaven, Glory, Transfiguration

God of truth,
we have seen with our eyes
and touched with our hands
the bread of life.
Strengthen our faith
that we may grow in love for you
and for each other;
through Jesus Christ our risen Lord.

6J18

Heaven
God and Father of our Lord Jesus Christ,   6J19
bring us to the dwelling which your Son
is preparing for all who love you.
Give us the will each day
to live in life eternal.

Let our citizenship be in heaven
with your blessed and beloved,
the whole company of the redeemed;
and with countless angels,
praising, worshipping and adoring him
who sits upon the throne for ever and ever. Amen.

Heaven
To him who is able to keep us from falling   6J20
and to present us without blemish
before the presence of his glory with rejoicing,
to the only God, our Saviour through Jesus Christ our Lord,
be glory, majesty, dominion and authority,
before all time and now and for ever.
Jude 24,25

Ascension
O God our Father,   7J21
you have raised our humanity in Christ
and have fed us with the bread of heaven.
Mercifully grant that with such spiritual blessings
we may set our hearts in the heavenly places;
through Jesus Christ our Lord.

Spirit, Pentecost, Gifts, Healing, Baptism and Confirmation
Holy and blessed God,   8J22
as you give us the body and blood of your Son,
fill us with your Holy Spirit,
that we may honour you not only with our lips
but also in our lives.
This we ask in the name of Jesus Christ our Lord.

Spirit, Pentecost, Gifts, Healing, Baptism and Confirmation
Almighty and ever-living God,   8J23
who fulfilled the promises of Easter
by sending us your Holy Spirit
and opening to every race and nation

the way of life eternal,
open our lips by your Spirit,
that every tongue may tell of your glory;
through Jesus Christ our Lord.

Spirit, Pentecost, Gifts, Healing, Baptism and Confirmation

Father, in baptism we die to sin, 8J24
rise again to new life
and find our true place in your living body.
Send us out sealed in Christ's blood of the new covenant,
to bring healing and reconciliation to this wounded world,
through Jesus Christ our Lord.

Spirit, Pentecost, Gifts, Healing, Baptism and Confirmation

God of power, 8J25
may the boldness of your Spirit transform us,
may the gentleness of your Spirit lead us,
may the gifts of your Spirit
equip us to serve and worship you
now and always.

Trinity

O God our mystery, 9J26
you bring us to life,
call us to freedom,
and move between us with love.
May we so participate
in the dance of your Trinity
that our lives may resonate with you,
now and for ever. **Amen.**

Creation, Harvest, Bread, Vine

Creator God, 10J27
you give seed for us to sow,
and bread for us to eat;
make us thankful for what we have received;
make us able to do those generous things
which supply your people's needs;
so all the world may give you thanks and glory.

Word

Almighty God, 11J28
we thank you for the gift of your holy word.
May it be a lantern to our feet,

a light to our paths,
and a strength to our lives.
Take us and use us
to love and serve
in the power of the Holy Spirit
and in the name of your Son,
Jesus Christ our Lord.

Word

Lord God,   11J29
you feed us with the living bread from heaven;
you renew our faith,
increase our hope,
and strengthen our love.
Teach us to hunger
for Christ who is the true and living bread,
and to live by every word
that comes from your mouth,
through Jesus Christ our Lord.

Church, Mission and Ministry, Unity

Eternal Giver of love and life,   12J30
your Son Jesus Christ has sent us into all the world
to preach the gospel of his kingdom.
Confirm us in this mission,
and help us to live the good news we proclaim,
through Jesus Christ our Lord.

Church, Mission and Ministry, Unity

Lord God,   12J31
the source of truth and love,
keep us faithful to the apostles' teaching and fellowship,
united in prayer and the breaking of bread,
and one in joy and simplicity of heart,
in Jesus Christ our Lord.

Church, Mission and Ministry, Unity

Keep us, Father, in this community of faith,   12J32
the Church of your Son Jesus Christ,
and help us to confess him as Messiah and Lord
in all we say and do.
We ask this in his name.

Church, Mission and Ministry, Unity

Lord God, 12J33
thank you for the unity you give us in your presence:
draw your Church together,
into one great company of disciples,
together following our Lord Jesus Christ
into every walk of life,
together serving him in his mission to the world,
and together witnessing to his love
on every continent and island,
in the power of your Spirit,
to your praise and glory.

Unity

Great God, you are one God, 12J34
and you bring together what is scattered
and mend what is broken.
Unite us with the scattered peoples of the earth
that we may be one family of your children.
Bind up all our wounds,
and heal us in spirit
that we may be renewed as disciples
of Jesus Christ, our Master and Saviour.

Unity

Fill us, good Lord, with your Spirit of love; 12J35
and as you have fed us with the one bread of heaven,
so make us one in heart and mind,
in Jesus Christ our Lord.

Mission, Unity

Eternal God and Father, 12J36
whose Son at supper
prayed that his disciples might be one,
as he is one with you;
draw us closer to him,
that in common love and obedience to you
we may be united to one another
in the fellowship of the one Spirit,
that the world may believe that he is Lord,
to your eternal glory;
through Christ our Lord.

City, World and Society

Father of lights, 13J37
from whom comes every good and perfect gift:
keep us in the light of Christ,
to shine in your world,
that all may believe in you
through Jesus Christ our Lord.
James 1.17

Family

Father of all, you gathered us here 14J38
around the table of your Son;
we have shared this meal with the saints
and the whole fellowship of the household of God.
In that new world
where the fulness of your peace will be revealed,
gather people of every race, language and way of life
to share in the one eternal banquet
of Jesus Christ the Lord.

Saints

Lord of heaven, 15J39
in this Eucharist you have brought us near
to an innumerable company of angels,
and to the spirits of saints made perfect.
As in this food of our earthly pilgrimage
we have shared their fellowship,
so may we come to share their joy in heaven,
for ever and ever.

Love, Peace

Lord God, 17J40
you hold both heaven and earth in a single peace.
Let the design of your great love
shine on the waste of our anger and sorrows,
and give peace to your Church,
peace among nations,
peace in our homes, and peace in our hearts,
in Jesus Christ our Lord.

General

Heavenly Father, 0J41
we share together
the blessing of your presence.

Give us in this life knowledge of your truth,
and in the world to come life everlasting;
through Jesus Christ our Lord.

General
Lord,
we have broken your bread.
We have received your life.
By the power of your Spirit
keep us always in your love.

0J42

General
Eternal Father,
we thank you for refreshing us
with these heavenly gifts:
may our communion
strengthen us in faith,
build us up in hope
and make us grow in love,
for the sake of Jesus Christ our Lord.

0J43

General
We thank you, Lord,
that you have fed us in this sacrament,
united us with Christ,
and given us a foretaste
of the heavenly banquet.

0J44

General
May holy Wisdom,
kind to humanity,
steadfast, sure and free,
the breath of the power of God;
may she who makes all things new, in every age,
enter our souls, and make us friends of God,
through Jesus Christ.

0J45

General
O Almighty Lord, and everlasting God,
vouchsafe, we beseech thee, to direct, sanctify, and govern
both our hearts and bodies, in the ways of thy laws,
and in the works of thy commandments;

0J46

that through thy most mighty protection, both here and for ever,
we may be preserved in body and soul;
through our Lord and Saviour Jesus Christ.

Morning
Eternal God,
our beginning and our end,
be our starting point and our haven,
and accompany us in this day's journey.
Dawn on our darkness,
open our eyes to praise you for your creation
and to see the work you set before us today.
Take us and use us
to bring to others the new life you give
in Jesus Christ our Lord.

0J47

Evening
Gracious God,
you have given us much today;
grant us also a thankful spirit.
Into your hands we commend ourselves
and those we love.
Stay with us, and when we take our rest
renew us for the service of your Son Jesus Christ.

0J48

Evening
**In darkness and in light,
in trouble and in joy,
help us, heavenly Father,
to trust your love,
to serve your purpose,
and to praise your name,
through Jesus Christ our Lord.**

0J49

Evening
Lord, you have brought us through this day
to a time of reflection and rest.
Calm us,
and give us your peace to refresh us.
Keep us close to Christ
that we may be closer to one another
because of his perfect love.
In his name we pray.

0J50

Evening

God, you are everything to us, OJ51
giving us life,
filling it with love,
and setting us free from sin
that we might live in you.
Accept the work of our hands this day,
take our lives,
give us your peace
and renew us in the service of Jesus Christ our Lord.

PRAISE

K Short acclamations and responses _____

These may be used at the beginning or end of worship. They may be used after a reading, or repeated at various points in a service as a reminder of the theme.

Christ in you, the hope of glory: 1K1
This is the gospel we proclaim!
Colossians 1.27

The word was made flesh and lived among us: 2K2
and we have seen his glory.
John 1.14

The Son of man came not to be served, but to serve: 2K3
to give up his life as a ransom for many.
Mark 10.45

Christ has brought us out of darkness: 3K4
to dwell in the light of his glory.
1 Peter 2.9

Jesus Christ is the Light of the world: 3K5
a light no darkness can quench.
John 8.12

Jesus is the Lamb of God: 4K6
who takes away the sins of the world.
Alleluia!
John 1.29

God forbid that we should glory: 5K7
save in the cross of Christ our Lord.
Galatians 6.14

Jesus is the resurrection and the life: 6K8
those who believe in him shall never die.
Alleluia!
John 11.25

We have a great high priest who has passed through the heavens.   7K9
We come boldly to the throne of grace.
Hebrews 4.14,16

Jesus said, 'Receive the Spirit: 8K10
as the Father sent me, so I send you.'
John 20.21,22

We have died together with Christ.   8K11
We rise united with him.
Romans 6.5

Your word is a lantern to my feet: 11K12
and a light upon our path.
Psalm 119.105

There is one body and one Spirit: 12K13
one Lord, one faith, one baptism.
Ephesians 4.4,5

The love of Christ compels us.   12K14
We are ambassadors for him.
2 Corinthians 5.14,20

A city on a hill cannot be hidden.   13K15
We are the light of the world.
Matthew 5.14

Rejoice in the Lord always: 0K16
and again I say, 'Rejoice!'
Philippians 4.4

L Acclamations and responses

NOTES

1. Responses

Most of these are suitable for use at Section 3 in *A Service of the Word*, or at the beginning of worship.

2. Songs

Sections marked * may be said together as a song, rather than in responsive form.

Advent

* Restore us, Lord God of hosts: 1L1
show us the light of your face, turned towards us.

Will you not give us life again:
that your people may rejoice in you?

Show us your mercy, O Lord:
and grant us your salvation.

Blessed is the King who comes in the name of the Lord!
Peace in heaven and glory in the highest.

Incarnation

* Blessed be the Lord, the God of Israel: 2L2
may the whole earth be filled with his glory.

Light has sprung up for the righteous:
and joyful gladness for those who are faithful.

Glory to God in the highest:
and peace to his people on earth.

Epiphany

Blessed are you, Lord our God, King of the universe!   3L3
To you be glory and praise for ever.

From the rising of the sun to its setting
your name is proclaimed in all the world.
To you be glory and praise for ever.

When the time had fully come
you sent the Sun of Righteousness.
In him the fulness of your glory dwells.
To you be glory and praise for ever.

He was unconquered: nothing could overcome him.
He called us out of darkness into his own marvellous light.
To you be glory and praise for ever.

You gave him as a light to the nations,
and by the outpouring of his anointing Spirit
you establish us as your royal priesthood.
To you be glory and praise for ever.

According to the riches of his glory
strengthen us through his Spirit.
Root us and ground us in love,
that our lives may be a witness to your truth,
and our lips never cease to proclaim your praise.
To you be glory and praise for ever. Amen.
Note: The congregation may respond with both the variable
responses and the refrain, or with the refrain alone.

Lent, Penitence

* Cast your burden upon the Lord: 4L4
and he will sustain you.
Create in us clean hearts, O God:
and renew a right spirit within us.
Cast us not away from your presence:
and take not your Holy Spirit from us.
Give us the joy of your saving help:
and sustain us with your life-giving Spirit.
(Blessed be the Lord day by day:
the God of our salvation, who bears our burdens.)

Cross

* Christ became obedient unto death for us: 5L5
even death upon a cross.
He was pierced for our sins:
bruised for no fault but our own.
His punishment has brought us peace:
and by his wounds we are healed.
Worthy is the Lamb that was slain
to receive power and riches and wisdom:
strength, honour, glory, and praise. Amen.

Cross

O Lord, open my lips: 5L6
and my mouth shall proclaim your praise.
When we were still helpless:
Christ died for the ungodly.
The proof of God's amazing love is this:
while we were still sinners, Christ died for us.
Romans 5.6,8

Baptism, Cross

Since we have died with Christ, 5L7
we believe that we will also live with him.
For we know that Christ has been raised from death:
and will never die again.
We were baptized into union with his death:
and have set out on a new life with the risen Christ.
Romans 6.4,8,9

Resurrection

Alleluia! Christ is risen: 6L8
he is risen indeed. Alleluia!
Praise the God and Father of our Lord Jesus Christ:
he has given us new life and hope!
He has raised Jesus from the dead!
God has claimed us as his own:
he has brought us out of darkness!
He has made us light to the world!
Alleluia! Christ is risen:
he is risen indeed. Alleluia!

Resurrection

Christ is risen: 6L9
he is risen indeed. Alleluia!

Blessed are those who have not seen him and yet have believed:
he is our Lord and our God. Alleluia!

We have seen his glory:
glory as of the only Son from the Father, full of grace and truth.
Alleluia!

The Lord says to us, 'Do you love me?'
Our hearts reply, 'You know that we love you!' Alleluia!

Jesus says, 'Whoever comes to me shall never hunger.
Whoever believes in me shall never thirst!' Alleluia!

This is the Lamb of God:
who takes away the sins of the world. Alleluia!

Jesus is the resurrection and the life:
those who believe in him shall never die. Alleluia!

Yes – Christ is risen:
he is risen indeed. Alleluia!

Resurrection
Here are words you may trust.   6L10
Remember Jesus Christ, risen from the dead:
he is our salvation, our eternal glory.

If we die with him, we shall live with him:
if we endure we shall reign with him.

If we deny him, he will deny us:
if we are faithless, he keeps faith.

For he has broken the power of death:
and brought life and immortality to light through the gospel.
2 Timothy 2.11-13

Ascension
(Christ has gone up on high.   7L11
Alleluia!)

God raised Christ from the dead
and enthroned him at his right hand in the heavenly realms.
God put all things in subjection beneath his feet
and gave him as head over all things to the Church.
We died, and our life lies hidden with Christ in God.
We set our minds on things above.
When Christ, who is our life, is revealed,
then we too will be revealed with him in glory.

(Christ has gone up on high.
Alleluia!)

Spirit, Pentecost, Gifts, Healing, Baptism and Confirmation
* There are varieties of gifts: 8L12
but the same Spirit.
There are varieties of service:
but the same Lord.
There are different kinds of working:
but the same God is at work in all.
1 Corinthians 12.4-6

Spirit, Pentecost, Gifts, Healing, Baptism and Confirmation
(may be used with 8L12 above)

* There is one body, one Spirit, one hope in God's call:
one Lord, one faith, one baptism.
There is one God, Father of all, over all and in all:
to whom Christ ascended on high.
And through his Spirit he gives us gifts:
some are apostles, some are his prophets.
Evangelists, pastors and teachers he gives us:
so we can minister together
to build up his body:
to be mature in the fulness of Christ.
Ephesians 4.4-13

8L13

Spirit, Pentecost, Gifts, Healing, Baptism and Confirmation
* The love of God has been poured into our hearts
through the Holy Spirit who has been given to us:
we dwell in him and he in us.

8L14

Give thanks to the Lord and call upon his name:
make known his deeds among the peoples.

Sing to him, sing praises to him:
and speak of all his marvellous works.

Holy, holy, holy, is the Lord God almighty:
who was and is and is to come!

Spirit, Pentecost, Gifts, Healing, Baptism and Confirmation
* I saw water flowing from the threshold of the temple:
where the river flows everything will spring to life.

8L15

On the banks of the river grow trees bearing every kind of fruit:
their leaves will not wither nor their fruit fail.

Their fruit will serve for food,
their leaves for the healing of the nations:
for the river of the water of life
flows from the throne of God and of the Lamb.
Ezekiel 47.1,9; Revelation 22.1-3

Spirit
Now that we have been put right with God through faith,
we have peace with God through our Lord Jesus Christ.
He has brought us by faith into the grace of God.

8L16

We rejoice in the hope of sharing God's glory!
This hope does not deceive us:
for God has poured his love into our hearts
by the gift of his Spirit.
Romans 5.1-2

Trinity

You are worthy, our Lord and God: 9L17
to receive glory and honour and power.

For you created all things:
and through your will they have their being.

You are worthy, Lamb of God, for you were slain:
and by your blood you ransomed us for God.

From every tribe and tongue and people and nation:
you made us a kingdom of priests to serve our God.

To him who sits upon the throne, and to the Lamb:
be blessing and honour and glory and might
for ever and ever. Amen.
Revelation 4.11; 5.9,10,13

Creation
(especially suitable for penitence)

Lord, we are clay: 10L18
and you are the potter.

We are all the work of your hand:
do not remember our sins for ever.

Look upon us in your mercy:
for we are your people.
Isaiah 64.8,9

Creation
Blessed are you, Lord God, King of the universe! 10L19
Your word brings on the dusk of evening.
Your wisdom creates both night and day.
You determine the cycles of time.
You arrange the succession of seasons
and establish the stars in their heavenly courses.
Lord of the starry hosts is your name.
Living and eternal God, rule over us always.
Blessed be the Lord, whose word makes evening fall.

Saints

* Great is the Lord and greatly to be praised:
there is no end to his greatness.
One generation shall praise your works to another:
and shall declare your power.
All your works praise you, Lord:
and your faithful servants bless you.
They make known the glory of your kingdom:
and speak of your power.
My mouth shall speak the praise of the Lord:
let all flesh bless his holy name for ever and ever.
Psalm 145.3,4,10,11,12

15L20

Saints

Blessed are you, Lord our God, King of the universe!
**You have given us a share
in the inheritance of the saints in light.**

In the darkness of this age
your saints proclaim the glory of your kingdom.
Chosen as lights in the world,
they surround our steps as we journey on
towards that eternal city of light
where they sing the triumphal song.
Open our eyes to behold your glory
and free our tongues to join their song:

**Great and wonderful are your deeds,
Lord God almighty;
just and true are your ways, King of the ages.
To you be praise and glory, now and for ever. Amen.**

15L21

Saints

In the city of God, night shall be no more:
the people of God need no light of lamp or sun.
For the Lord God will be their light:
and they will reign for ever and ever.
Revelation 22.5

15L22

Love

* This is love, not that we loved God,
but that he loved us and sent his Son.
He is the sacrifice for our sins,
that we might live through him.

17L23

If God loves us so much
we ought to love one another.
If we love one another
God lives in us.
1 John 4.12

Light, Evening
Jesus Christ is the light of the world: OL24
a light no darkness can quench.

Stay with us, Lord, for it is evening:
and the day is almost over.

Even the darkness is not dark for you:
and the night shines like the day.

Let your light scatter the darkness:
and fill your church with your glory.
John 1.5, 8.12; Luke 24.29

Light, Evening
God is light. OL25
In him there is no darkness.
If we live in the light,
as God is in the light,
we have fellowship with one another,
and the blood of Jesus, his Son, purifies us from all sin.
1 John 1.5,7

General
Let us give thanks to the God of our Lord Jesus Christ: OL26
who has blessed us in Christ with every spiritual blessing.
Before the world was made, God chose us in Christ:
that we might be holy and blameless before him.
Let us praise God for the glory of his grace:
for the free gift he gave us in his dear Son.
To Father, Son and Holy Spirit:
give praise and dominion, honour and might,
for ever and ever. Amen.
Ephesians 1.3-6

General

O Lord, open my lips: OL27
and my mouth shall proclaim your praise.
Sing psalms, hymns and sacred songs:
let us sing to God with thanksgiving in our hearts.
Let everything you do or say be done in the name of the Lord Jesus,
giving thanks to God through Jesus Christ.
Colossians 3.16-17

M Longer acclamations and responsive scriptures

NOTES

Songs

Sections marked * may be said together as a song, rather than in responsive form.

Responsive scriptures

Sections marked + may be used in the Ministry of the Word, where they may take the place of a song or reading; or they may, with appropriate texts, be used as thanksgivings, for instance as the climax to A Service of the Word. Others may be added to the selection here, provided care is taken to choose texts, and versions, which are rhythmical, and to choose responses which are short, easy to say congregationally, and contribute to reflection on the inner meaning of the scripture.

Praise responses

The following four **Praise responses** should be regarded as standard responses, to be used after biddings or in litanies in a similar way to the **Prayer responses** (see section G):

1   Praise him:
praise him!

2   We give you thanks:
we praise your holy name.

3   Father in heaven:
we give you thanks and praise.

4   Jesus, Lord of all:
we worship and adore you.

(The first line of this may be appropriately varied, within the same rhythm, e.g. Jesus, Son of God; Jesus, born of Mary; Jesus, conqueror of death; Jesus, servant of all; Jesus, Lord of heaven; Jesus, redeemer of the world. . .)

Advent

+ My soul is waiting for the Lord:
in his word is my hope.

1M1

My soul is waiting for the Lord:
in his word is my hope.

Out of the depths have I called to you, O Lord.
Lord, hear my voice.
In his word is my hope.

There is forgiveness with you:
therefore you shall be feared.
In his word is my hope.

My soul is longing for the Lord,
more than those who watch for daybreak.
In his word is my hope.

O Israel, wait for the Lord,
for with the Lord there is mercy.
In his word is my hope.

Glory to the Father, and to the Son, and to the Holy Spirit.
My soul waits for the Lord;
in his word is my hope.

Psalm 130

Christmas

The Word of Life which was from the beginning
we proclaim to you.

2M2

The darkness is passing away
and the true light is already shining:
the Word of Life which was from the beginning.

That which we heard, which we saw with our eyes,
and touched with our own hands,
we proclaim to you.

For our fellowship is with the Father,
and with his Son Jesus Christ our Lord.
The Word of Life which was from the beginning
we proclaim to you.

Epiphany, Light

* Jesus Christ is the Light of the world:
a light no darkness can quench.
Stay with us, Lord, for it is evening:
and the day is almost over.
Let your light scatter the darkness:
and fill your Church with your glory.

3M3

You, Christ, are the King of glory,
the eternal Son of the Father.
You overcame the sting of death
and opened the kingdom of heaven to all believers.
Come then, Lord, and help your people,
bought with the price of your own blood,
and bring us with your saints
to glory everlasting. Amen.

Lent, Penitence

Incline your ear to me;
be swift to answer when I call. 4M4

Incline your ear to me;
be swift to answer when I call.

Lord, hear my prayer,
and let my cry come before you:
be swift to answer when I call.

Hide not your face from me
in the day of my trouble:
be swift to answer when I call.

You, Lord, endure for ever,
and your name from age to age:
be swift to answer when I call.

You will arise and have compassion on Zion,
for it is time to have pity on her:
be swift to answer when I call.

Glory to the Father, and to the Son, and to the Holy Spirit.
Incline your ear to me;
be swift to answer when I call.
Psalm 102.1,2,12,13

Cross

Father, you loved the world so much that you sent
your only Son to die that we might live through him. 5M5

(For his words from the cross, we bring you thanks and praise:)

('Forgive them. . .')
He forgave in the face of bitter hatred.
We give you thanks:
we praise your holy name.

('Today you shall be with me in paradise.')
He promised heaven to the forgiven sinner.
We give you thanks:
we praise your holy name.

('Mother, behold your Son. . .')
He loved his Mother to the last.
We give you thanks:
we praise your holy name.

('I thirst.')
He shared in our physical suffering and longing.
We give you thanks:
we praise your holy name.

('Why have you forsaken me?')
He entered into our testing and desolation.
We give you thanks:
we praise your holy name.

('It is finished!')
He completed his saving work,
and made the new covenant of love between God and his world.
We give you thanks:
we praise your holy name.

('Into your hands I commit my spirit.')
He won the victory over sin and death for ever.
We give you thanks:
we praise your holy name.
*(The quotations in brackets are best used only when there has been
specific reference in the service to Jesus' words from the cross. Not
every section need be used.)*

Resurrection
Our Lord Jesus Christ, risen from death,
we praise you for changed lives and new hopes at Easter.

6M6

You come to Mary in the garden, and turn her tears into joy.
For your love and mercy we give you thanks:
we praise your holy name.

You come to the disciples in the upper room,
and turn their fear into courage.
For your love and mercy we give you thanks:
we praise your holy name.

You come to the disciples by the lakeside,
and turn their failure into faith.
For your love and mercy we give you thanks:
we praise your holy name.

You come to the disciples on the Emmaus road,
and turn their despair into hope.
For your love and mercy we give you thanks:
we praise your holy name.

You come to your people now,
and turn our weakness into triumph.
For your love and mercy we give you thanks:
we praise your holy name.

Resurrection
Let the voice of God's praise resound.
He is the source of our life.

Let the voice of God's praise resound.
He is the source of our life.

Be joyful in God, all you lands;
sing the glory of his name.
He is the source of our life.

Come now and see the work of God,
how wonderful he is toward all people.
He is the source of our life.

He turned the sea into dry land,
so that they went through the water on foot.
He is the source of our life.

There we rejoiced in him.
In his might he rules for ever.
He is the source of our life.

Glory to the Father, and to the Son, and to the Holy Spirit.
Let the voice of God's praise resound.
He is the source of our life.

Psalm 66.4-8

6M7

Resurrection, Heaven, Glory, Transfiguration, Death, Funerals
+ **Lord, we remember you, our creator.**
You sent your Son to win the victory over death for ever.

6M8

Before sun and light and moon and stars grow dark,
and the clouds return after the rain:

Lord, we remember you, our creator.
You sent your Son to win the victory over death for ever.

We see the day when those who keep the house tremble
and strong women are bowed.
When men grind no longer at the mill,
because day is darkening at the windows
and the street doors are shut:

Lord, we remember you, our creator.
You sent your Son to win the victory over death for ever.

When the sound of the mill is faint,
when the voice of the bird is silenced,
and song notes are stilled,
when to go uphill is an ordeal
and a walk is something to dread:

Lord, we remember you, our creator.
You sent your Son to win the victory over death for ever.

Yet the trees are in flower
and insects are fat with food,
while we go to our everlasting home,
and the mourners are already walking up and down in the street:

Lord, we remember you, our creator.
You sent your Son to win the victory over death for ever.

Before the silver cord has snapped,
or the golden lamp has broken,
or the pitcher shattered at the spring,
or the pulley cracked at the well:

Lord, we remember you, our creator.
You sent your Son to win the victory over death for ever.

Before the dust returns to the earth
and the breath to God who gave it:

Lord, we remember you, our creator.
You sent your Son to win the victory over death for ever: Alleluia!

Ecclesiastes 12.1-8

Creation

+ **You are the eternal Father:**
all creation worships you.

Who decided the dimensions of the earth?
Or who stretched the measuring line across it?

What supports its pillars at their bases?
Who laid its cornerstone
when all the stars of the morning were singing with joy,
and the children of God in chorus were chanting praise?

You are the eternal Father:
all creation worships you.

Who pent up the sea behind closed doors
when it leapt tumultuous out of the womb,
when I wrapped it in a robe of mist
and made black clouds its swaddling bands;
when I marked the bounds it was not to cross
and made it fast with a bolted gate?
Come thus far, I said, and no farther:
here your proud waves shall break.

You are the eternal Father:
all creation worships you.

Have you ever visited the place where the snow is kept,
or seen where the hail is stored up,
which I keep for times of stress,
for days of battle and war?

You are the eternal Father:
all creation worships you.

From which direction does the lightning fork
when it scatters sparks over the earth?
Who carves a channel for the downpour,
and hacks a way for the rolling thunder,
so that rain may fall on lands where no one lives,
and the deserts void of human dwelling,
giving drink to the lonely wastes
and making grass spring where everything was dry?

You are the eternal Father:
all creation worships you.

Have the rain or dew a father?
Who is mother of the ice or frost
which turn the water to stone?

You are the eternal Father:
all creation worships you.
Job 38

Church, Mission and Ministry, Unity

Sovereign Lord, creator of heaven and earth and sea,   12M10
and everything in them,
we are your people, we give you thanks.
We praise your holy name.

You shake us and fill us with your Spirit,
you stretch out your hand to heal,
to do signs and wonders through the name of Jesus.
We are your people, we give you thanks.
We praise your holy name.

He is the author of life,
handed over to be killed for us.
You raised him from the dead,
and made us whole in him.
We are your people, we give you thanks.
We praise your holy name.

Not many of us are wise by human standards,
not many are influential,
not many of noble birth.
We are your people, we give you thanks.
We praise your holy name.

You choose the foolish to shame the wise,
you choose the weak to shame the strong,
the lowly and despised,
so no one may boast before you.
We are your people, we give you thanks.
We praise your holy name.

Your strength is made perfect in our weakness.
Your grace is enough for us.
We are your people, we give you thanks.
We praise your holy name.
Acts 4.24,30,31; 3.15,13; 1 Corinthians 1.26-29; 2 Corinthians 12.9

General

In my mouth he has put a new song: 0M11
praise to our God!

In my mouth he has put a new song:
praise to our God!

I waited patiently upon the Lord;
he stooped to me and heard my cry:
praise to our God!

Many shall see, and stand in awe,
and put their trust in the Lord:
praise to our God!

I love to do your will, Lord God;
your law is deep in my heart:
praise to our God!

I proclaimed righteousness in the great congregation;
behold, I did not restrain my lips:
praise to our God!

Glory to the Father, and to the Son, and to the Holy Spirit.
In my mouth he has put a new song:
praise to our God!

Psalm 40

Morning

The Lord is with us, he is our stronghold;
God will help at the break of day.

OM12

The Lord is with us, he is our stronghold;
God will help at the break of day.

God is our refuge and strength,
a very present help in trouble:
God will help at the break of day.

We will not fear, though the earth be moved,
and though the mountains be toppled into the depths of the sea:
God will help at the break of day.

Come now and look upon the works of the Lord,
what awesome things he has done on earth:
God will help at the break of day.

Be still and know that I am God;
I will be exalted among the nations;
I will be exalted in the earth:
God will help at the break of day.

Glory to the Father, and to the Son, and to the Holy Spirit.

The Lord is with us, he is our stronghold:
God will help at the break of day.
Psalm 46

*Thanksgiving may be extempore, for example a series of lines
beginning with 'For. . .' followed by a response. Two examples follow.*

General
We thank God for the world he has made, OM13
and for all his love and care:

For the warmth of the sun,
Father in heaven:
we give you thanks and praise.

For the rain which makes things grow,
Father in heaven:
we give you thanks and praise.

For the woods and the fields,
Father in heaven:
we give you thanks and praise.

For the sea and the sky,
Father in heaven:
we give you thanks and praise.

For the flowers and the animals,
Father in heaven:
we give you thanks and praise.

For families and holidays,
Father in heaven:
we give you thanks and praise.

For all your gifts,
Father in heaven:
we give you thanks and praise. Amen.

General
We give thanks to God for all his gifts to us: OM14
For birth and life and strength of body,
for safety and shelter and food,
we give you thanks:
we praise your holy name.

For sight and hearing and the beauty of nature,
for words and music and the power of thought,
we give you thanks:
we praise your holy name.

For work and leisure and the joy of achieving,
for conscience and will and depth of feeling,
we give you thanks:
we praise your holy name.

For grace and truth in Jesus Christ,
for the gifts of the Spirit and the hope of heaven,
we give you thanks:
we praise your holy name.

Holy, holy, holy Lord,
God of power and might,
heaven and earth are full of your glory.
Hosanna in the highest.

N Proper prefaces

These seasonal or thematic Proper prefaces are for use at the
appropriate points in any authorized Eucharistic Prayer on suitable
occasions.

Advent

And now we give you thanks
as we look forward to the day when
you will make all things new
as you come to judge the world.

1N1

Advent

And now we give you thanks
as we await the promise of salvation,
the desire of all the nations,
and the fulfilment of your good purposes
before the world began.

1N2

Advent

And now we give you thanks
because your Son our Lord was awaited by the prophets,
announced by an angel, conceived by a virgin,
and proclaimed at last to men and women of every race.

1N3

Incarnation

And now we give you thanks because
he shared our life in human form
from the warmth of Mary's womb to the stillness of the grave.

2N4

Incarnation

And now we give you thanks because
he was born in the poverty of a stable,
to make known the riches of your kingdom.

2N5

Epiphany

And now we give you thanks because
you have brought us from darkness to light
and made your light shine in our hearts.
You bring us to know your glory
in the face of Jesus Christ.

2 Corinthians 4.6

3N6

Epiphany, Light

And now we give you thanks because
in the wonder of the incarnation
your eternal Word has brought to the eyes of faith
a new and radiant vision of your glory.
In him we see our God made visible
and so are caught up in the love of God we cannot see.

3N7

Lent, Penitence

And now we give you thanks because
by his death he broke the power of sin
and made us holy through his blood.

4N8

Cross

And now we give you thanks because
he is the true passover lamb offered for us,
to take away the sin of the world.

5N9

Cross

And now we give you thanks because
for our sins he was lifted up on the cross
that he might draw the whole world to himself.

5N10

Cross

And now we give you thanks because
Christ is the victim who dies no more,
the Lamb, once slain, who lives for ever,
our advocate in heaven to plead our cause,
exalting us there to join the angels and archangels,
with all the company of heaven for ever praising you and saying:

5N11

Resurrection

And now we give you thanks because
by his death he has destroyed death,
and by his rising again
he has restored to us eternal life.

6N12

Resurrection

And now we give you thanks because
by his victory over the grave
he burst the gates of death for ever.

6N13

Ascension

And now we give you thanks because
he humbled himself to die on a cross;
but you raised him high
and gave him the name above all other names,
Jesus Christ our Lord.
Philippians 2.8,9

7N14

Pentecost

And now we give you thanks because
through him we receive the Spirit of adoption,
affirming us as your children,
and crying 'Abba, Father'.
Romans 8.15

8N15

Spirit, Pentecost

And now we give you thanks because
he breathed upon his disciples the power of your Spirit
to proclaim the good news to all peoples.
John 20.21,22

8N16

Healing

And now we give you thanks
because you provide medicine to heal our sickness,
and the leaves of the tree of life
for the healing of the nations,
anointing us with your healing power
so that we may be the first-fruits of your new creation.

8N17

(handwritten annotations: your strength to help in our weakness to bring wholeness; and ...)

Baptism

And now we give you thanks because
through him we are saved for ever
and baptized into your service.

8N18

Creation, Harvest

And now we give you thanks because
all things are of your making,
all times and seasons obey your laws,
but you have chosen to create us in your own image,
setting us over the whole world in all its wonder.
You have made us stewards of your creation,
to praise you day by day for the marvels of your wisdom and power:
so earth unites with heaven
to sing the new song of creation:

10N19

Bread of Life

And now we give you thanks because 10N20
he broke bread with those whom others scorned
and when the multitude were hungry
he fed them abundantly.

The Vine

And now we give you thanks because 10N21
he is the true vine, your chosen one,
in whom we are joined to bear fruit in plenty.

Word and Wisdom

And now we give you thanks because 11N22
the wisdom of your word sustains all things,
and reveals you to us in your fulness.

City, World and Society

And now we give you thanks because 13N23
you call us to live in your city,
while we look for the city which is to come,
designed and built by you,
with eternal foundations,
to which we journey as citizens of heaven.
Hebrews 13.14; 11.10

City

And now we give you thanks because 13N24
he gave up his life outside the city gate
and opened for all the way to heaven.
Hebrews 13.12

Family

And now we give you thanks because 14N25
a man leaves his father and mother
and is joined to his wife:
you make them one flesh.
You put us together in families,
to grasp your love and forgiveness,
reflected in those around us.
And as we grow, you prepare to bring us
into the glorious freedom of your children,
as brothers and sisters of Jesus Christ.
Genesis 2.24; Romans 8.17,22

Saints

And now we give you thanks because
in him you have received us as your sons and daughters,
joined us in one fellowship with the saints,
and made us citizens of your kingdom.

15N26

Kingdom

And now we give you thanks because
he came among us as a servant,
to be Emmanuel, your presence with us.

16N27

Kingdom, Ascension

And now we give you thanks because
Jesus has been given all authority
in heaven and on earth,
to present to you, his Father,
a kingdom of truth, holiness and everlasting love.

16N28

Marriage, Love

And now we give you thanks because
in the covenant of marriage
you show us your divine love,
a mirror of your will for all creation
made new and united to you for ever.

17N29

General

And now we give you thanks because
as a mother tenderly gathers her children,
you embraced a people as your own,
that with all the powers of heaven
we may find a voice to sing your praise.

0N30

P Thanksgivings _____

NOTES

1. These may be used as part of, or the climax to, *A Service of the Word*. When used as a preface (for example in Eucharistic Prayer 2 in Rite A), the introduction 'Father, we give you thanks and praise through Jesus Christ our Lord' should be used only where indicated.

2. The *Benedictus* may be added to the *Sanctus* in these thanksgivings.

3. If it is desired to shorten the Thanksgivings, the lines in brackets may be omitted.

Incarnation, Christmas, Annunciation, Mary

Blessed are you, God of all glory,   2P1
through your Son the Christ.
His name is Jesus:
because he saves his people from their sins.

He will be called Emmanuel:
God is with us. Alleluia!

Let us praise the Lord, the God of Israel:
he has come to his people and set them free.

He gave up all the glory of heaven:
and took the nature of a servant.

In humility he walked the path of obedience:
to die on the cross.

God raised him to the highest place above
and gave him the name above every name:
Jesus Christ is Lord!

So all beings in heaven and earth will fall at his feet,
and proclaim to the glory of God:
Jesus Christ is Lord!

Today Christ is born:
Alleluia!

Today the Saviour has come:
Alleluia!

Today the angels sing on earth:
Alleluia! Glory to God in the highest!

So, with angels and archangels, and all the company of heaven,
we praise you for ever, saying:
Holy, holy, holy Lord,
God of power and might,
heaven and earth are full of your glory.
Hosanna in the highest.
Matthew 1.21,23; Philippians 2.9-11

Incarnation

Father, we give you thanks and praise
for Jesus Christ our Lord:
he was the Word before all creation.
Through him all things come to be;
not one thing has its being but through him.

Jesus, Light of the world:
we worship and adore you.

His life is the light that shines in the dark,
a light that darkness cannot overpower.

Jesus, Light of the world:
we worship and adore you.

(The Word was the true light coming into the world.
He was in the world
that had its being through him,
and the world did not know him.

Jesus, Light of the world:
we worship and adore you.)

He came to his own, and they did not accept him.
But to all who accept him
he gives power to become children of God.

Jesus, Light of the world:
we worship and adore you.

The Word was made flesh and lived among us,
and we have seen his glory,
as the only Son of the Father,
full of grace and truth.

Jesus, Light of the world:
we worship and adore you.

To him be all praise and glory.
We join with all the heavenly host saying:

2P2

Holy, holy, holy Lord,
God of power and might,
heaven and earth are full of your glory.
Hosanna in the highest.
John 1

Incarnation, Christmas, Annunciation, Mary

Blessed are you, God of all glory, 2P3
through your Son Jesus Christ.

He is the heavenly King, born of Mary;
Jesus is the Son of God:
we worship and adore you.

He is the Word of the Father, crying as a baby,
Jesus is the Son of God:
we worship and adore you.

He is robed in glory, wrapped in infant clothes;
Jesus is the Son of God:
we worship and adore you.

Lord of heaven and earth, laid in a manger;
Jesus is the Son of God:
we worship and adore you.

Strong in weakness,
glorious in humility,
to him be all praise and glory.
We join with all the company of heaven, saying:
Holy, holy, holy Lord,
God of power and might,
heaven and earth are full of your glory.
Hosanna in the highest.
Blessed is he who comes in the name of the Lord.
Hosanna in the highest.

Incarnation, Christmas, Annunciation, Mary

Glory to Christ, Son of Mary; 2P4
born a child,
he shares our humanity:
glory to God in the highest.

Glory to Christ, Son of David;
born to rule,
he receives gifts from the wise:
glory to God in the highest.

Glory to Christ, Son of Man;
born our Saviour,
you are the light of the world:
glory to God in the highest.

We celebrate the coming of our God
with all the voices of heaven:
Holy, holy, holy Lord,
God of power and might,
heaven and earth are full of your glory.
Hosanna in the highest.
Blessed is he who comes in the name of the Lord.
Hosanna in the highest.

Lent, Penitence

We give you thanks and praise, Father in heaven,
through Jesus Christ, your only Son, our Lord.
Through him you created the world.
Through his word the universe is sustained.

Father in heaven:
we give you thanks and praise.

Through him we come near to you,
with sincere heart and sure faith.
Because of the death of Jesus
we come into the holy place.

Father in heaven:
we give you thanks and praise.

(He is our high priest.
He knows and feels our weaknesses.
He was tempted in every way,
like us, but did not sin.

Father in heaven:
we give you thanks and praise.)

By his own blood
he entered once and for all into the holy place.
He obtained eternal salvation for us.
He is our perfect sacrifice.

Father in heaven:
we give you thanks and praise.

4P5

So we come by that living way,
the new way he opened for us,
to receive mercy and grace,
and to join with angels and archangels
and all the company of heaven, saying:
Holy, holy, holy Lord,
God of power and might,
heaven and earth are full of your glory.
Hosanna in the highest.
Hebrews 1.3; 4.15,16; 9.12; 10.19-22

Cross

Blessed are you, God of pain and mercy, 5P6
through your Son Jesus Christ:

Surely he has borne our griefs;
he has carried our sorrows.
Surely he has borne our griefs;
he has carried our sorrows.

He was despised; he was rejected,
a man of sorrows and acquainted with grief:
he has carried our sorrows.

He was pierced for our sins,
bruised for no fault but ours:
he has carried our sorrows.

His punishment has bought our peace,
and by his wounds we are healed:
he has carried our sorrows.

We had all strayed like sheep,
but the Lord has laid on him the guilt of us all:
he has carried our sorrows.

Glory to the Father, and to the Son, and to the Holy Spirit:
surely he has borne our griefs;
he has carried our sorrows.

So, with angels and archangels,
and all the company of heaven,
we praise you for ever, saying:
Holy, holy, holy Lord,
God of power and might,
heaven and earth are full of your glory.
Hosanna in the highest.
Isaiah 53

Cross

5P7

Thanks and praise be to you, almighty God.
You justify us through faith
and give us peace in our Lord Jesus Christ.

Through faith:
we are saved by grace.

Through him you brought us by faith
into this experience of grace in which we live,
where we rejoice in the hope of sharing your glory.

Through faith:
we are saved by grace.

Not only so, but we also rejoice in our sufferings,
because we know that suffering produces perseverance;
perseverance, character; and character, hope.

Through faith:
we are saved by grace.

And hope does not disappoint us,
because you have poured out your love
into our hearts by the Holy Spirit.

Through faith:
we are saved by grace.

You show us how much you love us:
while we were helpless, Christ died for the ungodly.
While we were still sinners, Christ died for us.

Through faith:
we are saved by grace.

And through faith we stand in heaven and worship you
with angels and archangels, saying:
Holy, holy, holy Lord,
God of power and might,
heaven and earth are full of your glory.
Hosanna in the highest.

Romans 5.1-9

Resurrection, Baptism

6P8

Blessed are you,
God and Father of our Lord Jesus Christ!
By your great mercy
we have been born anew

to a living hope
through the resurrection of your Son
from the dead,
and to an inheritance
which is imperishable,
undefiled, and unfading.
Once we were no people,
but now we are your people,
declaring your wonderful deeds in Christ,
who called us out of darkness
into his marvellous light.

By the baptism
of his death and resurrection
you gave birth to your Church,
delivered us from slavery
to sin and death,
and made with us a new covenant.
At his ascension
you exalted him to sit at your right hand,
where according to his promise
he is with us always,
baptizing us with the Holy Spirit
and with fire.

The joy of resurrection fills the whole world,
and therefore we join with angels and archangels
and the whole company of heaven,
in the song of unending praise, saying:
Holy, holy, holy Lord,
God of power and might,
heaven and earth are full of your glory.
Hosanna in the highest.

Resurrection

We give you thanks and praise 6P9
for the gospel we have received.
Christ died for our sins: Alleluia!
He is risen indeed. Alleluia!

Death comes to all through Adam,
and sin reigns for a time.
New life without end comes through Christ,
and he reigns for ever: Alleluia!
He is risen indeed. Alleluia!

Death, where is your victory?
Death, where is your sting?
Death is swallowed up in victory –
the victory you give us in Christ: Alleluia!
He is risen indeed. Alleluia!

We have been crucified with Christ,
and live his risen life,
to praise you for ever with angels and archangels:
Holy, holy, holy Lord,
God of power and might,
heaven and earth are full of your glory.
Hosanna in the highest.
1 Corinthians 15

Ascension, Kingship
Thanks and praise to you,   7P10
Jesus Christ, Lord of all,
given the name above every other name.

Jesus, Lord of all:
we worship and adore you.

King of righteousness, King of peace,
enthroned at the right hand of Majesty on high;
Jesus, Lord of all:
we worship and adore you.

Great high priest, living for ever to intercede for us;
Jesus, Lord of all:
we worship and adore you.

Pioneer of our salvation, you bring us to glory
through your death and resurrection;
Jesus, Lord of all:
we worship and adore you.
Every knee bows to you;
every tongue confesses:
you are Lord,
to the glory of God the Father.
Blessed is he who comes in the name of the Lord.
Hosanna in the highest.

*(If this Thanksgiving is used with a Eucharistic Prayer, it should
follow this form:*

Thanks and praise be to you, Lord of heaven,
for Jesus Christ your Son our Lord.
You gave him the name above every name,
so that we say:

Jesus is Lord of all:
we worship and adore you.

King of righteousness, King of peace,
enthroned at the right hand of Majesty on high;
Jesus is Lord of all:
we worship and adore you.

Great high priest, living for ever to intercede for us;
Jesus is Lord of all:
we worship and adore you.

Pioneer of our salvation, bringing us to glory
through death and resurrection;
Jesus is Lord of all:
we worship and adore you.
Every knee bows to him;
every tongue confesses, Jesus is Lord,
to the glory of God the Father.
Blessed is he who comes in the name of the Lord.
Hosanna in the highest.)

Ascension, Kingship, Trinity

Father, we are in your Spirit and hear your voice:
'I am the first and the last, who is, who was,
and who is to come.'
Before the worlds were made,
Jesus Christ the living one was reigning with you
and the Holy Spirit.
Through Christ you created everything in heaven and earth,
the whole universe created through him and for him.

Lord of glory:
we worship and adore you.

You sent him, the visible likeness
of the invisible God,
to reflect the brightness of your glory,

7P11

to sustain the universe with his word of power,
to achieve forgiveness for the sins of all.

Lord of glory:
we worship and adore you.

And now he rules in heaven, mighty risen Lord,
(his hair as white as snow, his eyes like fire,
his feet like polished brass, his hands full of stars,
his face bright as the noonday sun,)
his voice like a roaring waterfall:
'I am the living one!
I was dead but now I am alive for ever and ever.'

So, with angels and archangels,
and all the company of heaven,
we praise you for ever, saying:
Holy, holy, holy Lord,
God of power and might,
heaven and earth are full of your glory.
Hosanna in the highest.

Colossians 1.15-20; Hebrews 1.3; Revelation 1.14-18

(The acclamation 'We worship and adore you' may be repeated
between each line of the penultimate paragraph.)

Spirit, Pentecost, Gifts, Healing, Baptism and Confirmation   8P12
Father, while all your creation groans with pain
like the pain of childbirth,
and longs to share the freedom of the children of God,
your Spirit pleads for us
in groans words cannot express.

Father in heaven:
we give you thanks and praise.

The law of the Spirit brings us life in Christ,
and sets us free from the law of sin and death.

Father in heaven:
we give you thanks and praise.

Like all who are led by your Spirit,
we are your children.
By your Spirit's power we cry, 'Abba, Father.'

Father in heaven:
we give you thanks and praise.

(The Spirit confirms that we are your children,
fellow-heirs with Christ,
sharing his suffering now,
that we may share his glory.

Father in heaven:
we give you thanks and praise.)

So by your Spirit we praise you for ever
and proclaim your glory with all the company of heaven, saying:
Holy, holy, holy Lord,
God of power and might,
heaven and earth are full of your glory.
Hosanna in the highest.

Romans 8.2,14-25

Spirit, Baptism and Confirmation

Father, for your gift of water in creation: 8P13
we give you thanks and praise.

For your Spirit, sweeping over the waters,
bringing light and life:
we give you thanks and praise.

For your Son, Jesus Christ our Lord,
baptized in the river Jordan:
we give you thanks and praise.

For your new creation,
brought to birth by water and the Spirit:
we give you thanks and praise.

For your grace bestowed upon us your children,
washing away our sins:
we give you thanks and praise.

* So, Father, accept our sacrifice of praise;
by the power of your life-giving Spirit
bless these waters of your new creation:
Lord, receive our prayer.

* May your servants who are washed in them
be made one with your Son,
who took the form of a servant:
Lord, receive our prayer.

* May your Holy Spirit, who has brought us to new birth
in the family of your Church,

raise us in Christ, our anointed Lord,
to full and eternal life:
Lord, receive our prayer.

For all might, majesty and dominion are yours,
now and for ever. **Alleluia! Amen.**

*Paragraphs marked * should be omitted when this section is not
being used in connection with sacramental water.*

Trinity

1. Glory to the Holy and Undivided Trinity;   9P14
2. Father, Son and Holy Spirit;
3. Three persons and one God.

1. Perfectly one from before time began;
2. One in being and one in glory;
3. Dwelling in love; three persons, one God.

1. Incarnate Son, in suffering forsaken;
2. Father, giving and forgiving;
3. Spirit, bond in joy and pain.

1. Eternal Father, the Fountain of Life;
2. Risen Son, the Prince of Life;
3. Spirit of freedom, Giver of Life.

1. Truth, Word and Power;
2. Lover, Beloved and Friend;
3. Hope without end; Joy beyond words;

All Glory to God, Father, Son and Holy Spirit.

This may be said or sung in three voices.

Creation

You, Christ, are the image of the unseen God,   10P15
the first-born of all creation.
You created all things in heaven and on earth:
everything visible and everything invisible,
thrones, dominions, sovereignties, powers –
all things were created through you and for you.

Lord of all creation:
we worship and adore you.

You are the radiant light of God's glory:
you hold all creation together by your word of power.

Lord of all creation:
we worship and adore you.

You are the first to be born from the dead.
All perfection is found in you,
and all things were reconciled through you and for you,
everything in heaven and everything on earth,
when you made peace by your death on the cross.

Lord of all creation:
we worship and adore you.

The Church is your body,
you are its head.
You take your place in heaven
at the right hand of the divine majesty,
where we worship and adore you with all
your creation, singing:
Holy, holy, holy Lord,
God of power and might,
heaven and earth are full of your glory.
Hosanna in the highest.
Blessed is he who comes in the name of the Lord.
Hosanna in the highest.

Colossians 1.15-18

If this Thanksgiving is used with a Eucharistic Prayer it should be in
this form:

Father, we give you thanks and praise   10P16
for your Son, Jesus Christ our Lord.
He is the image of the unseen God,
the first-born of all creation.
He created all things in heaven and on earth:
everything visible and everything invisible,
thrones, dominions, sovereignties, powers –
all things were created through him and for him.

Lord of all creation:
we worship and adore you.

He is the radiant light of your glory:
he holds all creation together by his word of power.

Lord of all creation:
we worship and adore you.

He is first to be born from the dead.
All perfection is found in him,
and all things were reconciled through him and for him,
everything in heaven and everything on earth,
when he made peace by his death on the cross.

Lord of all creation:
we worship and adore you.

The Church is his body,
he is its head.
He takes his place in heaven
at your right hand,
where we worship you with all of your creation, singing:
Holy, holy, holy Lord,
God of power and might,
heaven and earth are full of your glory.
Hosanna in the highest.
Blessed is he who comes in the name of the Lord.
Hosanna in the highest.)

Colossians 1.15-18

City, World and Society

Father, you gave up your Son for us all:
you give us all things with him;
you call us, justify us, glorify us.

13P17

Father in heaven:
we give you thanks and praise.

Jesus Christ died, was raised to life,
and pleads for us at your right hand.
Who can separate us from your love?

Father in heaven:
we give you thanks and praise.

For your sake we face death all day long.
In your world we face trouble and hardship,
persecution, famine, nakedness, danger and death.

Father in heaven:
we give you thanks and praise.

But nothing separates us from your love:
neither death nor life,
neither angels nor demons,
neither the present nor the future,

nor any heavenly powers,
neither the world above nor the world below:
nothing in all creation can separate us
from your love in Jesus Christ.

Father in heaven:
we give you thanks and praise.

In all these things we are more than conquerors
through him who loves us,
and has freed us from our sins
and made us a kingdom and priests
to serve you for ever,
with all the company of heaven, saying:
Holy, holy, holy Lord,
God of power and might,
heaven and earth are full of your glory.
Hosanna in the highest.
Romans 8.23-39

City, World and Society

Living God, Father of light,   13P18
Hope of nations, Friend of sinners,
Builder of the city that is to come;
your love is made visible in Jesus Christ,
you bring home the lost, restore the sinner
and give dignity to the despised.
In the face of Jesus Christ
your light shines out,
flooding lives with goodness and truth,
gathering into one a divided and broken humanity.
With people from every race and nation,
with the Church of all the ages,
with apostles, evangelists and martyrs
we join the angels of heaven
in their unending song:
Holy, holy, holy Lord,
God of power and might,
heaven and earth are full of your glory.
Hosanna in the highest.
Blessed is he who comes in the name of the Lord.
Hosanna in the highest.

Saints

Blessed are you, gracious God: 15P19
creator of heaven and earth.
In the multitude of your saints,
you have surrounded us with a great cloud of witnesses.
The glorious company of apostles praise you.
The noble fellowship of prophets praise you.
The white-robed army of martyrs praise you.
We your holy Church acclaim you.
In communion with angels and archangels,
and with all those who have served you in every age,
and worship you now in heaven,
we raise our voices to proclaim your glory,
for ever praising you and saying:
Holy, holy, holy Lord,
God of power and might,
heaven and earth are full of your glory.
Hosanna in the highest.
Blessed is he who comes in the name of the Lord.
Hosanna in the highest.

Reconciliation

(Father, we give you thanks and praise 16P20
through Jesus Christ our Lord
because you are God almighty,
creator of the world and everything in it. . .)

Almighty God, creator of the world
and everything in it,
Lord of heaven and earth,
you made the whole human race.
You have shown to us in Christ the mystery
of your purpose:
you chose us all in Christ
to praise his glory.

You will bring all things together under Christ,
all things in heaven, all things on earth,
under him as head:
you chose us all in Christ
to praise his glory.

We have heard the word of truth, the good news of salvation,
you have stamped us with the seal of your Spirit of promise:
you chose us all in Christ
to praise his glory.

We who once were far away
have been brought near by the blood of Christ:
you chose us all in Christ
to praise his glory.

He is the peace between us,
and has broken down the barrier of hostility.
He has made us one new humanity
and reconciled us to you by the cross:
you chose us all in Christ
to praise his glory.

He killed hostility and brought peace,
peace to all near at hand, peace to all far away:
you chose us all in Christ
to praise his glory.

Through him we come, by the Spirit,
to you, our Father in heaven, singing:
Holy, holy, holy Lord,
God of power and might,
heaven and earth are full of your glory.
Hosanna in the highest.

Acts 17.25,26; Ephesians 1.9-13; 2.13-17

General

Father, we give you thanks and praise   0P21
through Jesus Christ your Son, our Lord.

Jesus is Lord of all creation:
we worship and adore you.

* A   Jesus made his home among us:
         we worship and adore you.

B   Jesus died to set us free:
       we worship and adore you.

C   Jesus was raised to life again:
       we worship and adore you.

D   Jesus reigns in glory now:
       we worship and adore you.

We worship and adore you with angels and archangels
and all the company of heaven, saying:

Holy, holy, holy Lord,
God of power and might,
heaven and earth are full of your glory.
Hosanna in the highest.

** One or more sentences in the following form, with the response 'we
worship and adore you' may be used at the points indicated by these
letters in the text above. This will provide the opportunity for
seasonal and thematic emphasis.*

A   Jesus, born of the Virgin Mary:

        Jesus, cradled in a manger:

        Jesus, Saviour, Christ our Lord:

        Jesus, God in human flesh:

        Jesus our Emmanuel:

B   Jesus lifted up for us:

        Jesus stretches out his arms:

        Jesus died for a dying world:

        Jesus bore our sins and griefs:

C   Jesus lay within the tomb:

        Jesus rose to life in triumph:

        Jesus conquers death for us:

D   Jesus, Lord of life and death:

        Jesus, Lamb upon the throne:

        Jesus crowned, in glory seated:

        Jesus, always pleading for us:

        Jesus comes again in glory:

        Jesus claims his kingdom here:

B,C,D   Jesus is the Son of God:

        Jesus, Light of all the world:

        Jesus is the bread of heaven:

Jesus, our way, our truth, our life:

Jesus is the door to life:

Jesus is the first and last:

Jesus is the Lord of all:

Jesus our wisdom from above:

Jesus is the King of kings:

Jesus is our friend and brother:

Jesus, healer of the sick:

Alleluia! Praise the Lord!

Q Scriptural songs

Note 6 in *A Service of the Word* says that the psalm may occasionally be replaced by a song or canticle, the words of which are taken directly from scripture, a 'scriptural song'. More examples may be found in *The Promise of His Glory*.

NOTES

1. It is not necessary always to end each song with 'Glory to the Father. . .' It may be omitted as required.

2. A song may be said responsively with the suggested response after each verse or pair of verses. Alternatively, a song may be said, or sung, by all the worshippers either together, or responsively by half verses or verses.

3. A metrical version of a song may provide an alternative method of saying or singing the song.

Advent
A SONG OF THE WILDERNESS   1Q1
Response: **The ransomed of the Lord shall return with singing.**

1   The wilderness and the dry land shall rejoice:
    the desert shall burst into song.

2   They shall see the glory of the Lord:
    the splendour of our God.

3   Strengthen the weary hands:
    make firm the feeble knees.

4   Say to the anxious, be strong, fear not:
    your God is coming in judgement to save you.

5   Then shall the eyes of the blind be opened:
    and the ears of the deaf unstopped;

6   Then the lame shall leap like the deer:
    and the tongue of the dumb shall sing for joy.

7   For waters shall spring up in the wilderness:
    and streams flow in the desert.

8   The ransomed of the Lord shall return with singing:
    crowned with everlasting joy.

9   They shall obtain joy and gladness:
    and sorrow and sighing shall flee away.

Glory to the Father, and to the Son,
and to the Holy Spirit:
as it was in the beginning, is now,
and shall be for ever. Amen.

Isaiah 35.1 – 6.10

Advent

A SONG OF THE BRIDE

Response: **He has clothed me with the garments of salvation.**

1   I will greatly rejoice in the Lord:
my soul shall exult in my God.

2   For he has clothed me with the garments of salvation:
he has covered me with the cloak of integrity,

3   as a bridegroom decks himself with a garland:
and as a bride adorns herself with her jewels.

4   For as the earth puts forth her blossom:
and as seeds in the garden spring up,

5   so shall the Lord God make righteousness and praise:
blossom before all the nations.

6   For Zion's sake, I will not keep silence:
and for Jerusalem's sake, I will not rest,

7   until her deliverance shines forth like the sunrise:
and her salvation as a burning torch.

8   The nations shall see your deliverance:
and all kings shall see your glory.

9   Then you shall be called by a new name:
which the mouth of the Lord will give.

10 You shall be a crown of glory in the hand of the Lord:
and a royal diadem in the hand of your God.

Glory to the Father, and to the Son,
and to the Holy Spirit:
as it was in the beginning, is now,
and shall be for ever. Amen.

Isaiah 61.10-11; 62.1-3

Incarnation, Christmas, Annunciation, Mary
2Q3
Response: **To us a child is born, to us a son is given.**

1   The people who walked in darkness have seen a great light:
    those who dwelt in a land of deep darkness,
    upon them the light has dawned.

2   You have increased their joy and given them great gladness:
    they rejoiced before you as with joy at the harvest.

3   For you have shattered the yoke which burdened them:
    the collar that lay heavy upon their shoulders.

4   For to us a child is born, to us a son is given:
    and the government will be upon his shoulder.

5   And his name will be called 'Wonderful Counsellor,
    the Mighty God:
    the everlasting Father, the Prince of Peace.'

6   Of the increase of his government and of peace:
    there will be no end,

7   upon the throne of David, and over his kingdom:
    to establish and uphold it with justice and righteousness.

8   From this time forth and for evermore:
    the zeal of the Lord of hosts will do this.

    Glory to the Father, and to the Son,
    and to the Holy Spirit:
    as it was in the beginning, is now,
    and shall be for ever. Amen.

Isaiah 9.2-7 adapted

Incarnation, Christmas, Annunciation, Mary
A SONG OF PROPHECY 2Q4
Response: **The Spirit of the Lord shall rest upon him.**

1   There shall come forth a shoot from the stump of Jesse:
    and a branch shall grow out of its roots,

2   and the Spirit of the Lord shall rest upon him:
    the spirit of wisdom and understanding,

3   the spirit of counsel and might:
    the spirit of knowledge and the fear of the Lord.

4   He shall not judge by what his eyes see:
     or decide by what his ears hear,

5   but with righteousness he shall judge the poor:
     and decide with equity for the meek of the earth.

6   The wolf shall dwell with the lamb:
     and the leopard shall lie down with the kid,

7   the calf and the young lion together:
     with a little child to lead them.

     Glory to the Father, and to the Son,
     and to the Holy Spirit:
     as it was in the beginning, is now,
     and shall be for ever. Amen.

Isaiah 11.1-4,6

Epiphany, Light
A SONG OF THE NEW JERUSALEM   3Q5
Response: **Arise, shine out, for your light has come.**

1   Arise, shine out, for your light has come:
     the glory of the Lord is rising upon you.

2   Though night still covers the earth:
     and darkness the peoples,

3   above you the Lord now rises:
     and above you his glory appears.

4   The nations will come to your light:
     and kings to your dawning brightness.

5   Your gates will always stand open:
     shut neither by day nor by night.

6   They will call you 'The City of the Lord':
     'Zion of the Holy One of Israel'.

7   The sound of violence shall be heard no longer in your land:
     or ruin and destruction within your borders.

8   You will call your walls 'Salvation':
     and your gates 'Praise'.

9   No more will the sun give you daylight:
     nor the moonlight shine upon you.

10   But the Lord will be your everlasting light:
     your God will be your splendour.

Glory to the Father, and to the Son,
and to the Holy Spirit:
as it was in the beginning, is now,
and shall be for ever. Amen.

Isaiah 60.1-3,11,14,18-19

Epiphany, Light
A Song of Restoration   3Q6
Response: **I, the Lord, will comfort my people.**

1   Listen to me you islands:
    and people who live far away.

2   My servant, in the time of my favour I will answer you:
    and in the day of salvation I will help you.

3   I will restore the land:
    and share out afresh its desolate fields;

4   I will say to the prisoners, 'Go free':
    and to those in darkness,
    'Come out to the light.'

5   They will feed beside the way:
    and find pasture on every barren hill.

6   They will never hunger nor thirst:
    sun and desert heat will never plague them,

7   For he who loves them will guide them:
    and lead them beside springs of water.

8   Shout for joy, you heavens and exult, you earth:
    mountains, break into song;

9   for I the Lord will comfort my people:
    and will have compassion on my own in their distress.

Glory to the Father, and to the Son,
and to the Holy Spirit:
as it was in the beginning, is now,
and shall be for ever. Amen.

Isaiah 49:1,8-10,13

Lent, Penitence

A Song of Hosea

Response: **Come, let us return to the Lord.**

1   Come, let us return to the Lord:
    for he has torn us and will heal us.

2   He has stricken us:
    and he will bind up our wounds.

3   After two days, he will revive us:
    on the third day he will raise us up,
    that we may live in his presence.

4   Let us humble ourselves, let us strive to know the Lord:
    for his justice dawns like the morning light,
    and its dawning is as sure as the sunrise.

5   He will come to us like the showers:
    like the spring rains that water the earth.

6   Ephraim, how shall I deal with you?
    How shall I deal with you, Judah?

7   Your love for me is like the morning mist:
    like the dew that vanishes early.

8   Therefore I have cut them in pieces by the prophets:
    and my judgement goes forth as the light.

9   For loyalty is my desire, and not sacrifice:
    and the knowledge of God rather than burnt offerings.

Glory to the Father, and to the Son,
and to the Holy Spirit:
as it was in the beginning, is now,
and shall be for ever. Amen.

Hosea 6.1-6

Cross

A Song of the Servant

Response: **By his wounds we are healed.**

1   He was despised, he was rejected:
    a man of sorrows, acquainted with grief.

2   As one from whom people hide their faces:
    he was despised, and we did not esteem him.

3   He bore our sufferings:
    he endured our torments,

4   while we thought he was being punished:
    and struck by God, brought low.

5   He was pierced for our sins:
    bruised for no fault but our own.

6   His punishment has won our peace:
    and by his wounds we are healed.

7   We have all strayed like sheep:
    each taking their own way.

8   But the Lord has laid on him:
    the guilt of us all.

    Glory to the Father, and to the Son,
    and to the Holy Spirit:
    as it was in the beginning, is now,
    and shall be for ever. Amen.

Isaiah 53.3-6

Cross

A SONG OF CHRIST THE SERVANT   5Q9
Response: **We die to sin and live to righteousness.**

1   Christ suffered for you leaving you an example:
    that you should follow in his steps.

2   Christ committed no sin, no guile was found on his lips:
    when he was reviled, he did not revile in turn.

3   When he suffered, he did not threaten:
    but he trusted in God who judges justly.

4   Christ himself bore our sins in his body on the tree:
    that we might die to sin and live to righteousness.

5   By his wounds you have been healed,
    for you were straying like sheep:
    but have now returned to the Shepherd and Guardian of your souls.

1 Peter 2.21-25

Resurrection, Heaven, Glory, Transfiguration, Death, Funerals
THE SONG OF MOSES   6Q10
Response: **The Lord is my strength and my song.**

1   I will sing to the Lord,
     for he has triumphed gloriously:
     he has thrown the horse and its rider into the sea.

2   The Lord is my strength and my song:
     and he has become my salvation.

3   This is my God, and I will praise him:
     the God of my father and I will exalt him.

4   Lord, who among the gods is like you:
     majestic in holiness and working wonders?

6   In your unfailing love you will lead the people you have
        redeemed:
     in your strength you will guide them to your holy dwelling.

7   You will bring them in and plant them on your mountain:
     the place you have made for your dwelling.

8   In the sanctuary that your hands have established:
     you, Lord, will reign for ever and ever.

     Glory to the Father, and to the Son,
     and to the Holy Spirit:
     as it was in the beginning, is now,
     and shall be for ever. Amen.

Exodus 15.1,2,11,13,17

Resurrection, Heaven, Glory, Transfiguration, Death, Funerals
A SONG OF PETER   6Q11
Response: **Praise be to the God and Father of our Lord Jesus Christ.**

1   Praise be to the God and Father of our Lord Jesus Christ:
     who in his great mercy gave you new birth as his children.

2   He has raised Jesus Christ from the dead:
     so that you have a sure hope in him.

3   You have the promise of an inheritance that can never be spoilt:
     because it is kept for you in heaven.

4   The ransom that was paid to free you:
     was not paid in silver or gold;

5   but in the precious blood of Christ:
     the Lamb without spot or stain.

6   God raised him from the dead and gave him glory:
     so that you would have faith and hope in God.

     Glory to the Father, and to the Son,
     and to the Holy Spirit:
     as it was in the beginning, is now,
     and shall be for ever. Amen.

1 Peter 1.3-4,18-21

Ascension

A SONG OF GOD'S GRACE   7Q12

Response: **You have blessed us in Christ Jesus.**

1   Blessed be the God and Father of our Lord Jesus Christ:
     for you have blessed us in Christ Jesus
     with every spiritual blessing in the heavenly places.

2   You chose us to be yours
     before the foundation of the world:
     that we should be holy and blameless in your sight.

3   In love you destined us to be your children,
     through Jesus Christ:
     such was your pleasure and your purpose,

4   to the praise of your glorious grace:
     which you have freely given us in the Beloved.

5   We have redemption through the blood of Christ:
     the forgiveness of our sins,

6   according to the riches of the grace:
     which you have freely lavished upon us.

7   You have made known to us in all wisdom and insight:
     the mystery of your will,

8   according to your purpose
     which you revealed in Christ Jesus:
     as a plan for the fulness of time,

9   to unite all things in Christ:
     things in heaven and things on earth.

Ephesians 1.3-10

Spirit, Pentecost, Gifts, Healing, Baptism and Confirmation
A SONG OF HOPE   8Q13
Response: **I will greatly rejoice in the Lord.**

1   The Spirit of the Lord God is upon me:
     because the Lord has anointed me
     to bring good tidings to the afflicted.

2   The Lord has sent me to bind up the broken-hearted:
     to proclaim liberty for the captives,
     and release for those in prison,

3   to comfort all who mourn:
     to bestow on them a crown of beauty instead of ashes,

4   the oil of gladness instead of mourning:
     a garment of splendour for the heavy heart.

5   They shall be called trees of righteousness:
     planted for the glory of the Lord.

6   Therefore I will greatly rejoice in the Lord:
     my soul shall exult in my God.

7   For God has robed me with salvation as a garment:
     and clothed me with integrity as a cloak.

8   For as the earth brings forth its shoots:
     and as a garden causes the seeds to spring up,

9   so the Lord God will cause righteousness and praise:
     to spring forth before all the nations.

     Glory to the Father, and to the Son,
     and to the Holy Spirit:
     as it was in the beginning, is now,
     and shall be for ever. Amen.

Isaiah 61.1-3,10,11

Creation, Harvest, Bread, Word
(especially suitable for use at the Eucharist)
A SONG OF THE BREAD OF HEAVEN   10Q14
Response: **Jesus Christ is the bread of heaven.**

1   You gave your people the food of angels:
     and sent them bread from heaven.

2   It was ready to eat, though they did no work:
     it was rich in delights, suiting every taste.

3   The food which you gave:
    showed your sweetness toward your children.

4   It satisfied the desire of those who ate:
    and was flavoured as each one wished,

5   that the children you love might learn, Lord God:
    that they are not fed by crops of many kinds.

6   It is your word which sustains:
    all those who trust in you.

    Glory to the Father, and to the Son,
    and to the Holy Spirit:
    as it was in the beginning, is now,
    and shall be for ever. Amen.

Wisdom 16.20-21,26

Creation, Harvest
THE CANTICLE OF THE SUN   10Q15
Response: **Praised be my Lord by all his creatures.**

1   O most high, almighty, good Lord, God:
    to you belong praise, glory, honour and all blessing.

2   Praised be my Lord by all his creatures:
    and chiefly by our brother the sun,
    who brings us the day and brings us the light.

3   Fair is he, and shines with a very great splendour:
    he points us, O Lord, to you.

4   Praised be my Lord by our sister the moon:
    and by the stars which you have set clear and lovely in heaven.

5   Praised be my Lord by our brother the wind:
    and by air and clouds, calms and all weather,
    by which you uphold life in all creatures.

6   Praised be my Lord by our sister water:
    who is very useful to us and humble and precious and clean.

7   Praised be my Lord by our brother fire,
    through whom you give light in the darkness:
    and he is bright and pleasant and very mighty and strong.

8   Praised be my Lord by our mother the earth,
    who sustains us and keeps us:
    and brings forth fruit of different kinds,

flowers of many colours, and grass.

9   Praised be my Lord by all who pardon one another
for your love's sake:
and all who endure weakness and trials.

10   Blessed are they who calmly endure:
for you, O most high, shall give them a crown.

11   Praised be my Lord by our sister the death of the body,
from which no one escapes:
blessed are those who are found walking by your most holy will.

12   Praise and bless the Lord, and give thanks to him:
and serve him with great humility.

Word

A Song of the Word   11Q16
Response: **Seek the Lord while he may be found.**

1   Seek the Lord while he may be found:
call on him while he is near.

2   Let the wicked abandon their ways:
and the unrighteous their thoughts.

3   Turn back to the Lord, who will have mercy:
to our God, who will richly pardon.

4   'For my thoughts are not your thoughts:
neither are your ways my ways,' says the Lord.

5   'As the heavens are higher than the earth:
so are my ways higher than your ways
and my thoughts than your thoughts.

6   As the rain and snow come down from heaven:
and return not again but water the earth,

7   bringing forth life and giving growth:
seed for sowing and bread to eat,

8   so is my word that goes out from my mouth:
it does not return to me empty,

9   but it will accomplish my purpose:
and succeed in the task I give it.'

Glory to the Father, and to the Son,
and to the Holy Spirit:
as it was in the beginning, is now,
and shall be for ever. Amen.

Isaiah 55:6-11

Mission, Unity, Kingdom
A SONG OF A HERALD
Response: **Lift up your voice with strength.**

12Q17

1   Go up to a high mountain,
     herald of good tidings to Zion:
     lift up your voice with strength,
     herald of good tidings to Jerusalem.

2   Lift it up, fear not:
     say to the cities of Judah, 'Behold your God!'

3   See the Lord coming with might:
     coming to rule with his mighty arm.

4   He brings his reward with him:
     his recompense before him.

5   He will feed his flock like a shepherd:
     and gather the lambs in his arms.

6   He will hold them to his breast:
     and gently lead those with young.

     Glory to the Father, and to the Son,
     and to the Holy Spirit:
     as it was in the beginning, is now,
     and shall be for ever. Amen.

Isaiah 40.9-11

City, World and Society
(also suitable for Advent)
A SONG OF THE HOLY CITY
Response: **Behold, I make all things new.**

13Q18

1   I saw a new heaven and a new earth:
     for the first heaven and the first earth had passed away
     and there was no longer any sea.

2   I saw the holy city, new Jerusalem,
     coming down out of heaven from God:
     prepared as a bride adorned for her husband.

3   I heard a great voice from the throne saying:
'Behold, the dwelling place of God is with his people.

4   He will dwell with them and they shall be his own:
and God himself will be with them.

5   He will wipe away every tear from their eyes:
and death shall be no more.

6   There shall be no mourning
nor crying, nor pain any more:
for the former things have passed away.'

7   And he who sat upon the throne said:
'Behold, I make all things new.'

Glory to the Father, and to the Son,
and to the Holy Spirit:
as it was in the beginning, is now,
and shall be for ever. Amen.

Revelation 21.1-5a

Saints

A Song of Wisdom

Response: **Glory to the one who gives me wisdom.**

1   Wisdom freed a holy people and a blameless race:
from a nation of oppressors.

2   She entered the soul of a servant of the Lord:
and withstood fearsome rulers with wonders and signs.

3   To the saints she gave the reward of their labours:
and led them by a marvellous road.

4   She was their shelter by day:
and a blaze of stars by night.

5   She brought them across the Red Sea:
she led them through mighty waters.

6   She swallowed their enemies in the waves:
and spat them out from the depths of the sea.

7   Then, Lord, the righteous sang the glories of your name:
and praised together your protecting hand.

8   For wisdom opened the mouths of the silent:
and gave speech to the tongues of her children.

Glory to the Father, and to the Son,
and to the Holy Spirit:
as it was in the beginning, is now,
and shall be for ever. Amen.

Wisdom 10.15-19,20b-21

Kingdom, Freedom, Reconciliation
THE SONG OF HANNAH
Response: **My heart rejoices in the Lord.**

16Q20

1   My heart rejoices in the Lord:
      my strength is exalted in my God.

2   There is no one holy like the Lord:
      there is no one like you, no rock like our God.

3   For you, Lord, are a God who knows:
      and by you our actions are weighed.

4   The bows of the mighty are broken:
      but the feeble gird on strength.

5   You, Lord, make poor and make rich:
      you bring low and you also exalt.

6   You raise up the poor from the dust:
      and lift the needy from the ash-heap.

7   You make them sit with princes:
      and inherit a seat of honour.

8   For the foundations of the earth are yours, Lord:
      and on them you have set the world.

Glory to the Father, and to the Son,
and to the Holy Spirit:
as it was in the beginning, is now,
and shall be for ever. Amen.

1 Samuel 2.1-4,7,8

Kingdom, Freedom, Reconciliation
A SONG OF SALVATION
Response: **I will trust and will not be afraid.**

16Q21

1   Behold God is my salvation:
      I will trust and will not be afraid.

2   For the Lord God is my strength and my song:
      and he has become my salvation.

3   With joy you will draw water:
      from the wells of salvation.

4   On that day you will say:
      'Give thanks to the Lord, call upon his name.

5   Make known his deeds among the nations:
      proclaim that his name is exalted.

6   Sing praises to the Lord, for he has triumphed gloriously:
      let this be known in all the earth.

7   Shout and sing for joy, you that dwell in Zion:
      for great in your midst is the Holy One of Israel.'

Glory to the Father, and to the Son,
and to the Holy Spirit:
as it was in the beginning, is now,
and shall be for ever. Amen.

Isaiah 12.2-6

Peace

17Q22

A SONG OF PEACE

Response: **Let us walk in the light of the Lord.**

1   'Let us go up to the mountain of the Lord,
      to the house of the God of Jacob,

2   that he may teach us his ways:
      that we may walk in his paths.'

3   For the law shall go out from Zion:
      and the word of the Lord from Jerusalem.

4   He shall judge between the nations:
      and settle disputes for many peoples.

5   They shall beat their swords into ploughshares:
      their spears into pruning hooks.

6   Nation shall not lift up sword against nation:
      nor ever again be trained for war.

7   People of Jacob, come:
      let us walk in the light of the Lord.

Glory to the Father, and to the Son,
and to the Holy Spirit:
as it was in the beginning, is now,
and shall be for ever. Amen.

Isaiah 2.2-5

Love, Peace

THE PROMISE OF THE NEW JERUSALEM

Response: **Rejoice with Jerusalem and exult in her.**

1   Rejoice with Jerusalem and exult in her:
    all you who love her;

2   Share her joy with all your heart:
    all you who mourn over her.

3   Then you may suck and be fed from her breasts:
    delighting in her plentiful milk.

4   For thus says the Lord:
    'I will send peace flowing over her like a river,
    and the wealth of nations like a stream in flood.

5   Jerusalem shall suckle you:
    and you shall be carried in her arms
    and rocked upon her knees.

6   As a mother comforts her child:
    so will I myself comfort you,
    and you shall find strength in Jerusalem.

7   This you shall see and be glad at heart:
    your limbs shall be as the fresh grass in spring.

8   Then I myself will gather all nations:
    and they shall come and behold my glory.'

    Glory to the Father, and to the Son,
    and to the Holy Spirit:
    as it was in the beginning, is now,
    and shall be for ever. Amen.

Isaiah 66.10-14a,18b

Love, Peace

A SONG OF GOD'S LOVE

Response: **Let us love one another, for love is from God.**

1   Let us love one another:
    for love is from God.

2   Those who love are born of God and know God:
    but those who do not love
    know nothing of God, for God is love.

3   Those who dwell in love:
    are dwelling in God and God in them.

4   There is no room for fear in love:
    perfect love banishes all fear.

5   We love because God first loved us:
    if anyone who hates another
    says, 'I love God', that person is a liar.

6   If we do not love those whom we have seen:
    we cannot love God whom we have not seen.

7   This commandment we have from God:
    that those who love God must also love their neighbour.

    Glory to the Father, and to the Son,
    and to the Holy Spirit:
    as it was in the beginning, is now,
    and shall be for ever. Amen.

1 John 4.7,8,16,18-21

General
THE BEATITUDES   0Q25
Response: **Rejoice and be glad, for your reward is great in heaven.**

1   Blessed are the poor in spirit:
    for theirs is the kingdom of heaven.

2   Blessed are those who mourn:
    for they shall be comforted.

3   Blessed are the gentle:
    for they shall inherit the earth.

4   Blessed are those who hunger and thirst for what is right:
    for they shall be satisfied.

5   Blessed are the merciful:
    for mercy shall be shown to them.

6   Blessed are the pure in heart:
    for they shall see God.

7   Blessed are the peacemakers:
    for they shall be called children of God.

8   Blessed are those who are persecuted in the cause of right:
    for theirs is the kingdom of heaven.

9   Blessed are you when others revile you and persecute you:
    and utter all kinds of evil against you falsely for my sake.

10 Rejoice and be glad:
    for your reward is great in heaven.

    Glory to the Father, and to the Son,
    and to the Holy Spirit:
    as it was in the beginning, is now,
    and shall be for ever. Amen.

Matthew 5.3-12

General

A Song of Salvation

0Q26

Response: **Blessed be the God and Father of our Lord Jesus Christ.**

1   Blessed are you, God and Father of our Lord Jesus Christ:
    you have blessed us in Christ
    with all the spiritual blessings of heaven.

2   Even before the world was made
    you chose us to be yours in Christ:
    to be holy and without blame.

3   In love you planned to adopt us:
    as your children through Jesus Christ,

4   that we might praise your glorious grace:
    your free gift to us in your beloved Son.

5   In Christ we gain redemption;
    through his blood our sins are forgiven:
    how rich is your grace!

    Glory to the Father, and to the Son,
    and to the Holy Spirit:
    as it was in the beginning, is now,
    and shall be for ever. Amen.

Ephesians 1.3-7

General

A Song of Anselm

0Q27

Responses: **Jesus, as a mother you gather your people to you** *or*
In your love and tenderness remake us.

1   Jesus, as a mother you gather your people to you:
    you are gentle with us as a mother with her children;

2   Often you weep over our sins and our pride:
     tenderly you draw us from hatred and judgement.

3   You comfort us in sorrow and bind up our wounds:
     in sickness you nurse us, and with pure milk you feed us.

4   Jesus, by your dying we are born to new life:
     by your anguish and labour we come forth in joy.

5   Despair turns to hope through your sweet goodness:
     through your gentleness we find comfort in fear.

6   Your warmth gives life to the dead:
     your touch makes sinners righteous.

7   Lord Jesus, in your mercy heal us:
     in your love and tenderness remake us.

8   In your compassion bring grace and forgiveness:
     for the beauty of heaven may your love prepare us.

     Glory to the Father, and to the Son,
     and to the Holy Spirit:
     as it was in the beginning, is now,
     and shall be for ever. Amen.

General

A SONG OF PILGRIMAGE   0Q28
Response: **Glory to the one who gives me wisdom!**

1   While I was still young, before I began my travels:
     I sought for wisdom openly in my prayers.

2   I asked for her outside the temple sanctuary:
     and I will seek her to the end.

3   She has been the delight of my heart:
     from first blossom to early fruit.

4   I have kept firmly to the true path:
     I have followed her steps since my youth.

5   I bowed my ear a little and received her:
     I found wisdom and was well instructed.

6   Glory to the one who gives me wisdom!
     I will live according to her way.

7   From the beginning I gained understanding from her:
     therefore I will never be deserted.

8   Because I longed to find her with all my heart:
     I have gained a good possession.

9   As my reward the Lord has given me a tongue:
     with which I shall sing his praises.

     Glory to the Father, and to the Son,
     and to the Holy Spirit:
     as it was in the beginning, is now,
     and shall be for ever. Amen.
Ecclesiasticus 51.13-18a,20b-22

R Introductory words to the Peace _____

Note 20 in the ASB Rite A Holy Communion provides for the Peace to
be used at other points than the one provided. It can be used at the
beginning of the service, or at the end of Holy Communion or a family
service. Section 30 in Rite A provides for other suitable words to be
used instead of those in the service; some are provided in section 83,
and more here. The pattern is easy to copy, for instance to provide
words for special occasions or to echo some particular teaching in the
sermon. The introductory words should not be a prayer, but an
encouragement, based on scripture, to minister peace to one another.
The second sentence, 'The peace of the Lord be always with you' is
best kept as a standard introduction to the response, but may be
seasonally varied, as for example, 'The peace of the risen Lord be
always with you.'

Advent   1R1

In the tender compassion of our God
the dawn from on high shall break upon us,
to shine on those who dwell in darkness and the shadow of death,
and to guide our feet into the way of peace:
The peace of the Lord be always with you. . .
Luke 1.78-79

Advent   1R2

The God of peace makes us holy in all things
that we may be ready at the coming of our Lord Jesus Christ.
The peace of the Lord be always with you. . .
1 Thessalonians 5.23

Incarnation, Christmas   2R3

Glory to God in the highest,
and peace on earth to all on whom his favour rests.
The peace of the Lord be always with you. . .
Luke 2.14

Incarnation, Christmas

To us a child is born, to us a child is given,
and his name shall be called the Prince of Peace.
The peace of the Lord be always with you. . .

2R4

Epiphany

Christ came and proclaimed the gospel,
peace to those who are far off
and peace to those who are near.
The peace of the Lord be always with you. . .

3R5

Cross

Being justified by faith,
we have peace with God through our Lord Jesus Christ.
The peace of the Lord be always with you. . .
Romans 5.1

5R6

Cross

Now in union with Christ Jesus
you who once were far off
have been brought near
through the shedding of Christ's blood;
for he is our peace.
The peace of the Lord be always with you. . .
Ephesians 2.13

5R7

Spirit, Pentecost, Baptism and Confirmation

We are baptized into Christ:
live in the Spirit of Christ.
The peace of the Lord be always with you. . .

8R8

Spirit, Pentecost

The mind of sinful nature is death;
The mind controlled by the Spirit is life and peace.
The peace of the Lord be always with you. . .
Romans 8.6

8R9

Trinity

Peace to you from God our heavenly Father.
Peace from his Son Jesus Christ who is our peace.
Peace from the Holy Spirit the lifegiver.
The peace of the Lord be always with you. . .

9R10

Harvest

Peacemakers who sow in peace raise a harvest of righteousness.
The peace of the Lord be always with you. . .

James 3.18

10R11

Church, Mission and Ministry, Unity

We are the body of Christ.
By one Spirit we were baptized into one body.
Keep the unity of the Spirit in the bond of peace.
We are bound by the love of Christ.
The peace of the Lord be always with you. . .

1 Corinthians 12.13

12R12

Church, Mission and Ministry, Unity

We are all one in Christ Jesus.
We belong to him through faith,
heirs of the promise of the Spirit of peace.
The peace of the Lord be always with you. . .

Galatians 3.28

12R13

Family

Jesus said, 'Whoever does the will of God
is my brother, and sister and mother.'
As we have opportunity, let us work for good to all,
especially members of the household of faith.
The peace of the Lord be always with you. . .

14R14

Kingdom, Freedom, Reconciliation

God calls us to peace:
in God's justice is our peace.
Christ calls us to be God's people:
in Christ is our peace.
The peace of the Lord be always with you. . .

Ephesians 2.14-15

16R15

Kingdom, Freedom, Reconciliation

Blessed be Christ, the Prince of Peace.
He breaks down the walls that divide us:
praise Christ who is our peace!
The peace of the Lord be always with you. . .

16R16

Kingdom, Freedom, Reconciliation

God has reconciled us to himself through Christ

16R17

and given us the ministry of reconciliation.
The peace of the Lord be always with you. . .

2 Corinthians 5.18

Love, Peace

Love one another.
As I have loved you,
so you are to love one another.
The peace of the Lord be always with you. . .

17R18

John 15.12

Wedding

We have celebrated the love of *N* and *N*.
We now celebrate God's love for all of us.
Greet one another with a kiss of love.
Peace in Christ to all of you. . .

17R19

1 Peter 5.14

Love, Peace

Let love be genuine. Never pay back evil for evil.
As far as it lies with you, live at peace with everyone.
The peace of the Lord be always with you. . .

17R20

Romans 12.9,17,18

Love, Unity

To crown all things there must be love,
to bind all together and complete the whole.
Let the peace of Christ rule in your hearts.
The peace of the Lord be always with you. . .

17R21

Colossians 3.14

General, Memorials and in Times of Trouble

Jesus says to his disciples,
'Peace I leave with you; my peace I give you.
Not as the world gives do I give to you.
Let not your hearts be troubled or afraid.'
The peace of the Lord be always with you. . .

0R22

John 14.27

General

Blessed are those who make peace:
they shall be called sons and daughters of God.
We meet in the name of Christ and share his peace.

0R23

The peace of the Lord be always with you. . .
Matthew 5.9

General

God will speak peace to his people,
to those who turn to him in their hearts.
The peace of the Lord be always with you. . .
Psalm 85.8; 1 Samuel 12.20

0R24

At an Agape

The kingdom of God is not a matter of eating and drinking,
but of righteousness, peace and joy in the Holy Spirit.
The peace of the Lord be always with you. . .
Romans 14.17

0R25

General

God has called us to live in peace.
The peace of the Lord be always with you. . .
1 Corinthians 7.17

0R26

General

Aim for perfection,
be of one mind, live in peace.
Greet one another with a holy kiss.
And the God of love and peace be with you. . .
2 Corinthians 13.11

0R27

General

Let the peace of Christ rule in your hearts,
since as members of one body you are called to peace.
The peace of the Lord be always with you. . .
Colossians 3.15

0R28

General

Sovereign Lord, your word has been fulfilled;
my eyes have seen your salvation:
now you let your servant go in peace.
The peace of the Lord be always with you. . .
Luke 2.29

0R29

S Words for dedication

These, or other similar responses, may be used at the beginning of the service, at the intercessions, at the presentation of the gifts, or before the blessing and dismissal. Gifts of money or tokens of the life and work of the people, or of some particular aspect of service, may be placed on a table in the middle of the congregation or presented to the presiding minister. Some of these responses might also be used for the dedication of church officers and leaders, PCC members, stewardship or mission visitors, etc. This may take place at the intercessions or at the Peace, and the minister may first say, 'As mission visitors (or whatever. . .) we dedicate *ourselves/you* to God's service.'

Christ has offered for all time a single sacrifice for sins.   0S1
He is seated at the right hand of God.

Through him let us offer up a sacrifice of praise to God:
the fruit of lips that acknowledge his name.

Do not forget to do good and share what you have.
Such sacrifices are pleasing to God.

The free gift of God is eternal life in Christ Jesus our Lord.   0S2
By his mercy we present our whole lives to God
as a living sacrifice.

Lord Jesus Christ, you emptied yourself,   0S3
taking the form of a servant.
Through your love, make us servants of one another.

Lord Jesus Christ, for our sake you became poor.
May our lives and gifts enrich the life of your world.

The free gift of God is eternal life in Christ Jesus our Lord.   0S4
By his mercy we present our whole lives to God
as a living sacrifice.

Though many, we form one body in Christ.
We belong to one another.

By God's grace we have different gifts.
We will use them in faith.

Rejoice in hope, stand firm in trouble, be constant in prayer.
Filled with his Spirit we will serve the Lord.

T BLESSINGS AND ENDINGS

Section 54 of the ASB Rite A Holy Communion permits the president to say an alternative blessing. Some are provided in Section 77, and two more as Sections 18 and 19 in 'Prayers for Various Occasions'. The ASB structure is easy to copy, to provide a blessing to fit with a special occasion or some particular emphasis in the worship or teaching: an opening sentence which is a prayer that God will do something, followed by that form of the blessing popularized by medieval bishops:

> '. . . and the blessing of God almighty,
> the Father, the Son, and the Holy Spirit,
> be among you and remain with you always.'

Some further examples of this form are provided here, together with some alternative structures, one of which is the three-part solemn blessing. This focuses on a biblical story or doctrine, relates that to what we believe, and prays for a deepening of our experience of that aspect of God's work, summed up in the same form of blessing.

The Peace may also be used as an ending: see Section R (page 171).

The dismissal, ending or blessing should always be the last item in any service, and should not be followed by a hymn or more prayers.

Advent

May God the Father,   1T1
who loved the world so much that he sent his only Son
to come among us in great humility,
open your eyes to look for his coming again. **Amen.**

May God the Son
give you grace to live
in the light of his coming as redeemer and judge. **Amen.**

May God the Holy Spirit
free you from sin,
make you holy,
and bring you to eternal life. **Amen.**

And the blessing. . .

Advent

Christ the Sun of righteousness shine upon you,
scatter the darkness from your path,
and make you ready to meet him when he comes in glory.
And the blessing. . .

1T2

Advent

May God himself, the God of peace,
make you perfect and holy;
and keep you all safe and blameless, in spirit, soul and body,
for the coming of our Lord Jesus Christ.
And the blessing. . .

1T3

1 Thessalonians 5.23

Incarnation, Christmas, Annunciation, Mary

God sent his angels from glory to bring to shepherds
the good news of our Saviour's birth. **Amen**

2T4

You have seen his glory,
the glory of the Father's only Son. **Amen.**

May he fill you with joy
and send you out from his glory
to bring this good news to others today. **Amen.**

And the blessing. . .

Incarnation, Christmas, Annunciation, Mary

May the Father,
who has loved the eternal Son
from before the foundation of the world,
shed that love upon you his children. **Amen.**

2T5

May Christ,
who by his incarnation gathered into one
things earthly and heavenly,
fill you with joy and peace. **Amen.**

May the Holy Spirit,
by whose overshadowing Mary became the God-bearer,
give you grace to carry the good news of Christ. **Amen.**

And the blessing. . .

Incarnation, Christmas, Annunciation, Mary

May the eagerness of the shepherds,   2T6
the joy of the angels,
the perseverance of the wise men,
the obedience of Joseph and Mary,
and the peace of the Christ-child
be yours this Christmas.

And the blessing. . .

Incarnation, Christmas

Jesus Christ was born of the Virgin Mary: 2T7
revealed in his glory;
worshipped by angels:
proclaimed among the nations;
exalted to the highest heavens:
believed in throughout the world.
Blessed be God, our strength and our salvation:
now and for ever. Amen

Mothering Sunday, Mary

When the Word became flesh   2T8
earth was joined to heaven in the womb of Mary:
may the love and obedience of Mary be your example. **Amen.**

May the peace of Christ
rule in your hearts and homes. **Amen.**

May you be filled with the joy of the Spirit
and the gifts of your eternal home. **Amen.**

And the blessing. . .

Epiphany, Light

May God the Father,   3T9
who led the wise men by the shining of a star
to find the Christ, the Light from light,
lead you in your pilgrimage to find the Lord. **Amen.**

May God who has brought us out of darkness
give us a place with the saints in light
in the kingdom of his Son. **Amen.**

May the light of the glorious gospel of Christ
shine in your hearts,
and transform your lives,

to bring his light to others. **Amen.**

And the blessing. . .
Colossians 1.13; 2 Corinthians 4.4

Epiphany, Light
May Christ draw you to humility and worship,   3T10
and bring you to see God at work.
And the blessing. . .

Epiphany, Wedding
May God, who sent his Son   3T11
to provide new wine at a wedding in Cana,
bring you the kindness and blessings of his presence. **Amen.**

May God who cares for us,
and whose power turned water into wine,
transform your lives and make glad your hearts. **Amen.**

May he work miracles in your lives,
fill you with his Spirit,
and change you day by day to reflect his glory,
until that day when you see him face to face. **Amen.**

And the blessing. . .
John 2.1-11

Lent, Penitence
May God the Father,   4T12
who does not despise the broken spirit,
give to you a contrite heart. **Amen.**

May Christ,
who bore our sins in his body on the tree,
heal you by his wounds. **Amen.**

May the Holy Spirit,
who leads us into all truth,
speak to you words of pardon and peace. **Amen.**

And the blessing. . .
Psalm 51; Isaiah 53

Cross
You believe that by his dying   5T13
Christ destroyed death for ever. **Amen.**

You have been crucified with Christ
and live by faith in the Son of God,
who loved you and gave himself for you. **Amen.**

May he send you out to glory in his cross,
and live no longer for yourselves but for him,
who died and was raised to life for us. **Amen.**

And the blessing. . .
Galatians 2.20; 2 Corinthians 5.15

Resurrection, Heaven, Glory, Transfiguration, Death, Funerals
You believe Jesus has been raised from the dead in glory. **Amen.**   6T14

You believe you have been raised with Christ. **Amen.**

May your hearts and minds be set on things above,
where Christ is seated at the right hand of God. **Amen.**

And the blessing. . .

Resurrection, Heaven, Glory, Transfiguration, Death, Funerals
God the Father,   6T15
by whose love Christ was raised from the dead,
open to you who believe the gates of everlasting life. **Amen.**

God the Son,
who in bursting the grave has won a glorious victory,
give you joy as you share the Easter faith. **Amen.**

God the Holy Spirit,
whom the risen Lord breathed into his disciples,
empower you and fill you with Christ's peace. **Amen.**

And the blessing. . .

Resurrection, Heaven, Glory, Transfiguration, Death, Funerals
May Christ, who out of defeat   6T16
brings new hope and a new future,
fill you with his new life.
And the blessing. . .

Ascension, Kingship
Christ our exalted King   7T17
pour upon you his abundant gifts
and bring you to reign with him in glory.
And the blessing. . .

Ascension, Kingship

God the Father,   7T18
who has given to his Son the name above every name,
strengthen you to proclaim Christ as Lord. **Amen.**

God the Son,
who is our great high priest passed into the heavens,
plead for you at the right hand of the Father. **Amen.**

God the Holy Spirit,
who pours out his abundant gifts upon the Church,
make you faithful servants of Christ our King. **Amen.**

And the blessing. . .

Ascension, Kingship

Yours, Lord, is the greatness, the power,   7T19
the glory, the splendour, and the majesty:
for everything in heaven and on earth is yours.

Yours, Lord, is the kingdom:
and you are exalted as head over all.
Alleluia! Alleluia! Amen.

1 Chronicles 29.11

Spirit, Pentecost, Gifts, Healing, Baptism and Confirmation

God poured out his promised Holy Spirit   8T20
on the day of Pentecost. **Amen.**

You have been baptized with the Spirit and with fire. **Amen.**

May his tongues of flame
burn out all evil from your hearts,
fill you with his love and peace,
and give you the gifts of his Spirit
and a voice to praise him for ever. **Amen.**

And the blessing. . .

Acts 2.1-4

Spirit, Pentecost, Gifts, Healing, Baptism and Confirmation

May the Spirit,   8T21
who hovered over the waters when the world was created,
breathe into you the life he gives. **Amen.**

May the Spirit,
who overshadowed the virgin when the eternal Son
    came among us,

make you obedient in the service of the Lord. **Amen.**

May the Spirit,
who inflamed the Church upon the day of Pentecost,
set the world on fire with the love of the risen Christ. **Amen.**

And the blessing. . .

Spirit, Pentecost, Gifts, Healing, Baptism and Confirmation
May Christ's holy, healing, enabling Spirit be with you   8T22
and guide you on your way at every change and turn.
And the blessing. . .

Spirit, Pentecost, Gifts, Healing, Baptism and Confirmation
May the God of hope fill us   8T23
with all joy and peace in believing,
through the power of the Holy Spirit. **Amen.**
Romans 15.13

Baptism
The Holy Trinity,   8T24
in whose name we were baptized,
preserve us,
members of Christ,
children of God,
inheritors of the kingdom of heaven,
saved by the waters,
and filled with the Spirit.
Glory to God,
Father, Son and Holy Spirit.

Trinity
The Lord bless you and keep you. **Amen.**   9T25

The Lord make his face to shine upon you,
and be gracious to you. **Amen.**

The Lord lift up his countenance upon you
and give you peace. **Amen.**

The Lord God almighty, Father, Son, and Holy Spirit,
the holy and undivided Trinity,
guard you, save you,
and bring you to that heavenly city,
where he lives and reigns for ever and ever. **Amen.**
Numbers 6.24-25

Trinity

9T26

To God the Father, who loved us,
and made us accepted in the Beloved:
to God the Son, who loved us,
and loosed us from our sins by his own blood:
to God the Holy Ghost,
who spreads the love of God abroad in our hearts:
to the one true God be all love and all glory
for time and for eternity. **Amen**.

Harvest, Creation

10T27

May God the Father of our Lord Jesus Christ,
who is the source of all goodness and growth,
pour his blessing upon all things created,
and upon you his children,
that you may use them to his glory and the welfare of all peoples.
And the blessing. . .

Harvest, Creation

10T28

May God who clothes the lilies and feeds the birds of the sky,
who leads the lambs to pasture and the deer to water,
who multiplied loaves and fishes and changed water into wine,
lead us, feed us, multiply us,
and change us to reflect the glory of our Creator
through all eternity.
And the blessing. . .

Harvest, Creation, Eucharist

10T29

May the Father,
who fed his children with bread and honey in the wilderness,
strengthen you in your pilgrimage to the Promised Land. **Amen**.

May the Son,
who gave his flesh for food and his blood for drink,
keep you in eternal life and raise you up on the last day. **Amen**.

May the Holy Spirit,
who leads us into all truth,
help you discern the Lord's body
and empower you to proclaim his death until he comes. **Amen**.

And the blessing. . .

Word

Hear the teaching of Jesus:
'Blessed are those who hear the word of God and obey it.'
Go now to do God's will.
And the blessing. . .

11T30

Word

Go now in peace,
knowing that you have been born again,
not of perishable seed,
but of imperishable,
through the living and enduring word of God.
And the blessing. . .

11T31

Church, Mission and Ministry, Unity

Glory to God:
**whose power, at work among us,
can do infinitely more
than all we can ask or conceive;
to him be glory in the Church and in Christ Jesus,
for ever and ever. Amen.**
Ephesians 3.20-21

12T32

Church, Mission and Ministry, Unity

May God, who gives patience and encouragement,
give you a spirit of unity
to live in harmony as you follow Jesus Christ,
so that with one voice you may glorify
the God and Father of our Lord Jesus Christ. **Amen.**
Romans 15.5,6

12T33

City, World and Society

God, who has prepared for you
a city with permanent foundations,
bring you to the eternal and triumphant joy
of that city of the great King.
And the blessing. . .

13T34

City, World and Society

Go forth into the world in peace;
be of good courage;
hold fast that which is good;
render to no one evil for evil;
strengthen the fainthearted; support the weak;

13T35

help the afflicted; honour everyone;
love and serve the Lord,
rejoicing in the power of the Holy Spirit.
And the blessing. . .

1 Thessalonians 5.13-22

Family

May the Father from whom every family   14T36
in earth and heaven receives its name
strengthen you with his Spirit in your inner being,
so that Christ may dwell in your hearts by faith,
and that, knowing his love,
broad and long, deep and high beyond our knowledge,
you may be filled with all the fulness of God.
And the blessing. . .

Ephesians 3.15-19

Saints

May God, who has given you in the lives of the saints   15T37
patterns of holy living and victorious dying,
strengthen you to follow them in the way of holiness. **Amen.**

May God, who has kindled the fire of his love
in the hearts of the saints,
pour upon you the riches of his grace. **Amen.**

May God, who calls you no longer strangers and aliens
but fellow-citizens with all the saints,
bring you to your home in heaven. **Amen.**

And the blessing. . .

Colossians 1.12; Ephesians 1.17,18; 2.14

Saints

May God, who kindled the fire of his love   15T38
in the hearts of the saints,
pour upon you the riches of his grace. **Amen.**

May he give you joy in their fellowship
and a share in their joy. **Amen.**

May he strengthen you to walk in the way of holiness
and to come to the full radiance of glory. **Amen.**

And the blessing. . .

Saints

May Christ, who makes saints of sinners, 15T39
who has transformed those we remember today,
raise and strengthen you that you may transform the world.
And the blessing. . .

Saints, Heaven

May God the Father bring us to the home 15T40
which his Son prepares for all who love him. **Amen.**

May God the Son give us the will
to live for him each day in life eternal. **Amen.**

May God the Holy Spirit give us the assurance
that our citizenship is in heaven
with the blessed and beloved,
and the whole company of the redeemed. **Amen.**

And the blessing. . .

Kingdom, Freedom, Reconciliation

Now may the blessing of God the Father, 16T41
who made from one every nation that occupies the earth;
of God the Son who bought us for God
from every tribe and language and people and nation;
and of God the Spirit who brings us together in unity,
be with us and remain with us always. **Amen.**

Acts 17.26; Revelation 5.9

Kingdom, Advent

May God the Father, Judge all merciful, 16T42
make us worthy of a place in his kingdom. **Amen.**

May God the Son, coming among us in power,
reveal among us the promise of his glory. **Amen.**

May God the Holy Spirit make us steadfast in faith,
joyful in hope and constant in love. **Amen.**

And the blessing. . .

Love, Marriage

May God the Father join you together 17T43
in mutual love and faithful living,
as he united Adam and Eve, our first parents. **Amen.**

May the Lord Jesus be present with you,
to bless your marriage with all his power
and gladden your hearts with the joy of Cana. **Amen**.

May the Holy Spirit fill you with a life of strength and patience,
and crown you with the blessing of his heavenly gifts. **Amen**.

And the blessing. . .

General

The Lord God almighty is our Father: OT44
he loves us and tenderly cares for us.
The Lord Jesus Christ is our Saviour:
he has redeemed us and will defend us to the end.
The Lord, the Holy Spirit, is among us:
he will lead us in God's holy way.
To God almighty, Father, Son and Holy Spirit,
be praise and glory today and for ever. Amen.

General

The almighty and merciful Lord, OT45
Father, Son, and Holy Spirit,
bless us and keep us. **Amen**.

General

Now may the Lord of peace himself OT46
give you peace at all times and in every way.
The Lord be with you all.
And the blessing. . .
2 Thessalonians 3.16

General

You are called and loved by God the Father OT47
and kept safe by Jesus Christ.
Mercy, peace and love be yours in abundance,
from God the Father, Son and Holy Spirit. **Amen**.
Jude 1,2

General

May God give to you and to all those you love OT48
his comfort and his peace,
his light and his joy,
in this world and the next.
And the blessing. . .

General

Let us bless the Lord:

OT49

thanks be to God.
Blessing, honour and glory be yours,
here and everywhere,
now and for ever. Amen.

General

Now unto the King eternal, immortal, invisible, the only wise God,

OT50

be honour and glory for ever and ever. **Amen.**

I Timothy 1:17

4

THE
COMMENTARY

Introduction to the commentary
	Why this is here	192
	How to use this commentary	192
	What is worship?	193

Preliminary factors
1	Imagination, vision and patterns: an introduction to St Ann's, St Bartholomew's, St Christopher's and St David's	194
2	Architecture, space and colour	197
3	Planning and preparation	201
4	Structures and 'specials'	203

Through the service
A	Introductions	206
B	Confessions	208
E	The Ministry of the Word	210
F	Affirmations of faith	212
G	Prayers of intercession	214
H	Collects	217
R	The Peace	219
S	Action and movement	222
	Distributing communion	224

Other issues
5	Additions and insertions	228
6	Producing a local service sheet	233
7	The law and common prayer	238

INTRODUCTION TO THE COMMENTARY

Why this is here

Worship is not worship until you do it.

It is no longer sufficient in the Church of England to produce a worship book which consists simply of texts, to say or sing. That is a bit like producing a recipe which is a list of ingredients without the instructions for putting them together.

But how do you offer advice and suggest questions to ask about the presentation of the liturgy without putting it all in rubrics, or mandatory stage instructions, in the services, or producing a separate manual? We decided the most digestible and least legalistic way of doing it would be to tell stories. So here you have the stories of four entirely imaginary churches, told in sections which correspond with the Resource Sections. As you read them, you will gather a little of the flavour and style of each church, town and country, with different spaces and resources. You may find you identify more with one than with another, but be prepared to learn from the others.

How to use this commentary

It is not necessary to read right through the commentary. Those wishing to look at the presentation of a particular aspect of worship might ask two or three people to read that particular section of the commentary. It might help to offer them some questions:

- Can you imagine being present in the situations described?
- What is good or bad about them?
- Do you feel nearer to the experience of one of the four churches? Which one?
- Make a list of suggestions which come to you as a result of reading this section.
- Are any of these suggestions possible for us
  a) right now?
  b) some time in the future?
- Do we need variety in how we handle this week by week, or do we need the security of being consistent?

● Do we need to consult with others before taking action – other church leaders, the PCC, musicians, choir, servers, etc?

What is worship?

A worship planning group, a PCC or church leaders' group would do well to have some discussion in general terms about worship. Are we agreed about what is worship and what is not, what the ingredients are, what kind of movement, physical, emotional and spiritual, we should expect in worship?

Try completing the sentence, 'Worship is. . .' Yes, it is giving God his worth, or what he deserves, or glory. 'The true end of man is to glorify God and enjoy him for ever', as they said in the seventeenth century. But explore the mechanics of that a bit more: do any of these sentences get near our experience?

Worship is a door open in heaven. We lift up our hearts, listen in to what God is saying, join the angels and archangels and all the saints in heaven in praising God's eternal holiness. We are there and he is here.

Worship is a door open to the inner depths of life. Suddenly, as we worship, there is wholeness, *shalom*, peace, as all the fragmented bits of our being are put into God's perspective. Things make sense, and there is something to hold on to which has hitherto seemed just beyond the grasp of our mind.

Worship is a door open to the rhythms of life. Through festivals, simple rituals, a weekly rhythm, worship marking morning and evening, the whole of life, time and space is claimed for God and given back to him. In the worship he gives it to us again, to use for him, and we know he is concerned with our hopes and fears, politics and problems, families and finance.

Worship is a door to our hearts open in obedience to God. He commands us to worship in spirit and in truth. We respond to the overwhelming majesty of his beauty revealed in creation, to his overwhelming love and grace revealed in his word and in his Son. And as we worship, we are changed. . .

Now, this is in no sense an agreed definition of worship. Rather, it is intended to stimulate local parish groups and worship leaders to arrive at some agreement on what they expect, or are longing for, in their worship. The next section, *Imagination, Vision and Patterns*, may help to clarify this vision.

PRELIMINARY FACTORS

1 Imagination, vision and patterns

St Ann's is a large urban/suburban church, with a mixed congregation of different ages and backgrounds. There is considerable lay involvement in the leadership of the church, and this is evident in the worship, too. The PCC recently spent a day away reviewing the church's worship, and one of the results of this was the setting up of a Worship Group (see box on the next page, and 'Planning and Preparation' on page 201).

Sunday worship is the centrepoint and focus of the whole life of this very active church, and a lot of energy is put into preparing for Sunday both by those involved in teaching the different adult and children's groups and by the music and drama groups. Sunday morning worship is on the Rite A Holy Communion pattern every week, but makes use of the provisions of *A Service of the Word* for the first half to give the flavour of a family service. There are regularly adult groups, video and other ways of doing the sermon, and a break at the Peace when the children come back from their groups and some non-communicants and enquirers can leave without embarrassment.

St Bartholomew's is a lovely medieval country church, small both in size and in congregation. Sharing a vicar with other churches in the group means that the Sunday pattern varies from week to week, and the main service is not always communion. The church is not as insular as it used to be, with one or two people sometimes going to services at other churches in the group, and some 'new' people in the village bringing experience of other churches. The main vision of the staff (vicar, deacon and an excellent Reader), is for worship that is accessible to everyone in the village, children included, and accurately reflects and sums up the life of the community. Some of the congregation would prefer it to be a little less related to the community, and more of a beautiful oasis away from the week's troubles – a kind of entering into eternity from which they can emerge refreshed to face the week.

St Ann's awayday agenda

1 Prayer

2 Share in twos or threes what is really good about our worship

3 Talk or Bible study or discussion:
'What is worship?'
'What should our Sunday worship include?'

4 From this, in twos and threes, list some principles which should govern our worship. Share these with the whole group, and see how much agreement there is. Sometimes we disagree on practical decisions about worship because we don't agree on the principles.

5 Next, consider in small groups practical questions such as: How does the worship meet the needs of:
● the elderly
● children of different ages
● the disabled
● those who find reading difficult
● those who need to be stretched intellectually?

Should there be more freedom (or less?) in our worship?
How should we expect to know the presence of God?
How could the intercessions be improved?
Then decide which two items should come top of the group's agenda.

6 With everyone together, list the suggested agenda items, see how much overlap there is, and start with the one with most 'votes'.
There will not be time to discuss everything.
Some items will need further research: two people could be briefed to bring items back to the PCC.

7 For each item, consider four questions:
● What resources do we need?
● What barriers or problems are there in the way of taking action on this?
● What is the timetable for action?
● Who is responsible for action?

St Christopher's is a large nineteenth-century mock Gothic building in the downtown part of the city. The parish priest lives in the vicarage adjoining the church – a high brick wall also encloses the disused school now used adventurously for a wide range of community activities – and he is the only professional living in the area. The small congregation spends a lot of time together: all of them live locally. Some of them help to run things in the community centre and every morning there are four or five praying, with more for late evening worship, and thirty for communion with hymns and sermon on Tuesday evening. Sunday worship is a culmination and gathering together of the activities, concerns and worship of the week. The social needs of the community are offered to God as easily as they are discussed practically in the pub after church – a kind of extended Peace attended by most of the congregation.

St Christopher's programme for Sunday evenings

6.00	1662 Evening prayer
6.45	A simple devotional or sacramental meditation
7.00	Coffee
7.15	Bible class
7.45	Singing and worship

Most people stay all the time, though some come just for the first or the second hour. Both the meditation and the informal singing and worship time are used for introducing new songs and material such as that in *Patterns*.

St David's is a church where worship is simply not one of the most important things the church does. It comes low on most people's agenda, though there are occasional heated discussions at the PCC. The demands of different factions and rival views in the church mean that the worship is very bitty, and there is a different kind of service each Sunday in the month, with very few people going every week. The vicar finds little time for preparation and feels he cannot involve others in preparing or helping to lead because of the need to keep the balance between the different factions.

2 Architecture, space and colour

St Ann's is a modern building with worshippers seated on moveable chairs in a semi-circle around the shallow open dais. The amplification system is excellent and none of the furniture in the building is fixed. A creative group in the church makes banners and throw-away paper visuals which focus on the season or the teaching theme – and the children's groups often contribute their own decorations. Using free-standing screens for some of these means that they need not always be in the same place, and can be moved according to the needs of the worship. It also avoids sticky messes on the walls, though occasionally the wall is used, as when they went for a year or so with the words 'Christ has died, Christ is risen, Christ will come again' in lovely paper letters on the wall behind the holy table.

St Bartholomew's found some years ago that they could increase the sense of space in their tiny church by removing the back row of the choir, moving the front stalls back, and putting carpet right across the chancel and sanctuary. At the same time, they moved the altar forward far enough for the president to get behind it.

More recently, they have looked at the need for somewhere for a very small group to worship on Sunday evenings or for less formal midweek occasions. The result of this has been the transformation of a small side-chapel. The floor has been levelled (a sanctuary step had been put in at some stage), an efficient independent heating system installed, and the old wooden chairs replaced by stacking cushioned stools, whose upholstery matches the carpet and the new pastel wash on the walls. Their small Jacobean table, restored and no longer boxed in with hangings, is a fitting focus for the seven or eight who gather round. Other 'focus' items include an icon of the Trinity and a single candle. Worshipping in this situation, with more personal relationship between the members of the congregation and the president, inevitably has an effect on what happens in the larger group on Sundays, and has been a suitable place for trying some of the less formal structures in *Patterns for Worship*.

St Christopher's have only been back in church for a month. They worshipped in the school hall while the church was being re-ordered and decorated, and found this a surprisingly valuable experience. They took a deliberate decision not to cart bits of furniture out of the church into the hall to make the place 'more like church' – they had seen the odd effect of this in another local church which used a community centre, with plastic chairs (each with its embroidered hassock) and metal tables (one of them with a Victorian frontal not quite fitting it), a heavy gothic lectern and sanctuary chairs to match.

Instead, they decided to use the school furniture as it was, with a white cloth on the table and all the links with church centred on the people and the colourful vestments of the ministers. Without hassocks, they stood for the whole of the Eucharistic Prayer – and quite a bit more in the worship – and decided to carry on doing this when they returned to church. Doing without the organ was a good experience, too, and opened up the possibility of using other instruments regularly. A group playing the flute, guitar and piano now practises each week for some of the items in each service, and taped music provides the background more often than the organ to receiving communion.

In the re-ordered St Christopher's, the choir stalls have been moved to the West end of the church, behind the congregation. The chancel, cleared of furniture, is made more spacious with a platform built forward of the chancel arch – with a carpet unifying the floor area. Gone are the heavy oak clergy desks and ornate bishop's chair, replaced by simple seats for the president and his assistants, facing the people. The lectern, too, is a simple design. The altar has been brought forward, under the arch, with plenty of space for movement round it. There is also space, at the side, for a modern one-piece font, big enough for an adult to stand in and have water poured over him, and incorporating a bowl at waist height for sprinkling.

St David's is a bit like an old-fashioned museum, with generations of furnishings and clutter which no one is allowed to touch. The sanctuary houses banners from long-departed church organizations, a large three-dimensional marble monument on one wall, a threadbare strip of carpet with brass fasteners, and a holy table which is not a table but a boxed-in wooden framework to hold ancient frontals (and behind which the flower vases, spare candles and watering can are kept). The light oak modern reading desks (given in memory of a benefactor twenty years ago and therefore immoveable – one reason why the table cannot be moved forward) contrast with the dark pine empty choir stalls. And there are some items taken from the now-demolished church in the next parish when it was amalgamated with St David's – an enormous carved oak lectern out of all proportion to the rest of the furnishings, and a large marble font. This was so heavy that a special concrete base had to be built for it at the back of the church (where it is never used). They even found space to cram in a few more pews at the same time, and all without thinking of seeking advice or getting a faculty.

St Ann's checklist

At their worship planning meeting, the leaders check through items to do with space, colour and the use of the building:

1 Should the seating be normal or do we need to change it – make the aisles wider for a procession or dancing, for example?
2 Are we making the best use of the different spaces? Could we, for example, do a dramatic reading from different parts of the building?
3 Can we visualize the different colours in use on any one day, in the dress of the ministers, banners and other hangings or visuals? Do we need to use the coloured stage lights?
4 How will people move? Are there clear 'ceremonial routes' for the ministers, e.g. moving to the font for a baptism with a family coming forward? Who is responsible for taking care of mechanical hiccups like moving a projector or microphone stand out of the way?
5 What does the church smell and look like? Do we need polish, air freshener or incense?

How St Christopher's moved

1 Some months of teaching about worship led to most people seeing that the present layout could be improved.
2 The vicar and churchwarden met the archdeacon, who outlined possibilities and offered a list of other churches who had made similar changes.
3 The PCC set up a small group to visit other churches, get ideas, take measurements and report back.
4 An on-site consultation was held between the PCC committee, architect and archdeacon. Members of the Diocesan Advisory Committee and the Diocesan Liturgical Committee looked at how the changes might help or hinder the worship – bearing in mind the need for flexibility as the exact ways of doing the worship might change.
5 The PCC rightly thought that it was important for people to have some idea of what it would be like before taking the final decision. They considered producing some artist's impressions to be mounted on large display boards. But they decided on an experimental moving of the furniture (by the congregation and therefore at no cost).
6 After a couple of months the PCC consulted every member of the congregation – which made raising the money easier, as everyone felt they had a stake in the decision.
7 The PCC agreed to apply for a faculty.

Small groups

Small groups at worship include not only small Sunday congregations, but those who gather midweek, church leaders and others praying daily, and one minister at prayer on his or her own.

St Bartholomew's discussed the importance of:

1   The scale of the worship area. A small group is de-scaled by a large and lofty building, and made to feel insignificant.
2   Warmth and comfort. It is easier to worship when people are comfortable.
3   Colour. Gentle colours are better for a group close to them, more strident colours for distant and dramatic viewing.
4   Flexible seating. This can be arranged so that people can look at each other or have as the focus: altar-table, icon, candle, banner, lectern or Bible.
5   Space, so that movement is possible, not only to come and go with ease, but to move during the worship.
6   The possibility of using the area for one-to-one counselling, the ministry of reconciliation, ministry to couples, spiritual direction.

3 Planning and preparation

St Ann's sent three lay leaders on a diocesan course on preparing worship. As a result they came back wanting to set up a planning group for worship. They brought back with them draft terms of reference for such a group, which were discussed and amended by the PCC (see box on page 202). The PCC recognized that this was a move away from the previous pattern, where a different housegroup had planned and led the worship each week. This had resulted in some inconsistency in the worship, though one good thing about it was that a very wide range of people had been involved, so the new planning group had quite a long list of people in the church who had worship gifts.

At **St Bartholomew's** the vicar recognized the difficulty of planning worship for several different country churches. In St Bartholomew's the monthly family service is planned and led by a group of young parents, two of whom teach in the small Sunday School, so that there is some link between the two. They plan the themes six months at a time with the vicar, decide on how to handle the theme in terms of teaching, readings, music, prayers, etc. In one village two people have been on a diocesan course on leading worship, and can plan and lead the first part of the Service of the Word until the vicar arrives. In another village the PCC is small enough to discuss worship easily and the vicar has been training some of them to lead the intercessions.

Planning at **St Christopher's** is in the hands of the staff. The vicar uses a blank form (specimen on page 202) which gradually gets filled in, from his initial ideas a couple of months ahead, through discussion with the staff and regular meetings with Sunday School leaders, organist and head server. Copies of the form, duly typed, give all concerned a complete menu for each service.

The vicar of **St David's** returned from a (compulsory) diocesan clergy conference at which worship had been on the agenda, keen to put into practice some of the things he had learnt others were doing. Next Sunday's worship was a different structure, with a new confession, creed and Eucharistic Prayer (and no time for the congregation to be taught about them or even to read quietly through them before having to join in). There were also new songs – which the choir hadn't seen before – in the order of service which had been badly duplicated on dark pink paper. The clearest liturgical refrain in the service was 'You'll find it on your pink slip' which amused everyone but the colour-blind. An angry PCC the next week invoked the provisions of the Worship and Doctrine Measure and insisted on a return to the traditional services. Everyone was hurt and the worship was fossilized.

St Ann's worship action group terms of reference

1 To review and evaluate all aspects of worship at St Ann's, including:
   - structures and patterns of worship on Sunday
   - the relationship between worship and the rest of the life of the church
   - the use of music, drama, teaching and preaching programme
   - the place of children and other groups.
2 To be responsible for the planning and preparation of Sunday worship, including working through other groups such as house groups, choir, music groups, drama group.
3 To ensure that the varied gifts of the congregation are being used in worship.
4 To plan developments in worship and to prepare for regular PCC discussion of worship.

St Christopher's service form:
10.30 a.m. Parish Eucharist

Season/mood:

President:

Assistants:

Standard service:

Setting:

Introit/introductory music /sentence:

Hymn:

Old Testament:

Canticle/song:

New Testament:

Psalm:

Gospel:

Sermon:

Intercessions:
· (who? add items. . .)

Any special requirements, e.g. tapes, visuals:

Variable items for eucharist (words/music for peace, preface, before and during distribution, post-communion sentence) :

Hymn:

Post-communion prayer:

Notices (list . . .)

Blessing/dismissal:

4 Structures and 'specials'

It's the fifth Sunday in the month, and each church is having a special family service, exploring how to use *A Service of the Word* to help them produce something a bit different from the regular worship.

There is a large number of children and young families present in **St Ann's** for another in their series of thematic services. They have been studying the *Children in the Way* report and trying to involve people of all ages in the action of the worship. As the service begins, everyone learns an acclamation:

> God has set his rainbow in the clouds:
> **He will remember his covenant for ever.**

Using the suggestion in Resource Section K, this is used as a 'shout' at intervals during the service, marking one section off from another. The drama group have rehearsed some small pieces of drama, one for each section, based on the Bible story, but the main thrust of the action is to involve the whole congregation. The first section, considering God's problem of confronting sin in the world, leads into the responsive confession for creation (10C6). The children in the drama saw and hammer to music, building the ark, and round up the animals into the ark, as the story is read. There is no sermon – the whole service is full of the Word – but there is time for two well-prepared testimonies to God's contemporary rescue operation before the service ends with a responsive thanksgiving for creation (10P15) and the sharing of the Peace.

At **St Bartholomew's** the planning group have been looking at Example 2 – the conversation structure (see page 24). They have been struck by the idea that Morning Prayer is like a conversation, with God speaking and then the congregation replying, and they have decided to use this to help people understand and benefit more from the regular services. Their service outline uses 'Hello, Sorry, Thank you, Please' as the headings for the main sections, held up on large visual-aid cards as the service proceeds. (See box on next page.)

There are two children being baptized at **St Christopher's**, so that provides the overall theme for the worship. The clergy have looked at the Baptism service in the ASB, and decided to have a service which is not eucharistic, and which involves people as much as possible. They take as their basis *Believe and Trust*, the Baptism sample service in *Patterns*, ending with the Peace. At the Ministry of the Word they put in those parts of the Baptism Service usually omitted when the service is combined with Morning Prayer or Holy Communion, one of the readings is dramatised, and a procession of children brings in the water, ceremonially poured from a large jug.

The vicar at **St David's** called a meeting of his worship planning group, which has representatives from every organization and interest in the church, many of them enthusiastic to take over the running of worship from the vicar. In generous mood, he said 'yes' to all their ideas for the fifth Sunday family service, but didn't think it possible to get them to agree on a common theme and also forgot to make a note of what each was offering. He thinks it's just a matter of adding a few things in to Morning Prayer, but as the service unfolds we are treated to a disorganized concert-like jostling for position between the Guides parading to the front with their flags, the women's group (they used to be 'Young Wives') anthem for St Cecilia's Day, a rogue drummer from the youth group who tries to get in on every hymn, three dramatized versions of the Good Samaritan, one in full costume with trip-over lighting effects. . . All agree it is a very special service.

St Bartholomew's Conversation Service

HELLO

| *Presentation* | **Word** | Introduction and Sentence on nature of God |
| *Response* | **Praise** | Hymn of approach |

SORRY

| *Presentation* | **Word** | Scripture sentence on sin |
| *Response* | **Prayer** | Responsive confession 0C10 |

| *Presentation* | **Prayer** | Absolution |
| *Response* | **Praise** | Hymn on forgiveness |

THANK YOU

Presentation	**Word**	Psalm paraphrase
		Readings
		Sermon
Response	**Praise**	Thanksgiving from Resource Section M

PLEASE

Response	**Prayer**	Collect and intercession
		Lord's Prayer
	Action	Peace: sharing with one another, commitment to go on praying

Wisdom lays her table: Proverbs 9

1 Call to worship

Blessed be the God and Father of our Lord Jesus Christ:
**for he has blessed us in Christ Jesus with every spiritual
blessing.**
God chose us in Christ before the foundation of the world:
that we should be holy and blameless before him.
He destined us in love to be his sons and daughters through
Jesus Christ:
to the praise of his glorious grace.
May God give us the Spirit of wisdom:
that we may know what is the hope of our calling.

2 Collect on the theme of wisdom and nourishment (e.g. 10J27)

3 Psalm 119.65-72

4 Proverbs 9.1-6

5 An address (either here or after section 6)

6 The laying of the table
A table is placed in the midst of the people. On it are placed a stack
of plates, and foodstuffs which are to be shared (grapes, biscuits,
dried fruit or other easily distributed foods).

Worshippers are invited to come and 'lay Wisdom's table', by setting
a plate and placing on it some of the food. As each worshipper does
so, they are also invited to name silently or aloud a person who has
been someone of wisdom to them or to their community. In effect,
they are laying 'their' place at Wisdom's table.

7 1 Corinthians 1.23-25

8 Prayers of thanksgiving and intercession

9 Canticle
A canticle may be said or sung either here or at section 12. A Song of
Wisdom (15Q19) is particularly appropriate.

10 The sharing of the food
The worshippers are invited to gather around the table, take the plate
which they each have prepared and share the food with each other; a
sign that the wisdom which we receive from God through others is a
gift to be shared, not hoarded.

The service may end with the sharing of food.

11 A canticle, song or hymn of thanksgiving

12 The service ends with a blessing or ending (Section T).

THROUGH THE SERVICE

A Introductions

While the large and lively mixed-age congregation arrive for worship, the **St Ann's** music group plays a selection of thematic hymns and choruses, in order to focus people's attention on worship, and to set the initial mood of the service.

The congregation join in the singing; the song numbers have been printed on the service sheet. The music stops three or four minutes before the ministers enter and take their places. The congregation becomes quiet, attentive and prayerful – a sense of expectancy is in the air. The minister rises to call the people to worship with a seasonal scripture sentence and congregational response. This is followed by the opening hymn of praise.

At **St Bartholomew's**, the organist quietly plays some simple Handel on the small village organ while the congregation arrive for worship. The minister has hurried from another village church in the parish, and makes his way to the vestry in order to robe and to have a few moments of prayer before the service begins. The sacristan has taken care to ensure that everything is prepared for worship before the minister arrives. The opening hymn is announced by the minister from the back of the church. As the congregation sing, he makes his way to his place. At the end of the hymn, he greets the congregation with a seasonal sentence, and invites them to join with him in some moments of silence before saying a prayer of preparation for worship.

At **St Christopher's**, good quality taped music is relayed gently through the amplification system as the multi-cultural, mixed-age congregation take their seats. The choir is already seated five minutes before the service is advertised to begin. As soon as the taped music ceases the opening song of praise is announced and a well-ordered procession of crucifer, acolytes and two ministers enters the church. They process without fuss to their seats while the choir leads the congregation in the song. As soon as the song is finished a minister welcomes the people with a responsive greeting, announces the theme of the service, and invites the people to make their confession.

It is Pentecost at **St David's**, and the clergy and choir are hurrying to prepare for worship as the congregation arrive. The organist starts to play a dreary voluntary five minutes before the service is advertised to begin. Four minutes after the service should have begun the minister appears at the front of the church, nods at the organist to stop playing, welcomes everyone, and realizes that the amplification system is not working. High-pitched feedback jolts everyone awake as the system comes to life. No one can hear the announcement of the number of the opening processional hymn. Choir and clergy process slowly in a ragged crocodile to their seats. The minister turns and greets the people again – this time with a liturgical sentence. He then tells everyone to be seated and announces the notices for the week at some length, before inviting the congregation to join him in a prayer of preparation for worship.

Other options which **St Ann's** have used for Introductions include:

- well-prepared notices, followed by the opening hymn and sentence/prayer of preparation
- the giving of the Peace
- a solo song or hymn
- a spoken verse of a song or hymn.

On Palm Sunday, the people of **St Bartholomew's** take full advantage of the provision in *Lent, Holy Week, Easter*. They gather in the village hall for the greeting, invitation to worship, prayer over the palms, and a Gospel reading. Accompanied by the local band, they then process through the village, singing, to the church where the service continues with the collect and Ministry of the Word.

B Confessions

At **St Ann's,** the deacon invites the congregation to kneel or sit in order to make their confession. Time is given for the people to settle down before the deacon invites the people to call to mind their sins against God and against their neighbour. After a time of silence for reflection, a sentence of scripture is read aloud and the people are invited to confess their sins in the words of an authorized form of confession from *Patterns for Worship*. The president prays for forgiveness using an authorized absolution in the 'us' form.

The confession at **St Bartholomew's** during Holy Communion is said after the prayers of intercession. The priest invites the people to sit or kneel and, after a pause, reads a seasonal sentence calling the people to repentance and to make their confession. As it is Lent, the responsive seasonal confession (5C3) from *Patterns for Worship* is used, the priest first reminding the congregation of the response: 'Lord, forgive: **Christ have mercy.'** After the confession, the priest pronounces the absolution.

The congregation at **St Christopher's** remain standing for the confession which takes place immediately after the introduction to worship. It is Lent, and the prayers of penitence are introduced with the Summary of the Law, followed by a Kyrie Confession on the *Patterns for Worship* model, with appropriate insertions. At the absolution, the sign of the cross is made by all the congregation, signalling their acceptance of God's forgiveness in Christ.

At **St David's,** it is the monthly family service and the minister has decided to use *Patterns for Worship* General Confession (0C12). No indication is given as to whether the congregation should sit or kneel and there is confusion as people look around to see what they should do. After a pause while the minister finds her service sheet, the people are asked to find their service sheets on which is printed the confession. The minister invites the congregation to be quiet and to remember their sins before God in silence. She then immediately and loudly lists a number of sins on which the people may care to reflect and begins the confession, inserting these sins into it as she goes along. The absolution is mumbled inaudibly while the minister continues to kneel in her stall.

At **St Ann's** and **St Christopher's,** several weeks are being devoted to teaching on repentance, confession and forgiveness. As a result their worship groups have recommended that the confession be used at different times during various services:

- at ASB Rite A Holy Communion the confession is normally near the beginning of the service, as part of the preparation for worship. Occasionally it now features after the intercessions as part of the people's response in prayer to the Ministry of the Word.

- in A Service of the Word, confession may be made: as a preparation for worship; as a response to the Word; towards the end of the service, as its climax.

- corporate preparation for confession may be made: in silence; whilst sentences or passages of scripture are read aloud; during the singing of a suitable hymn or song, either corporately or by a solo voice.

The **St Ann's** dance/drama group is also looking at mime and other possibilities for expressing repentance and forgiveness.

E   The Ministry of the Word _____

At **St Ann's** they are having an adult teaching series on Romans, while
the young people's groups continue with material based on the Gospel
in the lectionary. As the children depart before the Gospel and might
not follow the long reading from Romans, the Gospel today comes
immediately after the collect – everyone remains standing – and the
children go out after the psalm that follows. The Gospel is the story of
the breakfast on the seashore after the resurrection. It is read
dramatically by well-rehearsed people from different parts of the
building – the narrator at the lectern, Jesus by the communion table,
and the disciples coming forward from the congregation.

For the sermon time, which lasts just over half an hour, the adults at
St Ann's have a choice. Some go out to a discussion Bible study on
Romans, others to a well-structured adult education session on the
church and politics (linking up with Romans 13). The rest stay in
church for a sermon on the same passage, with visuals on an overhead
projector and questions at the end.

The four people who share the responsibility for reading at **St
Bartholomew's** have recently been on a deanery training day for those
who read, and as well as coming back with some good ideas for
varying the usual pattern, they are much more confident. There is a
card on the lectern reminding the reader how to announce the
reading. She introduces the reading with the paragraph heading and
the page number from the pew Bible, and leaves space for some
reflective silence before ending, 'This is the word of the Lord.'

At **St Christopher's**, the worship committee has asked one or two
artistic people in the church to produce something around the Gospel
theme this Sunday. There is a throwover frontal on the altar, picking
up the theme of bread and fishes. The Gospel procession, with the
deacon carrying the book of the Gospels, preceded by acolytes and
crucifer, comes today only to the front row of the congregation. This
is to keep people still facing towards the front, where on a screen
behind the lectern there is a beautiful sequence of slides of Galilee,
fishermen, bread and fishes. The sermon ends with some guided
meditation inviting people to put themselves into the Gospel story.

The president at **St David's** sits for the first reading. No one comes
forward to read so he glares at the churchwarden, moves to the
lectern and intones the lesson in a voice betraying boredom. There is
a bit of excitement, though, as – inevitably – two people come forward

to read the second reading and look like having a punch-up. The one who wins fails to announce where the reading comes from, which is a pity as it seems to have been changed from what is on the notice sheet. It would have helped to have been able to follow the reading, as the reader was speaking very quietly, on the mistaken assumption that the microphone was amplifying all he said. But no one had adjusted the height of it since one of the children read last Sunday.

St Ann's worship group plans how the readings are done, usually a month at a time to make sure that there is variety and that the 'unusual' element is not overdone. Different methods they have used include:

- gentle musical backing to the reading, on tape or live
- mime to the reading
- (especially at a family service) having the reading interrupted by someone asking questions, and putting in mistakes which the children are asked to spot
- memorizing a Gospel reading and telling it as a story.

The Sermon: what and where?

The 'Instructions' for *A Service of the Word* redefine the sermon and outline different possibilities:

- more than one person taking part
- the congregation dividing into groups for all (as at **St Ann's** here), or for part of the time (for example, getting people talking to each other about applying it)
- the sermon in, say, two parts at different points in the service
- time for silent – or guided – reflection after the sermon.

Add to this some further things to consider:

- the use of handouts, either of the whole sermon or to help people take action
- using overhead projector visuals in an integrated way, with pictures taking the application or story further, rather than merely summarizing the sermon in words
- sermons with deliberate interruptions and questions, or with pauses to pray or worship and sing
- the use of drama, as an integral part of the sermon.

Discussing these should open some new possibilities and also begin to answer the question 'Where?' Clearly not all of these sermon activities are suitable for the pulpit. Different areas of the church may be used. And even with a more traditional sermon there may be a case for leaving the pulpit, moving nearer a small congregation at the back, walking up and down, speaking from the lectern where the word has been read, or from under a window whose stained glass enshrines the story. . .

F Affirmations of faith

At **St Ann's**, after the sermon, the preacher announces a reflective chorus, and encourages people to use it to make their response to the preaching. She then introduces the creed from the pulpit as the second part of their response. She uses the interrogative form of the creed from Resource Section F, pointing out that the sermon was asking direct questions about their faith.

The sermon in **St Bartholomew's** (on today's theme of unity) mentions using the creed as a symbol of our unity in faith with the worldwide Church through the ages. The Nicene Creed is introduced formally by the first four words, without referring back to this. But it is clearly in the minds of many in church.

St Christopher's have recently been having some teaching on the creed. They have used one or two of the seasonal affirmations of faith in Resource Section F, to fit with the teaching subject. One of the points that has been highlighted is the 'doxological' use of the creed in Eastern churches, to gather together the praise of the congregation. So today the creed is postponed until after the intercessions, when the choir leads an outburst of praise in a glorious setting of the Nicene Creed.

Meanwhile, in **St David's** the choir attempts to sing the Nicene Creed to a tune too difficult for them, let alone for the congregation to join in. They falter in the middle, miss a few words and have to start again. The congregation haven't been told how to occupy their time, and spend it meditating on the obvious disagreement between some of the choir and the clergy over which way to face while singing it – to the East for reverence to tradition, to the 'audience' for effect, or to one another, to keep in time. . . The creed does not appear to be fulfilling its function of uniting the church in the faith.

Which creed?

St Christopher's have had a debate about whether to use the Nicene Creed or the Apostles' Creed.

- The Nicene Creed is traditional in the Holy Communion service and emphasizes the corporate: '*We* believe.'
- The Apostles' Creed has an individual emphasis, is shorter, and is in easier language.

Both **St Ann's** and **St Bartholomew's** regularly use the Renewal of Baptismal Vows from the ASB, at Easter and sometimes at New Year. Things have settled down now after the objections at St Bartholomew's because it was being used so frequently that it became meaningless.

What to use when from Resource Section F

- Affirmation 2F6 for the incarnation and Lent
- Affirmation 2F7 for the resurrection and for memorial services
- Affirmation 0F8 for Advent, Trinity and heaven
- Affirmation 2F4 for the Incarnation and Trinity

Can we use a credal hymn instead of the creed?

It is important for our unity in the catholic faith that any creeds used are not private or local compositions, but ones that are recognized by the wider Church. However, both in ASB Morning and Evening Prayer and in Rite A Holy Communion the creed may be omitted on weekdays, so it clearly does not make the service invalid in some way. Public recitation of the creed has not always been an essential part of the Church's worship. *A Service of the Word* allows for the occasional omission of the creed, provided it is replaced by one of the affirmations of faith (Resource Section F). Some of these are already set to music, and one of them is the specially commissioned hymn paraphrase of the Apostles' Creed, *We believe in God the Father* by Timothy Dudley-Smith. There is no provision for the use of any other credal hymn as a substitute, and where one is used on a Sunday it might well follow one of the shorter affirmations of faith.

G Prayers of intercession

At **St Ann's**, one of the elders comes forward to lead the intercessions, and asks the congregation to mention things to pray for. A series of people say 'Can we pray for. . .', usually mentioning things of a fairly personal and practical nature. The elder fits this list of requests into the litany prepared before the service. From the intercession that follows, it is clear that the elder has been awake during the notices and sermon. Both the sermon and the Bible reading on which it was based are clearly reflected in the prayers. St Ann's have tried other variations for the intercessions, and at the family service these are sometimes led by a family together (using the microphone for all of them). Once or twice for a special occasion they have used visuals, both with the overhead projector and a set of slides, inviting people to have their eyes open as they pray. Occasionally they pray in small groups, which they find a good way of including children in the intercessions. Occasionally, someone will suggest using extemporary prayer with the whole congregation free to join in, but this has posed severe difficulties with audibility.

A small group from **St Bartholomew's** went to a deanery course on praying in public and in private, and came back with a checklist (see box on page 216) of dos and don'ts. Intercessions at Evensong, where the congregation is small, are usually led by the preacher, who can most easily relate the contents of the prayers to the sermon. Recently in the mornings they have been following a pattern using traditional collects, each introduced with a bidding from a different person, followed by silence before the collect. Today, the intercession is based on the Lord's Prayer (in its traditional form), with a pause after each petition, into which another person (with a contrasting voice) inserts appropriate intercessions relating to the petition. Next week, they are going to do the same sort of thing with the lesser litany in Evening Prayer. Some of the topics come from the *Anglican Cycle of Prayer*, so that they get a wider – and international – view of the Church. And since going on the deanery course they have adopted the practice of the intercession leader joining the preacher and the person leading the worship in the vestry for prayer before the service.

As you enter **St Christopher's** today, there are display boards with some posters, newspaper cuttings and pictures which indicate the theme and some of the contents of the intercession. The person leading the intercessions is well prepared, and has arrived in time to look at the requests for prayer pinned on the board by the votive candle stand, and decide how many of these can be included within the Sunday intercessions – not all are suitable! The prayers are led from the centre of the church, among the people. The standard form of response to the intercessions, from *Patterns for Worship*, is sung to a Taizé-style chant. The congregation picks up the note and hums it while the intercession leader continues to the next response.

At **St David's**, the person leading the intercessions says 'Let us pray', but as he hasn't thought of what to say next, we can hear him turning the pages of *Patterns for Worship* during the ensuing silence. Unfortunately, he begins the responsive intercession for Harvest and Creation, which fits neither the readings nor the mood of the congregation. He fails to rehearse the response at the start and so has to stop at the first break and say 'When I say. . . you should say. . .' in a voice which implies that the congregation should have known this all along. He continues to make remarks addressed to the congregation throughout the intercessions: 'We really ought to pray for Ann ('Who is she?' half the congregation wonder) especially today because. . .' – and more of his views of the circumstances of members of the community follow.

St Bartholomew's checklist

1 **DO** read the readings. Sometimes they might be used as a basis for prayer ('Father, thank you for. . . (what the verse says); now please help us to. . .').

2 **DO** discover the theme (that of the day or season, or the readings, or the preaching). It may mean asking the preacher if there is something specific to pray for if the prayers follow the preaching.

3 **DO** find out about particular needs, who is ill or what church meetings or organizations need prayer this week. Watch the news, and vary the way in which international topics are prayed for. **DON'T** be out of date!

4 **DO** be aware of special events like baptisms or when there are large numbers of children or the Town Council present. **DON'T** focus on them (for example a group of bereaved people the week after a funeral) in a way which will embarrass them.

5 **DO** remember what was prayed for last week: should there be thanksgiving for answered prayer? What other thanksgiving should there be?

6 Decide what pattern of intercessions will be best, given what has been discovered and the pattern of the rest of the service:

  ● a series of set prayers and collects (introduced by biddings?)
  ● a series of biddings, 'Let us pray for. . .' followed by one summing-up prayer. Sometimes the Lord's Prayer may be used.
  ● a litany-style intercession: the main ASB Rite A form; one of the alternatives on page 166 of the ASB; one from *Patterns for Worship* or another book; one made up by the person leading the intercessions.

7 **DON'T** cram so much in that you have to rush. **DON'T** forget about the need for silences, and how and whether to introduce them.

8 **DON'T** preach at people ('We pray we may all give generously at Gift Day. . .').

9 **DO** pray the intercessions out loud before the service, especially if a home-grown form is being used. Watch the speed: will the congregation have time to pray, or will they be overwhelmed by the variety of images and topics? Will they know when to come in with the response: is it short enough to remember and introduced by the same 'trigger' words each time? Look at the examples in Resource Section G.

H Collects

Today, **St Ann's** are using *A Service of the Word* for the first part of the Holy Communion. They have seen that the rubric in the service allows them to use the collect as a summing-up prayer which draws together the intercessions and thanksgivings before the service moves on into the Holy Communion. This means that it need not be particularly linked with the readings or the Ministry of the Word. They have recently been printing it on the notice sheet, so that members of the church can use it at home during the week.

Children in the church school at **St Bartholomew's** have been learning this week how to write collects. They have used a very simple formula (see the box on page 218) which shows them how to take a verse of scripture, thank God for something about himself and then pray for something connected with that aspect of God's character. The teacher hopes it will help them in making up their own prayers at home (and the vicar secretly thinks some of the adults would find this a help, too!). He recently preached on the prayer of the believers in Acts 4.24-31, pointing out how many lines of the prayer were taken up with telling God how great he was and what he had done, using that as the reason why God should take notice of their request, which was to result in 'wonders and miracles. . . through the name of Jesus'. Compare this with the pattern in the 'Constructing collects' box. Four of the children's collects are going to be used in the worship this month.

The vicar and reader at **St Christopher's** have been particularly struck recently by how good some of the collects from the *Book of Common Prayer* still sound. They have been using them in less formal settings, in small groups and to open or close meetings, following the pattern: 'Let us pray (for. . .)' – silence – collect. They have also used them, where they fit the theme or season of the year, before the final prayer at the Eucharist. The congregation already know three alternative post-communion prayers by heart, so that they can join in from the first phrase of the prayer.

At **St David's**, the vicar announces the collect on page 738 of the ASB as if he intends people to join in with him, but then, despite blowing hard at the pages to try to separate them, he gives up the struggle and prays the collect a few pages earlier instead, which one or two remember from last week. He also announces that as it is St William Tyndale's day tomorrow, he is going to pray that prayer, too. There is another suitably long silence while he fumbles for the page in another book. The congregation are left with the impression that the collect is just a bit of mumbo-jumbo to be got through, rather than contributing to the movement of the worship.

Constructing collects

1	Address: *God, you are . . you say. . .*	ASH WEDNESDAY Almighty and everlasting God, you hate nothing that you have made
	you do. . . /have done. . .	and forgive the sins of all those who are penitent:
2	Petition or request: *Therefore, Lord, please. . .*	create and make in us new and contrite hearts that we, worthily lamenting our sins and acknowledging our wretchedness,
3	Result or reason: *So that. . .*	may receive from you, the God of all mercy, perfect remission and forgiveness;
4	Ending:	through Jesus Christ our Lord.

Guidelines on language

These guidelines may help those writing their own material, for collects or intercessions, for example, to be on the same level of language as the new writing in *Patterns*.

1 Use concrete visual images rather than language which is conceptual and full of ideas.
2 Avoid complicated sentence constructions.
3 If there is a choice, prefer the word with fewer syllables.
4 Address God as you.
5 Keep sentences as short as possible. Use full stops rather than semicolons.
6 Use language which includes women as well as men, black as well as white.
7 Watch the rhythm. The language should be rhythmic and flow easily, but take care not to have a repetitive poetic dum-de-dum!
8 Liturgical language should not be stark or empty. It is not wrong to repeat ideas or say the same thing twice in different words. Cranmer recognized that people need time and repetition to make the liturgy their own: we need to do it without a string of dependent clauses.
9 Be prepared to throw it away after using it, and to do it differently next time.

R The Peace

At **St Ann's**, the Peace is the climax to which the first half of the service moves. The President uses a sentence which echoes the theme of the service. Sometimes this is printed on the notice sheet as a versicle and response, which is used for a month or more during the same teaching theme or season of the Church's year. Members of the congregation are encouraged to use this when greeting one another outside the church – or even over the telephone! With the response 'and also with you' the signal is given for a lot of movement in the church as people shake hands, hug or greet one another in other ways. There is some sensitivity to people who want to remain on their own, though the PCC recently rejected a suggestion that one corner of the church be set aside as a Peace-free zone! The church leaders sometimes warn people against the exchange of greetings becoming too secular, and it is good to see some people using the time to share with three or four others something of what God has said to them through the preaching. This is sometimes shared with the younger members of the church as they talk about what has been going on in their groups, rather than entering a competition to see how many hands they can shake. People have been taught what the Peace is for, and how to use it (see box on page 220). The Peace at St Ann's is something which usually lasts for fifteen to twenty minutes, with coffee and refreshments being served and some people (who are not staying for the Eucharist) leaving. This has been found a useful way of encouraging enquirers and those seeking baptism for their children, for instance, to come to a more family-service style of service which does not commit them to receiving communion. The service begins again with some gentle music and chorus singing as people prepare for the thanksgiving.

At **St Bartholomew's** today the service has been led by one of the lay people. At the end of the intercessions she glances at her watch. The vicar is taking the service at one of the other churches in the group, and often arrives here towards the end of the intercessions. If he does, it is natural for him to say the words of the Peace and it acts partly as a greeting announcing his arrival. But he must have met sheep on the road, so the lay leader says the words of the Peace and the small congregation spend a few moments greeting one another. If they are stuck for time, the Peace can be briefer and more formal: living together in a village means they have already greeted one another today. Enter the vicar, at speed just as the hymn is being announced. 'Peace be with you all!' he shouts, with a wave of the hand, and they reply. Much better than 'Good morning, everyone!'

Some of the things people at **St Ann's** have been taught:

- time to get straight with God before coming to communion (so you may need to be on your own, perhaps grappling with something from the preaching)
- time to get straight with other people before coming to communion (so you may need to go and make your peace, or ask forgiveness from someone at the other end of the church). This is what the Prayer Book calls being 'in love and charity with your neighbour'.
- time to share with others something for prayer (so you may need to ask one of the leaders for the laying on of hands for healing, or some other individual ministry, later in the service)
- time to share with others something for praise (so you may have something that God has been doing with you during the week that will contribute to the praise of the whole church)
- time to greet people you do not know (so you may need to help someone else, perhaps someone new to the church, feel part of the Christian family at communion, rather than greeting only your close friends).

The clergy at **St Christopher's** use a full range of seasonal introductory words to the Peace, occasionally following the pattern of the Maundy Thursday service in *Lent, Holy Week, Easter*, using a short collect about peace instead of the introductory sentence. The deacon says, 'Let us offer one another a sign of peace' and sometimes wonders why people need this reminder what to do: why can't they just get on with it? But when they were moving away from the (bad old?) days when the Peace was first exchanged in the sanctuary and then brought down to the people by a server greeting the person at the end of each row, these action words were needed to give people permission to move on their own. And occasionally they have the Peace later in the service, before the distribution, and a general handshake is not appropriate at that point, so the 'Let us offer. . .' words are not used.

The vicar at **St David's** is used to commanding his congregation, but has been having a battle over the Peace, with some resisting his attempts to make it more demonstrative. 'We will all stand for the Peace. The Peace. . .' he bellows. 'We will **all** exchange a sign of Peace.' And when one couple on the front row remain kneeling (in peace), he marches over, lays a hand on each head and says, 'The Peace of the Lord be with you!' which is not quite a demonstration of peace. There has never been any teaching on why or how to exchange the Peace. There is embarrassment as one lady, taught in a more formal church, extends both hands tentatively towards a large man bearing down on her with arms flung out ready to hug her. She ducks. In one corner, some of the younger people don't seem to have been taught the difference between the Peace and snogging. And those who know one another well are engaging in noisy back-slapping and jolly handshaking, ignoring those who are not known to them who stand in sheepish silence waiting for the ordeal to be over. But that is the problem. The vicar is deep in (no doubt important) conversation with the church treasurer and has not thought how to announce the next hymn over the hubbub. So he shouts. . .

How to stop the Peace

- When announcing the Peace, announce the hymn after it: 'At the end of the Peace we shall sing. . .' Then all that is needed is a nod to the organist, or an agreement that the organist takes the decision when to start.
- The organist plays the opening bars of the hymn, and stops while the announcement is made.
- Some gentle music is played, perhaps a chorus which people can join in. As this ends the hymn is announced.

S Action and movement

Today is Whit Sunday at **St Ann's**. The church feels very different. Everyone is wearing something red, and it feels as if the whole church is ablaze. The focus is an enormous crown suspended over the communion table, which has been there for the Ascension and the theme of the kingship of Christ. Now there are flames all around and inside it as the theme moves on to the Lord, the Spirit. St Ann's have been having a discussion about the use of symbols and symbolic action, and divided them into three groups (see box opposite). Today, the small dance group interpret a hymn to the Holy Spirit while the congregation remain seated to sing, so that they can see and be involved in the movement.

At **St Bartholomew's**, just before the Peace, there is a noise at the back of the church, and the children enter in a procession with musical instruments (recorders, percussion, etc.). This used to happen during the hymn after the Peace, but was brought forward so that the children could share in exchanging the Peace. At the end are two children with bread and wine which they take up to the sanctuary. They have been learning about being on the move with children, and sometimes process outside the church, for example on Palm Sunday with a donkey.

At **St Christopher's** there is deliberate and systematic use of symbols. They have decided which need some teaching about and which are self-explanatory: they have learnt that taking too much time to explain to people what they are doing simply interrupts the worship, and that not everything needs explaining. They have also learnt not to be minimalistic about their symbols and actions. So, for instance, there was a large bonfire outside the church on Easter Saturday night,

---

Guidelines for processions

1 Where is the procession going from and where to?
2 How will they know the way? Is it obvious or do they need leading by crucifer/verger/musicians?
3 Processions should have a purpose, not just wander about. What is the purpose for this procession? What is going to happen when it 'arrives'? Is there a gift to receive, a banner to display, a prayer to say?
4 In what order are people to move off? There is no particular reason why the important people have to come at the end. It may often work best if they leave first.

Symbols

Symbols can be of very many different sorts:

1 **Symbols people bring with them.**
   For example, being the people of God, a crowd or smaller
   related groups; clothes symbolizing respectability or purity
   or some aspect of the season such as bonnets at Easter
   or something white worn at Christmas.

2 **Symbols and actions which are individual.**
   Holding a book for worship (what is the message of that?).
   Bowing, making the sign of the cross, distributing nails to
   people on Good Friday, or candles at Candlemas: though
   these are individual, they also express relationship and
   unity among the congregation.

3 **Symbols and actions uniting the congregation.**
   For example, some of the individual things done together
   at the same time such as standing and kneeling, exchanging
   the Peace, holding hands, etc.

Pictures, statues, icons, frontals and banners should be unitive and
gather the attention of the congregation towards God. They can
sometimes be fragmentary and disperse the congregation's
thoughts and responses. Should some things be moved away for
some sorts of service, as happens with the stripping of the Holy
Table on Maundy Thursday?

Dance is also something which can unite or divide. It might involve
one person or a group 'performing' something which is usually
rehearsed, for example as an interpretation of a reading, song or
prayer. It can involve spontaneous solo dancers: this is usually
easier during a hymn or song, expressing praise to God and often
assisting the congregation in gathering up their praise and worship,
too. Sometimes large numbers of a congregation might dance
spontaneously to praise God, sometimes moving out to occupy the
aisles and other spaces in the church.

from which the candles were lit as they followed the service in *Lent,
Holy Week, Easter*. Similarly, the movement in church is not over-
solemn and slow: they recognize that movement is necessary and
should be done well. Today, they are trying something different as, at
the offertory, people come from different corners of the church
carrying the altar cloth, chalice and ciborium, bread and wine, and
proceed to lay the table which has been bare until that point. The

church is sufficiently large for the whole congregation to get up and move to different parts of it in a procession: this turns out to be more like a moving group of people than a solemn two-by-two procession. They did this very successfully with the Epiphany service from *The Promise of His Glory*, and found that the children could take part more easily in something that moved from place to place.

Though the usual symbolism at **St David's** is that of dead flowers and failed light bulbs, things look brighter today with a fairly full church for the Christingle service. The children go to the sanctuary step to hand over money in return for lighted Christingles (no one seems to have thought through the implications of the symbolism of this exchange: see the alternative service in *The Promise of His Glory*). Because things seem to be moving very slowly, with small children finding it difficult to hold the Christingle orange upright, the vicar sends some of them off in one direction and some in another, and the two processions meet amid great and dangerous confusion towards the back of the church, where angry parents, afraid of the danger, have to intervene to sort things out. They remembered what happened on Palm Sunday a few years ago when an acolyte set fire to a palm frond with his candle. A server with great presence of mind picked up the burning palm but instead of throwing it on the floor and stamping the fire out, tried to (solemnly but with difficulty) process out of church holding it in front of him, with the result that his hair was very badly singed. Remember the rule: when processing out of church with a burning palm, walk backwards.

Distributing communion

At **St Ann's**, five of the elders come and stand around the table to receive communion, which they pass from one to the other. They then distribute communion, together with the president, in three pairs moving right round the rail, returning round the far side of the communion table to the point at which they started. The bread is part of a loaf, which they break as they go. (They have been taught that the breaking – 'fraction' – was something functional rather than ceremonial in the New Testament descriptions, and that the custom of chopping the bread into little bits before the service starts really undermines the strong image of unity in the body of 'We break this bread. . . Though we are many, we are one body. . .'). As they pass the children, they lay one hand on them and pray for them; one or two of the parents break a piece off their own bread to share with their children. At the side of the long rail, one or two people remain kneeling, waiting for the ministry of the laying on of hands for healing. This is usually done by the same group of elders, though others may join in or come forward to take over the distributing of communion if that seems in danger of being held up.

At **St Bartholomew's** the vicar is away, and the first part of the service is led by a reader. In the hymn at the offertory, the consecrated bread and wine are brought from the church in the next village, and placed on the altar. There is no consecration prayer, but the reader uses one of the prayers authorized by the bishop of the diocese for use on such occasions, which includes some thanksgiving and refers to the other congregation where the bread and wine were consecrated. The reader distributes the sacrament, following the local custom of saying the longer BCP words to the whole line of people at the rail, followed by brief words to each. The communicants at the rail wait until everyone has received, and all depart together. The sidesmen encourage forward only the right number to fill the rail each time, so there is no queue.

Blessings

Where children and adults who are not receiving communion are being blessed at the rail, it is good to vary the form of words used. Some possibilities are:

- The Lord bless you and keep you.
- The Lord bless you and give you joy in all you do for him.
- The Lord bless and take care of you *both* (for example, with a married couple when one of them is receiving communion and the other not).
- Christ fill you with his joy and peace.
- The blessing of Jesus Christ rest upon you.
- May God be with you.
- May Jesus Christ bless you.

(The last four may be more suitable for lay people to use in situations where there is some sensitivity about whether or not they may use a more direct form of blessing.)

As well as words there should be some gesture of inclusion. Some ministers prefer to lay a hand on the shoulder rather than the head, to avoid episcopal or priestly connotations, but laying hands on heads is a biblical gesture by no means confined to priests, and is unlikely to upset lay people. Another possibility is to make the sign of the cross, on the forehead for example. With very small children, rather than simply patting them on the head it may help to get down to their level and greet them briefly before blessing them. But it is best not to get into long conversations about teddy bears.

The distribution at **St Christopher's** is equally well organized, with sidesmen gradually moving back down the church so that people know when to go forward, and a server some yards from the rail to direct people where to go. The whole thing moves very smoothly. The two lay ministers of communion are deliberately in lay dress, and follow the president with the cup. All know that those who come to the rail holding a book are not receiving the sacrament. When there is a large service, the congregation have got used to receiving communion standing, from two stations, one at the front of the church and one half-way down the nave. Those who give the cup to people taller than themselves when standing up have realized that it is easier to put the cup into people's hands! At the end of the distribution, three people who have the bishop's permission to take communion to the sick come forward, with their pyxes, and after a prayer they go straight out to perform their ministry.

At **St David's**, no one is quite sure who is helping the president to distribute communion, so after a hurried conversation at the back of the church and rejecting one of the women who offers to do it because they think she is unsuitably dressed, one of the wardens moves forward as the president glares anxiously down the church. He has to lift the centre part of the rail out in order to get into the sanctuary, and by the time he arrives the president has begun to distribute wafers to the four members of the choir at one side of the rail. The warden is not quite sure whether he has the authority to take the cup from the table, so there is a hiatus. The delay puts a certain amount of pressure on the operation, so the distribution proceeds at a rapid pace, so much so that some people do not have any space to pray when they kneel down before the wafer is thrust at them. Those distributing also have no time to pray for each person, as disasters follow thick and fast. The president drops a wafer and the warden, following close behind, puts his foot on it (or was he trying to conceal it?). He then discovers a fly struggling to get out of the cup and tries to get it out with a flick of his finger, all still in full view of the waiting communicants! The warden next gives the cup to a young woman carrying a small child who immediately reaches out a violent arm, knocking the cup so that a quantity of wine spills down the woman's front. A considerable amount of embarrassment and mopping up with purificators ensues, all of which might have been avoided had the warden, perhaps wise from previous encounters, held the child's hand, or retained a firm hold over the cup. Before long, the wine runs out and he simply goes to the credence table and fills up with more.

Training for those who distribute communion

This should be theological, spiritual and practical. It might include:

- something on theology and history
- knowledge of differing approaches to the sacrament within the church, so that those who distribute are prepared for different customs, and can be sensitive to those with different views from their own
- knowing the words by heart
- prayer before and silently for each person during the distribution
- recognizing those in distress
- how to distribute bread without dropping crumbs
- the best way to cope with intinction (whether by the president or by the communicant taking the wafer and waiting until the cup comes round)
- giving the cup to women with wide-brimmed hats
- how to tell the president quietly and without attracting attention if the bread or wine is running out
- what to do when the distribution is finished.

Authorization of Ministers of the Sacrament

Canon B 12.3 says: 'No person shall distribute the holy sacrament of the Lord's Supper to the people unless he shall have been ordained in accordance with the provisions of Canon C 1, or is otherwise authorized by Canon or unless he has been specially authorized to do so by the bishop acting under such regulations as the General Synod may make from time to time.'

The Church Assembly Regulations made in 1969 are still in operation:

'1. *An application to the Bishop to authorize. . . a baptized and confirmed person to distribute the Holy Sacrament in any parish shall be made in writing by the incumbent or priest-in-charge of the parish and supported by the churchwardens, and shall specify the name and give relevant particulars of the person to whom the application relates.*

2. It shall be in the discretion of the Bishop to grant or refuse the application and to specify the circumstances or conditions in or on which the authority is to be available.'

OTHER ISSUES

5 Additions and insertions

Most churches add things into the standard pattern of Morning or Evening Prayer or Holy Communion from time to time. The ASB gives clear instructions about such things as combining the Marriage Service with Holy Communion, or putting a Thanksgiving or a Baptism and Confirmation into Holy Communion or Morning Prayer. Notes to the ASB services also express a certain amount of indifference about where to put in hymns, the offering, or even the Peace.

At **St Ann's** they usually have some kind of 'spot' which is particularly suitable for the children before they go out. Sometimes it is a fairly riotous action chorus which (depending on the mood of the service) usually fits best among the introductory choruses. Today there is a brief quiz (with scoring on the projection equipment) on the Old Testament story which is read in church and forms the basis of the teaching when they leave. This naturally comes straight after it is

---

Questions to ask when putting something different into the service

1   Is this something covered by the notes or tables in the ASB, or by the examples here?

2   Is it such a large item that it will change the feel of the whole service? If so, would it be better to construct a special service?

3   What is the effect of this item likely to be on the parts of the service around it? Where will it fit most naturally so that it contributes to and does not halt the flow of the worship? For example, if it is giving information, would this lead into prayer? If it is a special musical contribution, can it replace or be part of a Godward part of the worship? If a procession, can it happen at the beginning or end, or when there is movement anyway in the service?

4   Is it going to help or hinder the congregation's sense of God's presence and his purpose for them? If it is likely to hinder, is it really necessary?

---

read. Sometimes there is an interview with a member of the congregation, or a visitor or past member of the church (always done with a microphone). Some interviews are lively enough or of particular interest to be done when the children are present, and may come before or after one of the readings; others fit much better as part of the sermon or, more usually, just before the intercessions so that prayer follows naturally from them. Today a missionary couple are returning overseas after home leave, and the farewell prayer and commissioning takes place after communion, immediately before the blessing. Apart from the notices (before the intercessions today) the only other 'insertion' is the laying on of hands for healing, which happens in a non-intrusive way as people come forward to receive communion.

Today is Rogation Sunday at **St Bartholomew's** and the archdeacon is there for Evensong in the afternoon. The congregation have saved up for a new electric organ to replace the old harmonium, and it is dedicated after the second lesson, before the small choir sings an anthem. After the sermon, everyone goes out in a haphazard kind of procession to the lych gate, where a pair of new gates, given in memory of a young farmer killed last year, are blessed. There is prayer for the family, and conversation with them as the procession moves off to the highest point at the top of the churchyard for the rogationtide blessing of fields, crops, sheep and sea. The blessing of the people, present at the service and in the surrounding village, ends the service. Sometimes an insertion on this scale becomes the focus and climax towards which the worship moves.

The vicar at **St Christopher's** has studied Note 21 of ASB Rite A, so silences are inserted at the right points, and the service moves along with a clear and dignified rhythm of music, words and space for reflection. Today, ministers of the eucharist to take communion to the sick are being commissioned, and this is most appropriately done, with some words of explanation, questions to them and a prayer of commissioning, immediately before the Peace. This is the point in the service where the annual commissioning of the PCC and church leaders takes place in April, using some of the Words for Dedication in Resource Section S of *Patterns*, but other points are used when appropriate: a couple of weeks ago a new head chorister was installed after one of the readings before the choir led the singing of the psalms.

At **St David's**, the vicar knows he has a number of different things to get into the service, but has failed to sort out on paper where they should come. It is a Parade Service, and there is a baptism. He announces the first hymn and goes to the sanctuary to collect the assorted Scout and Guide flags which don't begin their slow procession from the back of the church until during the last verse. He gets impatient and flustered, and doesn't get back to his reading desk until after the Reader, trying to be helpful, has said 'Let us pray'. Oh dear! He had meant to welcome the baptism party and give a few notices. Never mind: there is plenty of time to do this after the second reading because the churchwardens (despite his frantic signalling during the psalm – what wouldn't he give for a radio phone in his pocket for such emergencies?) have failed to come forward with the stand, portable glass sugar-bowl font and water for the baptism. So, having begun the baptism part of the service he realizes people can't insert the child's name into the prayer (their usual custom) as he has not yet welcomed them or told people who they are. He invites the parents and godparents to the front and introduces them while the wardens get things ready. To fill in time, he asks them a couple of impromptu questions (he has heard that other churches sometimes do this), but they don't seem very prepared for it, and get embarrassed. To give himself time to think, he puts an extra hymn after the baptism, but forgets that the third hymn is always the one when the collection is taken and so is faced unexpectedly with an approaching column of plate-bearers. In the confusion, he forgets that he had promised one of the Guide leaders that they could present a gift to one of their leaders who is moving away. He remembers just as the flag party are half-way down the aisle to collect their flags in the last hymn and – rightly – judges it to be too late.

Notices

When in the service?
ASB Rite A Note 19 suggests three possible places:

At the beginning:
- Notices can be used to give the congregation some sense of unity, of being part of the same family, as family news and forthcoming events are shared.
- Some people might miss them by arriving late, saying 'It's only the notices'; on the other hand the notices may be so attractive and important that people get there in time for them.
- If not well done, they can get the service off to a bad start.
- If at the beginning, they could be done before the president enters (in which case they should not be done by the president but by someone else) or (possibly by the president) after the opening greeting. This might mark them out as part of the worship, and spiritually important.

Before the intercessions:
- People can be urged to pray for items of news or events to come.
- It may help to provide a bit of a break in the middle of the service.
- Notices here can disrupt the flow of the worship.

At the end:
- Everyone has arrived by then.
- The notices are seen as part of the Christian community going out to serve God in the world: things to fix our eyes on, to pray for, and times to meet again during the week.
- It is too late to pray for these things in this service.
- It may seem disruptive to those who want to go on quietly praying: notices are a community-centred activity, not easily mixed with private prayer. Which is most important at this point in this particular service?

How to do them?
- A printed weekly bulletin or notice sheet; if there are spoken notices as well, these should be used to highlight important items, not to add another long collection of details.
- Vary the person who gives the notices: why should it be the function of the person leading the worship?
- Try two people sharing the task as 'presenters', with media-style headlines.
- Use visuals, such as an overhead projector or some drama.
- Be enthusiastic; look at the congregation; remember there is a spiritual purpose to the notices.
- Evaluate and review both the place in the service and the method.

Interviews

Interviews have some advantages over inviting someone to talk for five minutes:

- The interviewer is in control of the time taken.
- The interviewer can direct the conversation to those things the congregation will be most interested in, and interrupt and curtail boring bits.
- The variety in voices makes it easier to listen to.

How to prepare:
- Don't meet to 'talk it over' hours or days beforehand. It will taste like leftovers and be like trying to recapture a spontaneous joke when the circumstances are different. Meeting the interviewee three or four minutes beforehand is plenty.
- Do some reading and thinking around the background to the interview. Decide on an 'angle'. Be selective in what you want to ask. The informed interviewer can select what is most interesting or relevant to the congregation.
- Have a simple outline you can hold in your mind, perhaps three or four basic questions which can be elaborated. Make sure they lead on from one to the next.

How to do it:
- Use a microphone if one is available.
- Be mobile: face the interviewee and also turn to the congregation.
- Above all, be interested. If the interviewer is not interested in the answers to the questions, no one else will be. If the interviewer yawns, so will everyone else.

6 Producing a local service sheet_____

Numbers in brackets refer to the flowchart on the next page.

The **St Ann's** PCC has decided to put some outline forms of service into its new loose-leaf worship book which also includes the text of hymns and songs. This is the result of some consultation which has been going on between the worship group and the rest of the church, including those who lead the children's and youth organizations. The forms of service (1) were worked out by the worship group and agreed by the PCC. For a year before this, they had a computer-produced leaflet for each Sunday. With the Bible readings printed on such a take-home sheet, together with topics for intercession, it had provided a link both with the midweek housegroup worship and with daily prayer in the home. But some people said that there were too many words, that the structure of the service was not clear enough and that it was changed too frequently. They had printed out the text of prayers and readings, including those used by the leader as well as the congregation, and at times had added bits of running commentary to explain what was happening: occasionally, people had wondered if these were to be spoken out loud! They now have a clearer structure, with bold headings and only the responses and prayers which the congregation say together printed out. Many of these are known by heart by the regular congregation.

At **St Bartholomew's**, they generally prefer to use prayerbooks and hymnbooks, but for the monthly family service they have a card with a simple outline of the service structure (so people can see where they are going) and the words the congregation say together. They now have a series of coloured cards for different seasons of the year – Advent, Epiphany, Lent, Easter, Pentecost. Someone in the village set these cards up on their computer, so that the printing looks good, and a local artist provided some illustrations which include local scenes (6). They are printed on coloured card (7), cut to the same size as the hymnbook, to fit inside it or alongside it on the shelf. St Bartholomew's decided to go for a seasonal variety of cards after their experience of having just one card for the previous three years. They found that this had limited the options which they could use and made it difficult to give the service a different 'feel'.

Aware of the dangers of fossilizing the worship by choosing one route through the many alternatives in the service and enshrining it in their own service booklet, the PCC at **St Christopher's** also decided to go for a series of seasonal cards, but with two differences. Because the

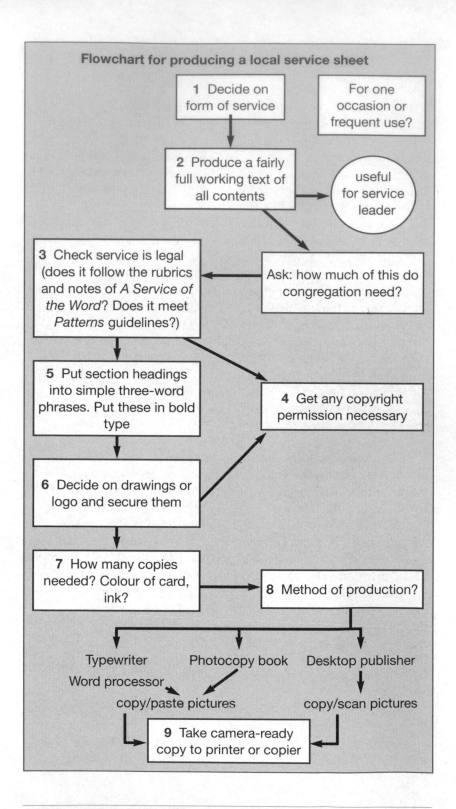

Flowchart for producing a local service sheet

1 Decide on form of service

For one occasion or frequent use?

2 Produce a fairly full working text of all contents

useful for service leader

3 Check service is legal (does it follow the rubrics and notes of *A Service of the Word*? Does it meet *Patterns* guidelines?)

Ask: how much of this do congregation need?

5 Put section headings into simple three-word phrases. Put these in bold type

4 Get any copyright permission necessary

6 Decide on drawings or logo and secure them

7 How many copies needed? Colour of card, ink?

8 Method of production?

Typewriter   Photocopy book   Desktop publisher
Word processor
          copy/paste pictures   copy/scan pictures

9 Take camera-ready copy to printer or copier

church is sometimes fairly dark, printing on coloured card might be difficult to see, so they use only white. And while each card has a different seasonal or thematic 'feel' (7) – one more penitential (especially for Lent), another full of resurrection joy (Easter season), another more on the theme of the Holy Spirit (Pentecost), another focusing on the incarnation (Christmas and Epiphany) – the PCC decided not to put seasonal names on them so as to make them easier to use at other times. There are drawings taken from the vicar's library of clipart, and clear, bold headings acting as 'signposts' through the services, following those in the ASB or those from the *Patterns* sample services which have been carefully thought out (5). They decided to use laminated plastic card to give a more 'professional' feel, and to enable sticky fingermarks to be wiped away easily. When the cards were introduced, more copies of the standard card were printed than the church needed, so that members of the congregation could have one at home to use in their home prayers and to learn by heart the opening and closing collects, the modern Lord's Prayer, *Gloria,* creed and *Sanctus.* They also use a commercially produced weekly take-home sheet with readings, psalm, collect and responses which provides another link between weekdays and Sundays.

St David's is entering a new era. For some years, people were often given a noticesheet (on to which the two opening choruses have been crammed at the end), an old duplicated sheet of dark-coloured paper with a hymn on it, a tatty five-year-old service booklet, and a hymnbook, out of which slips the all-important duplicated second hymn as you walk to your seat. The problem was that the booklet was clearly different from the service actually taken by the vicar, who jumped from place to place in it, holding it up and saying 'down here at the bottom of – er, is it the fourth page?' when he wanted people to join in, as there were no section numbers to refer to. But this week there is a new service sheet, produced by the vicar on his own late on Saturday night. Parts of it are typed (with a worn ribbon), parts are cut and pasted from hymnbooks and service books, with the lines showing where the paper has overlapped and many different sizes and styles of print. He hasn't had time to proofread it or to make sure that things are in the right order, which is why one line is missed out of one of the hymns. The thin economy paper, badly duplicated on both sides, makes the service difficult to follow, and as the responses are not in bold type the congregation are not sure where to come in. There is, of course, no copyright notice.

Copyright

The copyright laws ensure that a text is not altered without permission and that authors and publishers are fairly rewarded for their work. In liturgy, a particular text may have been very carefully thought out, debated and agreed, for example in the General Synod, as a text on which all shades of opinion in the Church can agree. For some churches to change that text without consultation could be seen as damaging the unity of the Church's worship. The copyright law makes people think before they take such action.

How to know what is copyright

Material may usually be freely copied if the writer (or composer or arranger) died more than 50 years ago and if the book from which the copy is to be taken was published more than 25 years ago. In all other cases, the material is probably copyright, unless there is a specific disclaimer, usually at the beginning of the book.

The copyright in the ASB and other authorized alternative or commended service books such as *Lent, Holy Week, Easter, Patterns for Worship* and *The Promise of His Glory* is held by the Central Board of Finance of the Church of England. For a copy of *Liturgical Texts for Local Use: Guidelines and Copyright Information* send a stamped self-addressed envelope 8$^1/_2$ x 6" to the Copyright Administrator, Central Board of Finance, Church House, Great Smith Street, London SW1P 3NZ. As well as containing helpful advice on other matters such as copyright arrangements for hymns and Bible versions and for video and audio recordings, the leaflet sets out the conditions under which local booklets and service leaflets, which are not for sale, and which are clearly marked with the name and the place in which they are to be used, may be produced without written application to the CBF. These must include a copyright notice in the following form:

'*The Alternative Service Book 1980*, (names of other books), material from which is included in this service, is/are copyright © The Central Board of Finance of the Church of England.'

Within these books there are prayers, excerpts from the Bible and other items whose copyright belongs not to the CBF but to other bodies and individuals. These are usually listed under 'copyright acknowledgements' (see p.330). The CBF has obtained the agreement of the copyright owners that all material in the official service books may be reproduced, with acknowledgement, in local editions which meet the conditions in *Liturgical Texts for Local Use*.

Permission to reproduce any part of the *Book of Common Prayer*, the rights of which are vested in the Crown, must be obtained from Cambridge University Press, The Edinburgh Building, Shaftesbury Road, Cambridge, CB2 2R2. They have, however, agreed that BCP texts included in the ASB and other official service books may be reproduced in local editions under the agreement outlined above.

Other ways of doing it

St Ann's have experimented with two other ways of doing things in the last few years. For some time they tried having all the congregational words of the service, hymns and choruses on an overhead projector. This helped the singing, as people were looking up, and those who wanted them could still have books if they needed that security. They stopped this, partly because some people at the back could never see the screen, partly because of the problem of having a double focus of attention, on the screen as well as the minister.

The second experiment was an enormous amount of work. They had a loose-leaf binder containing the order of service (they had several to choose from, like **St Christopher's**) and all the hymns and other congregational material just for that morning's service. This was much more 'seeker-friendly' than a collection of hymnbooks and prayerbooks: people new to the church found it easy to follow. There were sometimes problems because of the inflexibility: when the worship leader wanted to use a song not in that morning's folder. But what killed it was the slog of having a team of people on Saturdays collating the contents for 300 binders from the church's worship library.

Other ideas

Use bold headings or 'signposts' to indicate main sections. The headings in the ASB and in the sample services in *Patterns* have been carefully thought out and provide good examples to use. It is perfectly in order to print only the congregational parts of the service, so long as it is made clear that copies of the full text of the ASB, *Patterns for Worship*, *The Promise of His Glory*, *Lent, Holy Week, Easter* are available on request.

Follow the ASB convention of putting parts to be said by the congregation in bold type, not underlined or italic which are more difficult to see. Some of the congregational responses may need to be printed with a 'cue' phrase.

The typography of published editions of the ASB and other service books which are copyright The Central Board of Finance may be reproduced photographically for local use.

7 The law and common prayer

St Ann's PCC has had to discuss 'Who has the authority to change the worship in our parish church?' because there are a number of people in the church who would like to see a return to the *Book of Common Prayer* for some services. They have found a good description of the present legal position in *Public Worship in the Church of England* (available from Church House Bookshop). The provisions of Canon B 3 apply to *A Service of the Word*. This means in general that decisions as to which forms of service are used are taken jointly by the minister and the PCC. In cases of disagreement, the BCP or a form previously in use for two of the past four years is to be used. There is no provision for appeal to the bishop under Canon B 3, apart from cases where there is dispute over the form to be used for occasional offices. Matters under Canon B 5 can be referred to the bishop, where there is doubt about whether a variation in a service made by the minister is of substantial importance or not.

With *A Service of the Word* there is scope for Prayer Book material to be used, if desired, for some of the headings, and the St Ann's PCC thinks this might be a possible way forward. The diocesan bishop has issued guidelines, emphasizing that the spirit of the *Worship and Doctrine Measure* is that there should be local agreement. The PCC should have full discussion and agreement on questions such as:

- How often is *A Service of the Word* to be used? How often is it intended to combine it with Holy Communion? Is there to be, say, a monthly pattern which will involve the use of the *Book of Common Prayer* or the ASB?
- Does the PCC want to put specific limitations on the contents of the service?
- For what period of time will the PCC agree to *A Service of the Word* being used? When will the PCC review this pattern of worship?

St Bartholomew's group of churches have recently been looking at what authority is needed for lay people to conduct services. Canon B 11 (see box on page 240) speaks of two categories of lay person, as well as Readers: those authorized by the bishop of the diocese (in their diocese this is done after attendance at a group of diocesan courses on worship sponsored jointly by the adult training department and the diocesan liturgical committee), and other suitable lay persons, invited by the incumbent. Because of the existence of the course, the diocesan bishop has given directions that where lay people are to lead worship regularly, they should be those authorized by him. So St

Bartholomew's now has four lay people on the course! They realize that this provision includes *A Service of the Word*, which is alternative to Morning and Evening Prayer, the structure for their family service, frequently led by lay people.

In the church school attached to **St Christopher's** there is a real need for a eucharistic prayer which the children can understand. The vicar has a copy of some new prayers from a non-Anglican church, and has written to the bishop to ask 'Please will you authorize this eucharistic prayer for use with children in our church school?' The bishop replies warmly, enthusiastic about the work in the school, but counselling patience until new prayers are properly authorized by the Synod. He encloses a letter from his legal adviser, who says:

'It does not matter legally whether the service is in school or in church. Canon B 1 limits Church of England ministers to using only the services it covers, unless it is claimed that the provisions of Canon B 5 apply, namely that it is a service for which no provision is made in the *Book of Common Prayer* or under Canons B 2 or B 4. Our common understanding is that Canon B 5 cannot be stretched to cover services of Holy Communion even if they are for specific occasions, age groups, or places not specifically provided for in the BCP or Canons B 2 and B 4. So a service of Holy Communion for St Swithun's Day should be regarded primarily as a service of Holy Communion (and therefore coming under Canons B 1 and B 2), and not as a special liturgy for St Swithun (for which the BCP etc. makes no provision, thus leaving the minister to his own discretion under Canon B 5).'

The vicar of **St David's** complains at the Chapter meeting that the Rural Dean has used some illegal liturgy in the service which began the meeting. 'Where did that confession and absolution come from?' he asks, and is shown the Notes in *A Service of the Word* which allow any authorized confession and absolution, including the sixteen confessions and thirteen absolutions printed in Resource Sections C and D in *Patterns*. All the invitations to confession (Section B) are already allowed by Rite A Section 6, which allows 'other suitable words' to be used for the invitation to confession.

Common prayer in the Church of England

It may help to identify three aspects of the Anglican understanding of common prayer.

First, the valuing of patterns of worship which are recognized as the common possession of the people of God. This does not mean that nothing can change nor that every popular practice must prevail. It does not rule out any local variation. It does mean that worship must not simply be governed by the whim of the minister or the congregation. Corporate patterns of worship must exist and be developed which are recognized by worshippers as their corporate worship. It is therefore appropriate that these are approved and regulated by the Church.

Second, the patterns and forms of worship must not be determined purely at the level of the local congregation but must bear witness to participation in the wider common life of the Church. For this reason it is right that common forms such as creeds, collects, confessions and eucharistic prayers should be followed, as well as common approaches to the shape and content of Christian worship.

Third, patterns of common prayer play an important part in maintaining the unity of the Church in its confession of the Christian faith. For this reason:

(a)   Those authorized to lead worship promise 'to use only the forms of service which are authorized or allowed by canon'.

(b)   While ministers have considerable liturgical freedom under Canon B 5, they are charged to ensure that such services are 'neither contrary to, nor indicative of any departure from, the doctrine of the Church of England in any essential matter'. The same provision applies to services derived from *Patterns for Worship*. The next box sets out the things which need to be taken into account in assessing whether particular words and actions conform to the doctrine of the Church of England.

(c)   General Synod in recent years has taken great care that all liturgical forms it has authorized can be used with a good conscience by the different traditions in the Church of England. In compiling *Patterns for Worship* the Liturgical Commission, which is widely representative of the different traditions, has taken similar care. Similar care to respect others' traditions should be taken by those who compile services from these provisions.

The doctrine of the Church of England

1 Canon A 5, of the doctrine of the Church of England states:

'The doctrine of the Church of England is grounded in the Holy Scriptures, and in such teachings of the ancient Fathers and Councils of the Church as are agreeable to the said Scriptures. In particular such doctrine is to be found in the Thirty-nine Articles of Religion, the Book of Common Prayer, and the Ordinal.'

This canon is entrenched in the Worship and Doctrine Measure 1974 (5(1)). It is under this Measure that alternative forms of service to the *Book of Common Prayer* and new forms of declaration of assent for church office holders have been authorized.

2 The Worship and Doctrine Measure 1974 requires that 'every form of service. . . approved by the General Synod. . . shall be such as in the opinion of the General Synod is neither contrary to, nor indicative of any departure from, the doctrine of the Church of England in any essential matter' (S4(1)). S4(2) states: 'The final approval of the General Synod of any such Canon or regulation or form of service or amendment thereof shall conclusively determine that the Synod is of such opinion as aforesaid with respect to the matter so approved.'

3 In considering whether any rite is contrary to, or indicative of any departure from, the doctrine of the Church of England in any essential matter, reference should be made to:

(i)   the Holy Scriptures

(ii)   such teachings of the Fathers and the Councils of the Church as are agreeable to the said Scriptures

(iii)   the Thirty-nine Articles of Religion, the *Book of Common Prayer* and the Ordinal of 1662

(iv)   such forms of service, canons and regulations as have received the final approval of General Synod.

Attention will need to be paid to (iv) in weighing matters that have recently been in dispute in the Church of England. Where, in controversial matters, General Synod has taken care not to depart from the teachings or usage found in (iii), this should be respected.

Canon B 11.1

Morning and Evening Prayer shall be said or sung in every parish church at least on all Sundays and other principal Feast Days, and also on Ash Wednesday and Good Friday. Each service shall be said or sung distinctly, reverently, and in an audible voice. Readers, such other lay persons as may be authorized by the bishop of the diocese, or some other suitable lay person, may, at the invitation of the minister of the parish or, where the cure is vacant or the minister is incapacitated, at the invitation of the churchwardens say or sing Morning or Evening prayer (save for the Absolution).

5

SAMPLE
SERVICES

1	A Service of the Word	245
2	Word and Worship	249
3	For All the Church Family	252
4	Hear His Voice Today	255
5	An Evening Service of the Word	259
6	Christ is Our Peace: Holy Communion	265
7	Holy Communion	270
8	Holy Communion	275
9	The Lord is Here: The Eucharist	281
10	Come, Lord Jesus: Holy Communion during Advent	286
11	Peace to His People on Earth: Holy Communion at Christmas	291
12	In Penitence and Faith: Holy Communion during Lent	296
13	Alleluia! Christ is Risen: Holy Communion at Easter	301
14	The Day the Spirit Came: Holy Communion at Pentecost	308
15	All Creation Worships: Holy Communion	314
16	Believe and Trust: Celebrating Baptism at Holy Communion	319
17	A Service of Healing	325

Introduction

This section of the book contains a variety of sample services, both for *A Service of the Word* and for Holy Communion, for general and for seasonal use. These are offered:

- to provide examples of how to put together material from *Patterns for Worship* and the ASB following the rubrics, notes and guidelines in both books. They are not provided as 'ideal' services designed by the Liturgical Commission for everyone to use, but to show how the basic outlines work. This is the reason for the variety in headings, rubrics and illustrations, and also explains the variety of titles at the start of the services. Those who plan worship locally may find it helpful to consider a broad range of options as they learn how to adapt the material in *Patterns* for services they produce themselves.

- to provide, for those who wish to use them, services which can be photocopied off the page. For information on reproduction for local use see page 330. A selection of these are also available for purchase in packs of coloured cards ready for use.

A Service of the Word

We say together the lines in **bold type.**

The preparation

The minister welcomes the people with a liturgical greeting, which
may include:
The Lord be with you.
And also with you.

Prayers of penitence

The minister introduces the confession in suitable words.

Almighty God, our heavenly Father,
we have sinned against you and against our neighbour,
in thought and word and deed,
through negligence, through weakness,
through our own deliberate fault.
We are truly sorry,
and repent of all our sins.
For the sake of your Son Jesus Christ, who died for us,
forgive us all that is past;
and grant that we may serve you in newness of life
to the glory of your name. Amen.

The minister declares God's forgiveness.

Praise

This may include the *Venite*:

O come let us sing out to the Lord:
let us shout in triumph to the rock of our salvation.
Let us come before his face with thanksgiving:
and cry out to him joyfully in psalms.
For the Lord is a great God:
and a great king above all gods.
In his hand are the depths of the earth:
and the peaks of the mountains are his also.
The sea is his and he made it:
his hands moulded dry land.
Come let us worship and bow down:
and kneel before the Lord our maker.
For he is the Lord our God:
we are his people and the sheep of his pasture.
If only you would hear his voice today:
for he comes to judge the earth.
He shall judge the world with righteousness:
and the peoples with his truth.

Glory to the Father, and to the Son,
and to the Holy Spirit:
as it was in the beginning, is now,
and shall be for ever. Amen.

and

O Lord, open my lips:
and my mouth shall proclaim your praise.

Sing psalms, hymns and sacred songs:
let us sing to God with thanksgiving in our hearts.

Let everything you do or say be done in the name of the Lord Jesus,
giving thanks to God through Jesus Christ.

The ministry of the Word_____

This includes:

Readings (or a Reading) from Holy Scripture

After each reading:
This is the word of the Lord.
Thanks be to God.

A **Psalm** or a **Scriptural song**

Sermon

An authorized **Creed** or **Affirmation of Faith**

The Apostles' Creed
I believe in God, the Father almighty,
creator of heaven and earth.

I believe in Jesus Christ, his only Son, our Lord.
He was conceived by the power of the Holy Spirit
and born of the Virgin Mary.
He suffered under Pontius Pilate,
was crucified, died, and was buried.
He descended to the dead.
On the third day he rose again.
He ascended into heaven,
and is seated at the right hand of the Father.
He will come again to judge the living and the dead.

I believe in the Holy Spirit,
the holy catholic Church,
the communion of saints,
the forgiveness of sins,
the resurrection of the body
and the life everlasting. Amen.

The prayers_____

These include intercessions and thanksgivings, a Collect and the
Lord's Prayer.

One of these responses may be used:
Lord, in your mercy:
hear our prayer.

or

Jesus, Lord of. . .
in your mercy, hear us.

The intercessions may end with:
Merciful Father,
**accept these prayers
for the sake of your Son,
our Saviour Jesus Christ. Amen.**

The prayer of the day, the **Collect**

**The Lord's Prayer
Our Father in heaven,
hallowed be your name,
your kingdom come,
your will be done,
on earth as in heaven.
Give us today our daily bread.
Forgive us our sins
as we forgive those who sin against us.
Lead us not into temptation
but deliver us from evil.
For the kingdom, the power, and the glory are yours
now and for ever. Amen.**

The conclusion
The service concludes with a liturgical ending, which may include a
blessing and a dismissal.

Go in the peace of Christ.
Thanks be to God.

Word and Worship

We say together the lines in **bold type**.

The preparation

Singing, Introduction, Scripture sentence, or Prayer

This is the day which the Lord has made.
Let us rejoice and be glad in it.

Lord, direct our thoughts,
teach us to pray,
lift up our hearts to worship you
in Spirit and in truth,
through Jesus Christ. Amen.

Confession

Let us return to the Lord our God and say to him:

Father,
we have sinned against heaven and against you.
We are not worthy to be called your children.
We turn to you again.
Have mercy on us,
bring us back to yourself
as those who once were dead
but now have life through Christ our Lord. Amen.

The minister declares God's forgiveness.

Praise

O Lord, open our lips:
and our mouth shall proclaim your praise.

Let us worship the Lord:
all praise to his name.

Glory to the Father, and to the Son,
and to the Holy Spirit:
as it was in the beginning, is now,
and shall be for ever. Amen.

Other responses and songs may be used.

The ministry of the Word_____

Readings (or a Reading) from Holy Scripture

After each reading:
This is the word of the Lord.
Thanks be to God.

Psalms or **Songs**

Sermon

Affirmation of Faith
Do you believe and trust in God the Father,
who made all things?
We believe and trust in him.

Do you believe and trust in his Son Jesus Christ,
who redeemed the world?
We believe and trust in him.

Do you believe and trust in his Holy Spirit,
who gives life to the people of God?
We believe and trust in him.

This is the faith of the Church.
This is our faith.
We believe and trust in one God:
Father, Son and Holy Spirit. Amen.

The prayers_____

The prayers may include some of these responses:
Lord, in your mercy:
hear our prayer.

or

Jesus, Lord of. . .
in your mercy, hear us.

and end with:

Merciful Father,
accept these prayers
for the sake of your Son,
our Saviour Jesus Christ. Amen.

The prayer of the day, the **Collect**

The Lord's Prayer
Our Father in heaven,
hallowed be your name,
your kingdom come,
your will be done,
on earth as in heaven.
Give us today our daily bread.
Forgive us our sins
as we forgive those who sin against us.
Lead us not into temptation
but deliver us from evil.
For the kingdom, the power, and the glory are yours
now and for ever. Amen.

The conclusion

Either:

The **Peace**, introduced with suitable words

The peace of the Lord be always with you.
And also with you.

or:

The grace of our Lord Jesus Christ,
and the love of God,
and the fellowship of the Holy Spirit
be with us all evermore. **Amen.**

For All the Church Family

We say together the lines in **bold type**.

The preparation

Singing, Scripture sentence, Greeting, Introduction or Prayer

Grace, mercy and peace from God our Father
and the Lord Jesus Christ be with you.
And also with you.

Loving Lord,
fill us with your life-giving,
joy-giving, peace-giving presence,
that we may praise you now with our lips
and all the day long with our lives,
through Jesus Christ our Lord. Amen.

Cast your burden upon the Lord:
and he will sustain you.
Create in us clean hearts, O God:
and renew a right spirit within us.
Cast us not away from your presence:
and take not your Holy Spirit from us.
Give us the joy of your saving help:
and sustain us with your life-giving Spirit.
Blessed be the Lord day by day:
the God of our salvation, who bears our burdens.

We confess our sins.

O King enthroned on high,
filling the earth with your glory:
holy is your name,
Lord God almighty.
In our sinfulness we cry to you
to take our guilt away,
and to cleanse our lips to speak your word,
through Jesus Christ our Lord. Amen.

The minister declares God's forgiveness.

Praise

O Lord, open our lips:
and our mouth shall proclaim your praise.

Let us worship the Lord:
all praise to his name.

Glory to the Father, and to the Son,
and to the Holy Spirit:
as it was in the beginning, is now,
and shall be for ever. Amen.

Other responses, psalms and songs may be used.

The ministry of the Word

Readings (or a Reading) from Holy Scripture

There may be a special activity for children, psalms or songs. The sermon may come here or after the prayers.

Affirmation of Faith

Do you believe and trust in God the Father,
who made all things?
We believe and trust in him.

Do you believe and trust in his Son Jesus Christ,
who redeemed the world?
We believe and trust in him.

Do you believe and trust in his Holy Spirit,
who gives life to the people of God?
We believe and trust in him.

This is the faith of the Church.
This is our faith.
We believe and trust in one God:
Father, Son and Holy Spirit. Amen.

The prayers

Our Father in heaven,
hallowed be your name,
your kingdom come,
your will be done,
on earth as in heaven.
Give us today our daily bread.
Forgive us our sins
as we forgive those who sin against us.
Lead us not into temptation
but deliver us from evil.
For the kingdom, the power, and the glory are yours
now and for ever. Amen.

Other **prayers** follow, ending with the **Collect**, the prayer for the day.

The conclusion

Eternal Giver of love and life,
your Son Jesus Christ has sent us into all the world
to preach the gospel of his kingdom.
Confirm us in this mission,
and help us to live the good news we proclaim,
through Jesus Christ our Lord. Amen.

A blessing may be said, or all say:

The grace of our Lord Jesus Christ,
and the love of God,
and the fellowship of the Holy Spirit
be with us all evermore. Amen.

A service from *Patterns for Worship*. Text copyright © The Central Board of Finance of the Church of England 1989, 1995. Illustrated by Taffy © The Central Board of Finance 1995. Reproduced with permission for use in

Hear His Voice Today

Introduction

Singing, Scripture sentence, Greeting, Introduction or **Prayer**

The **Peace** may be exchanged.

After an introductory sentence, the president says:
The peace of the Lord be always with you.
And also with you.

This is the day which the Lord has made.
Let us rejoice and be glad in it.

**Lord, direct our thoughts,
teach us to pray,
lift up our hearts to worship you
in Spirit and in truth,
through Jesus Christ. Amen.**

We confess our sins.

Either:

**Lord God,
we have sinned against you;
we have done evil in your sight.
We are sorry and repent.
Have mercy on us according to your love.
Wash away our wrongdoing and cleanse us from our sin.
Renew a right spirit within us
and restore us to the joy of your salvation,
through Jesus Christ our Lord. Amen.**

Lord, we are clay:
and you are the potter.

We are all the work of your hand:
do not remember our sins for ever.

Look upon us in your mercy:
for we are your people.

or:

Almighty God, our heavenly Father,
we have sinned against you and against our neighbour,
in thought and word and deed,
through negligence, through weakness,
through our own deliberate fault.
We are truly sorry,
and repent of all our sins.
For the sake of your Son Jesus Christ, who died for us,
forgive us all that is past;
and grant that we may serve you in newness of life
to the glory of your name. Amen.

The minister declares God's forgiveness.

Praise

O Lord, open our lips:
and our mouth shall proclaim your praise.

Let us worship the Lord:
all praise to his name.

Glory to the Father, and to the Son,
and to the Holy Spirit:
as it was in the beginning, is now,
and shall be for ever. Amen.

Psalm or **Song**

The Word

This includes:

Readings (or a Reading) from Holy Scripture

After each reading:
This is the word of the Lord.
Thanks be to God.

Sermon after one of the readings

Psalms or **Songs**

The Apostles' Creed

Do you believe and trust in God the Father,
who made all things?
**I believe in God, the Father almighty,
creator of heaven and earth.**

Do you believe and trust in his Son Jesus Christ,
who redeemed the world?
**I believe in Jesus Christ, his only Son, our Lord.
He was conceived by the power of the Holy Spirit
and born of the Virgin Mary.
He suffered under Pontius Pilate,
was crucified, died, and was buried.
He descended to the dead.
On the third day he rose again.
He ascended into heaven,
and is seated at the right hand of the Father.
He will come again to judge the living and the dead.**

Do you believe and trust in the Holy Spirit,
who gives life to the people of God?
**I believe in the Holy Spirit,
the holy catholic Church,
the communion of saints,
the forgiveness of sins,
the resurrection of the body,
and the life everlasting. Amen.**

Prayers

The prayers may include the **Collect** and some of these responses:
Lord, have mercy upon us.
Christ, have mercy upon us.
Lord, have mercy upon us.

or

Lord, in your mercy:
hear our prayer.

or

Jesus, Lord of. . .
in your mercy, hear us.

and end with:

Merciful Father,
accept these prayers
for the sake of your Son,
our Saviour Jesus Christ. Amen.

Our Father in heaven,
hallowed be your name,
your kingdom come,
your will be done,
on earth as in heaven.
Give us today our daily bread.
Forgive us our sins
as we forgive those who sin against us.
Lead us not into temptation
but deliver us from evil.
For the kingdom, the power, and the glory are yours
now and for ever. Amen.

God of power,
may the boldness of your Spirit transform us,
may the gentleness of your Spirit lead us,
may the gifts of your Spirit
equip us to serve and worship you
now and always. Amen.

An Evening Service of the Word

Introduction

Song or **Hymn**

May the light and peace of Jesus Christ our Lord be with you.
The Lord bless you.

We have come together as the family of God in our Father's presence
to offer him praise and thanksgiving,
to hear and receive his holy word,
to bring before him the needs of the world,
to ask his forgiveness of our sins,
and to seek his grace,
that through his Son Jesus Christ
we may give ourselves to his service.

or

O Lord, we call to you: come to us quickly.
Hear us when we cry to you.
Let our prayer rise before you as incense,
the lifting up of our hands as the evening sacrifice.

We confess our sins.

God is light.
In him there is no darkness.
If we live in the light,
as God is in the light,
we have fellowship with one another,
and the blood of Jesus, his Son, purifies us from all sin.

Almighty God, our heavenly Father,
we have sinned against you and against our neighbour,
in thought and word and deed,
through negligence, through weakness,
through our own deliberate fault.
We are truly sorry,
and repent of all our sins.
For the sake of your Son Jesus Christ, who died for us,
forgive us all that is past;
and grant that we may serve you in newness of life
to the glory of your name. Amen.

The minister declares God's forgiveness.

The Word

Psalms or **Songs**

Readings (or a Reading) from Holy Scripture

At the end of each reading the reader may say:

This is the word of the Lord.
Thanks be to God.

Sermon

The Apostles' Creed

I believe in God, the Father almighty,
creator of heaven and earth.

I believe in Jesus Christ, his only Son, our Lord.
He was conceived by the power of the Holy Spirit
and born of the Virgin Mary.
He suffered under Pontius Pilate,
was crucified, died, and was buried.
He descended to the dead.
On the third day he rose again.
He ascended into heaven,
and is seated at the right hand of the Father.
He will come again to judge the living and the dead.

I believe in the Holy Spirit,
the holy catholic Church,
the communion of saints,
the forgiveness of sins,
the resurrection of the body
and the life everlasting. Amen.

Praise

Blessed are you, Lord God, King of the universe!
Your word brings on the dusk at evening.
Your wisdom creates both night and day.
You determine the cycles of time.
You arrange the succession of seasons,
and establish the stars in their heavenly courses.
Lord of the starry hosts is your name.
Living and eternal God, rule over us always.
Blessed be the Lord, whose word makes evening fall.

Psalm or **Song**

Prayers

The prayers may include some of these responses:
Lord, have mercy upon us.
Christ, have mercy upon us.
Lord, have mercy upon us.

or

Lord, in your mercy,
hear our prayer.

or

Jesus, Lord of. . .
in your mercy, hear us.

and end with:
Merciful Father,
accept these prayers
for the sake of your Son,
our Saviour Jesus Christ. Amen.

or this form may be used:
(We pray to the Lord, saying:
'in faith we pray:
we pray to you our God.')

That the rest of this day may be holy, peaceful
and full of your presence;
in faith we pray:
we pray to you our God.

That the work we have done and the people we have met today
may bring us closer to you;
in faith we pray:
we pray to you our God.

That we may hear and respond to your call to peace and justice;
in faith we pray:
we pray to you our God.

That you will sustain the faith and hope
of those who are lonely, oppressed and anxious;
in faith we pray:
we pray to you our God.

That you will strengthen us in your service,
and fill our hearts with longing for your kingdom;
in faith we pray:
we pray to you our God.

God of mercy,
**you know us and love us
and hear our prayer:
keep us in the eternal fellowship
of Jesus Christ our Saviour. Amen.**

The **Collect**

**The Lord's Prayer
Our Father in heaven,
hallowed be your name,
your kingdom come,
your will be done,
on earth as in heaven.
Give us today our daily bread.
Forgive us our sins
as we forgive those who sin against us.
Lead us not into temptation
but deliver us from evil.
For the kingdom, the power, and the glory are yours
now and for ever. Amen.**

Ending

Gracious God,
you have given us much today;
grant us also a thankful spirit.
Into your hands we commend ourselves
and those we love.
Stay with us, and when we take our rest
renew us for the service of your Son Jesus Christ. **Amen.**

**In darkness and in light,
in trouble and in joy,
help us, heavenly Father,
to trust your love,
to serve your purpose,
and to praise your name,
through Jesus Christ our Lord. Amen.**

Jesus Christ is the light of the world:
a light no darkness can quench.

Stay with us, Lord, for it is evening:
and the day is almost over.

Even the darkness is not dark for you:
and the night shines like the day.

Let your light scatter the darkness:
and fill your church with your glory.

and/or

You, Christ, are the King of glory:
you are the everlasting Son of the Father.
When you drew the sting of death:
you opened heaven to all who trust in you.
Come then, we pray, to the aid of your people:
we are bought at the price of your own precious blood.
When you make up the number of your saints:
reward us with them in glory for ever. Amen.

Mercy, peace and love be ours for ever:
from God the Father, Son and Holy Spirit. Amen.

The **Peace**

Sovereign Lord, your word has been fulfilled;
my eyes have seen your salvation:
now you let your servant go in peace.
The peace of the Lord be always with you.
And also with you.

Christ is our Peace
HOLY COMMUNION

We say together the lines in **bold type**.

We prepare

The minister welcomes the people with a liturgical greeting, which may include:
The Lord be with you.
And also with you.

Almighty God,
to whom all hearts are open,
all desires known,
and from whom no secrets are hidden:
cleanse the thoughts of our hearts
by the inspiration of your Holy Spirit,
that we may perfectly love you,
and worthily magnify your holy name;
through Christ our Lord. Amen.

We confess

Almighty God, our heavenly Father,
we have sinned against you and against our neighbour,
in thought and word and deed,
through negligence, through weakness,
through our own deliberate fault.
We are truly sorry,
and repent of all our sins.
For the sake of your Son Jesus Christ, who died for us,
forgive us all that is past;
and grant that we may serve you in newness of life
to the glory of your name. Amen.

The president declares God's forgiveness.

We praise

This song may be said or sung:
**Glory to God in the highest,
and peace to his people on earth.**

**Lord God, heavenly King,
almighty God and Father,
we worship you, we give you thanks,
we praise you for your glory.
Lord Jesus Christ, only Son of the Father,
Lord God, Lamb of God,
you take away the sin of the world:
have mercy on us;
you are seated at the right hand of the Father:
receive our prayer.**

**For you alone are the Holy One,
you alone are the Lord,
you alone are the Most High,
Jesus Christ,
with the Holy Spirit,
in the glory of God the Father. Amen.**

The president says the prayer for the day, the **Collect**.

We listen to God's word

Two or three **Readings, Psalms** or **Songs**, and a **Sermon** after one
of the readings.

After each reading:
This is the word of the Lord.
Thanks be to God.

Before the Gospel:
Glory to Christ our Saviour.

and at the end:
Praise to Christ our Lord.

**The Apostles' Creed
I believe in God, the Father almighty,
creator of heaven and earth.**

I believe in Jesus Christ, his only Son, our Lord.
He was conceived by the power of the Holy Spirit
and born of the Virgin Mary.
He suffered under Pontius Pilate,
was crucified, died, and was buried.
He descended to the dead.
On the third day he rose again.
He ascended into heaven,
and is seated at the right hand of the Father.
He will come again to judge the living and the dead.

I believe in the Holy Spirit,
the holy catholic Church,
the communion of saints,
the forgiveness of sins,
the resurrection of the body,
and the life everlasting. Amen.

We pray

The prayers sometimes include the response:
Lord in your mercy:
hear our prayer.

and end with:
Merciful Father,
accept these prayers
for the sake of your Son,
our Saviour Jesus Christ. Amen.

We sometimes say:
We do not presume
to come to this your table, merciful Lord,
trusting in our own righteousness,
but in your manifold and great mercies.
We are not worthy
so much as to gather up the crumbs under your table.
But you are the same Lord
whose nature is always to have mercy.
Grant us therefore, gracious Lord,
so to eat the flesh of your dear Son Jesus Christ
and to drink his blood,
that we may evermore dwell in him
and he in us. Amen.

The **Peace**

After the introductory words:
The peace of the Lord be always with you.
And also with you.

We give thanks _____

The Lord be with you.   or   The Lord is here.
And also with you.   **His Spirit is with us.**

Lift up your hearts.
We lift them to the Lord.

Let us give thanks to the Lord our God.
It is right to give him thanks and praise.

The president leads the **Thanksgiving**.

We join in the words:
Holy, holy, holy Lord,
God of power and might,
heaven and earth are full of your glory.
Hosanna in the highest.

This Anthem may also be used:
Blessed is he who comes in the name of the Lord.
Hosanna in the highest.

The words of Christ at the supper end:
. . . in remembrance of me.
Christ has died:
Christ is risen:
Christ will come again.

The Eucharistic Prayer ends with:
Amen.

or

Blessing and honour and glory and power
be yours for ever and ever. Amen.

We break bread and share in communion ____

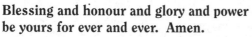

As our Saviour taught us, so we pray:
Our Father in heaven,
hallowed be your name,

your kingdom come,
your will be done,
on earth as in heaven.
Give us today our daily bread.
Forgive us our sins
as we forgive those who sin against us.
Lead us not into temptation
but deliver us from evil.
For the kingdom, the power, and the glory are yours
now and for ever. Amen.

The president breaks the consecrated bread.

We break this bread
to share in the body of Christ.
**Though we are many, we are one body,
because we all share in one bread.**

The president invites the people to receive communion.
Each communicant replies **Amen** to the words of distribution.

We prepare to go

Almighty God,
we thank you for feeding us
with the body and blood of your Son Jesus Christ.
Through him we offer you our souls and bodies
to be a living sacrifice.
Send us out in the power of your Spirit
to live and work
to your praise and glory. Amen.

The dismissal

A blessing may be said, and the service ends:
Go in peace to love and serve the Lord.
In the name of Christ. Amen.

or

Go in the peace of Christ.
Thanks be to God.

Holy Communion

Preparation

Singing, Scripture sentence, Greeting, Introduction or **Prayer**

Grace, mercy and peace from God our Father
and the Lord Jesus Christ be with you.
And also with you.

The president says the prayer of the day, the **Collect**.

The ministry of the Word

Readings from Holy Scripture, **Psalms** or **Songs,** and a **Sermon**
after one of the readings

After each reading:
This is the word of the Lord.
Thanks be to God.

Before the Gospel:
Glory to Christ our Saviour.

and at the end:
Praise to Christ our Lord.

The Nicene Creed

We believe in one God,
the Father, the almighty,
maker of heaven and earth,
of all that is,
seen and unseen.

We believe in one Lord, Jesus Christ,
the only Son of God,
eternally begotten of the Father,
God from God, Light from Light,
true God from true God,
begotten, not made,
of one Being with the Father.
Through him all things were made.

For us men and for our salvation
he came down from heaven;
by the power of the Holy Spirit
he became incarnate of the Virgin Mary,
and was made man.
For our sake he was crucified under Pontius Pilate;
he suffered death and was buried.
On the third day he rose again,
in accordance with the Scriptures;
He ascended into heaven
and is seated at the right hand of the Father.
He will come again in glory
to judge the living and the dead,
and his kingdom will have no end.

We believe in the Holy Spirit,
the Lord, the giver of life,
who proceeds from the Father and the Son.
With the Father and the Son he is worshipped and glorified.
He has spoken through the Prophets.

We believe in one holy catholic and apostolic Church.
We acknowledge one baptism for the forgiveness of sins.
We look for the resurrection of the dead,
and the life of the world to come. Amen.

Intercessions

The prayers sometimes include the response:

Lord, in your mercy: or   Lord, hear us.
hear our prayer.   **Lord, graciously hear us.**

and end with:
Merciful Father,
accept these prayers
for the sake of your Son,
our Saviour Jesus Christ. Amen.

Penitence

The **Commandments** or the **Summary of the Law** may be used,
with the response:
Amen. Lord, have mercy.

Almighty God, our heavenly Father,
we have sinned against you,

through our own fault,
in thought and word and deed,
and in what we have left undone.
For your Son our Lord Jesus Christ's sake,
forgive us all that is past;
and grant that we may serve you in newness of life
to the glory of your name. Amen.

The president declares God's forgiveness.

All may say:
We do not presume
to come to this your table, merciful Lord,
trusting in our own righteousness,
but in your manifold and great mercies.
We are not worthy
so much as to gather up the crumbs under your table.
But you are the same Lord
whose nature is always to have mercy.
Grant us therefore, gracious Lord,
so to eat the flesh of your dear Son Jesus Christ
and to drink his blood,
that we may evermore dwell in him and he in us. Amen.

The president may introduce the **Peace** with a suitable sentence,
and then say:
The peace of the Lord be always with you.
And also with you.

The holy table is prepared. Bread and wine are placed upon it, and
the president says:

The Eucharistic Prayer

The Lord be with you.   or   The Lord is here.
And also with you.   **His Spirit is with us.**

Lift up your hearts.
We lift them to the Lord.

Let us give thanks to the Lord our God.
It is right to give him thanks and praise.

The president leads the Thanksgiving, ending:
. . . for ever praising you and saying,

Holy, holy, holy Lord,
God of power and might,
heaven and earth are full of your glory.
Hosanna in the highest.

This Anthem may also be used:
Blessed is he who comes in the name of the Lord.
Hosanna in the highest.

The words of Christ at the supper end:
. . . in remembrance of me.
Christ has died:
Christ is risen:
Christ will come again.

The Eucharistic Prayer ends with:
Amen.

or

Blessing and honour and glory and power
be yours for ever and ever. Amen.

Breaking bread and sharing in communion __

As our Saviour taught us, so we pray:

Our Father, who art in heaven,
hallowed be thy name;
thy kingdom come;
thy will be done;
on earth as it is in heaven.
Give us this day our daily bread.
And forgive us our trespasses,
as we forgive those who trespass against us.
And lead us not into temptation;
but deliver us from evil.
For thine is the kingdom, the power, and the glory
for ever and ever. Amen.

The president breaks the consecrated bread.

We break this bread
to share in the body of Christ.
Though we are many, we are one body,
because we all share in one bread.

Either here or later we may pray:
**Lamb of God, you take away the sins of the world:
have mercy on us.
Lamb of God, you take away the sins of the world:
have mercy on us.
Lamb of God, you take away the sins of the world:
grant us peace.**

The president invites the people to receive communion.
Each communicant replies **Amen** to the words of distribution.

After communion

**Almighty God,
we thank you for feeding us
with the body and blood of your Son Jesus Christ.
Through him we offer you our souls and bodies
to be a living sacrifice.
Send us out in the power of your Spirit
to live and work
to your praise and glory. Amen.**

The dismissal

A blessing may be said, and the service ends.

Go in peace to love and serve the Lord.
In the name of Christ. Amen.

or

Go in the peace of Christ.
Thanks be to God.

Holy Communion

We prepare

Singing, Scripture sentence, Greeting, Introduction or **Prayer,**
which may include:

The Lord be with you.
And also with you.

Almighty God,
to whom all hearts are open,
all desires known,
and from whom no secrets are hidden:
cleanse the thoughts of our hearts
by the inspiration of your Holy Spirit,
that we may perfectly love you,
and worthily magnify your holy name;
through Christ our Lord. Amen.

We confess

Father eternal, giver of light and grace,
we have sinned against you and against our neighbour,
in what we have thought,
in what we have said and done,
through ignorance, through weakness,
through our own deliberate fault.
We have wounded your love,
and marred your image in us.
We are sorry and ashamed,
and repent of all our sins.
For the sake of your Son Jesus Christ, who died for us,
forgive us all that is past;
and lead us out from darkness
to walk as children of light. Amen.

The president declares God's forgiveness.

We praise

This song may be said or sung:

Glory to God in the highest,
and peace to his people on earth.

Lord God, heavenly King,
almighty God and Father,
we worship you, we give you thanks,
we praise you for your glory.
Lord Jesus Christ, only Son of the Father,
Lord God, Lamb of God,
you take away the sin of the world:
have mercy on us;
you are seated at the right hand of the Father:
receive our prayer.

For you alone are the Holy One,
you alone are the Lord,
you alone are the Most High,
Jesus Christ,
with the Holy Spirit,
in the glory of God the Father. Amen.

The president says the **Collect**, the prayer of the day.

We listen to God's word

Either two or three **Readings** follow.

At the end of each reading the reader may say:
This is the word of the Lord.
Thanks be to God.

Before the Gospel:
Glory to Christ our Saviour.

and at the end:
Praise to Christ our Lord.

Psalms or **Songs**

Sermon

We believe

Do you believe and trust in God the Father
who made all things?
We believe and trust in him.

Do you believe and trust in his Son Jesus Christ,
who redeemed the world?
We believe and trust in him.

Do you believe and trust in his Holy Spirit,
who gives life to the people of God?
We believe and trust in him.

This is the faith of the Church.
This is our faith.
We believe and trust in one God,
Father, Son, and Holy Spirit.

We pray

The prayers of the people may include the response:
Lord, in your mercy:
hear our prayer.

and end with:
Merciful Father,
accept these prayers
for the sake of your Son,
our Saviour Jesus Christ. Amen.

All may say:
Most merciful Lord,
your love compels us to come in.
Our hands were unclean,
our hearts were unprepared;
we were not fit
even to eat the crumbs from under your table.
But you, Lord, are the God of our salvation,
and share your bread with sinners.
So cleanse us and feed us
with the precious body and blood of your Son,

that he may live in us and we in him;
and that we, with the whole company of Christ,
may sit and eat in your kingdom. **Amen.**

The **Peace**

After the introductory words:
The peace of the Lord be always with you.
And also with you.

We give thanks in the Eucharistic Prayer____

The Lord be with you.   or   The Lord is here.
And also with you.   **His Spirit is with us.**

Lift up your hearts.
We lift them to the Lord.

Let us give thanks to the Lord our God.
It is right to give him thanks and praise.

The president leads the Thanksgiving, ending:
. . . for ever praising you and saying,
Holy, holy, holy Lord,
God of power and might,
heaven and earth are full of your glory.
Hosanna in the highest.

This Anthem may also be used:
Blessed is he who comes in the name of the Lord.
Hosanna in the highest.

The words of Christ at the supper end:
. . . in remembrance of me.
Great is the mystery of faith.
Christ has died:
Christ is risen:
Christ will come again.

The Eucharistic Prayer ends with:
Amen.

or

Blessing and honour and glory and power
be yours for ever and ever. Amen.

We break bread and share in communion _____

As our Saviour taught us, so we pray:

Our Father in heaven,
hallowed be your name,
your kingdom come,
your will be done,
on earth as in heaven.
Give us today our daily bread.
Forgive us our sins
as we forgive those who sin against us.
Lead us not into temptation
but deliver us from evil.
For the kingdom, the power, and the glory are yours
now and for ever. Amen.

The president breaks the consecrated bread.
Every time we eat this bread and drink this cup:
we proclaim the Lord's death
until he comes.

The president invites the people to receive communion.
Jesus is the Lamb of God
who takes away the sin of the world.
Happy are those who are called to his supper.
Lord, I am not worthy to receive you,
but only say the word, and I shall be healed.

Each communicant replies **Amen** to the words of distribution.

After communion _____

God of truth,
we have seen with our eyes
and touched with our hands
the bread of life.
Strengthen our faith
that we may grow in love for you
and for each other;
through Jesus Christ our risen Lord. Amen.

The dismissal

A blessing may be said, and the service ends.
Go in peace to love and serve the Lord.
In the name of Christ. Amen.

or

Go in the peace of Christ.
Thanks be to God.

The Lord is Here
THE EUCHARIST

We prepare

The minister welcomes the people with a greeting, which may
include:
Grace and peace to you from God.
May he fill you with truth and joy.

**Lord, direct our thoughts,
teach us to pray,
lift up our hearts to worship you
in Spirit and in truth,
through Jesus Christ. Amen.**

or

**Almighty God,
to whom all hearts are open,
all desires known,
and from whom no secrets are hidden:
cleanse the thoughts of our hearts
by the inspiration of your Holy Spirit,
that we may perfectly love you,
and worthily magnify your holy name;
through Christ our Lord. Amen.**

Let us return to the Lord our God and say to him:

Father,
we have sinned against heaven and against you.
We are not worthy to be called your children.
We turn to you again.
Have mercy on us,
bring us back to yourself
as those who once were dead
but now have life through Christ our Lord. Amen.

May God our Father forgive *us our* sins,
and bring *us* to the fellowship of his table
with his saints for ever. **Amen.**

We praise

This or a similar song may be sung:
Glory to God, glory to God,
Glory to the Father.
To him be glory for ever.
Alleluia! Amen.

Glory to God, glory to God,
Son of the Father,
To him be glory for ever.
Alleluia! Amen.

Glory to God, glory to God,
Glory Holy Spirit.
To him be glory for ever.
Alleluia! Amen.

The president says the prayer of the day, the **Collect**.

The ministry of the Word

Either two or three **Readings**

After each reading:
This is the word of the Lord.
Thanks be to God.

Before the Gospel:
Glory to Christ our Saviour.

and at the end:
Praise to Christ our Lord.

Psalms or **Songs**

Sermon

We believe

Do you believe and trust in God the Father,
who made all things?
We believe and trust in him.

Do you believe and trust in his Son Jesus Christ,
who redeemed the world?
We believe and trust in him.

Do you believe and trust in his Holy Spirit,
who gives life to the people of God?
We believe and trust in him.

This is the faith of the Church.
This is our faith.
We believe and trust in one God:
Father, Son and Holy Spirit. Amen.

We pray

The prayers sometimes include the response:
Lord, in your mercy:
hear our prayer.

and end with:
Merciful Father,
accept these prayers
for the sake of your Son,
our Saviour Jesus Christ. Amen.

We stand for the Peace.

After the introductory words:
The peace of the Lord be always with you.
And also with you.

After the gifts have been prepared, the president says:

The Eucharistic Prayer

The Lord is here.   or   The Lord be with you.
His Spirit is with us.   **And also with you.**

Lift up your hearts.
We lift them to the Lord.

Let us give thanks to the Lord our God.
It is right to give him thanks and praise.

The president leads the Thanksgiving, ending:
. . . for ever praising you and saying,
Holy, holy, holy Lord,
God of power and might,
heaven and earth are full of your glory.
Hosanna in the highest.

This Anthem may also be used:
Blessed is he who comes in the name of the Lord.
Hosanna in the highest.

The words of Christ at the supper end:
. . . in remembrance of me.
Great is the mystery of faith.
Christ has died:
Christ is risen:
Christ will come again.

The Eucharistic Prayer ends with:
Amen.

or

Blessing and honour and glory and power
be yours for ever and ever. Amen.

Silence should be kept.

As our Saviour taught us, so we pray:
Our Father in heaven,
hallowed be your name,
your kingdom come,
your will be done,
on earth as in heaven.

Give us today our daily bread.
Forgive us our sins
as we forgive those who sin against us.
Lead us not into temptation
but deliver us from evil.
For the kingdom, the power, and the glory are yours
now and for ever. Amen.

The president breaks the consecrated bread.
We break this bread
to share in the body of Christ.
Though we are many, we are one body,
because we all share in one bread.

The president invites the people to receive communion.
Each communicant replies **Amen** to the words of distribution.

After communion

Almighty God,
we thank you for feeding us
with the body and blood of your Son Jesus Christ.
Through him we offer you our souls and bodies
to be a living sacrifice.
Send us out in the power of your Spirit
to live and work
to your praise and glory. Amen.

The dismissal

A blessing may be said, and the service ends.

Go in peace to love and serve the Lord.
In the name of Christ. Amen.

or

Go in the peace of Christ.
Thanks be to God.

Come, Lord Jesus
HOLY COMMUNION DURING ADVENT

The preparation

Singing, Scripture sentence, Greeting, Introduction or **Prayer**,
which may include:
Praise God! For the Lord, our almighty God, is King!
Happy are those who have been invited
to the wedding-feast of the Lamb.
Alleluia!

We confess our sins.

O King enthroned on high,
filling the earth with your glory:
holy is your name,
Lord God almighty.
In our sinfulness we cry to you
to take our guilt away,
and to cleanse our lips to speak your word,
through Jesus Christ our Lord. Amen.

The president declares God's forgiveness.

The president says the prayer of the day, the **Collect**.

The ministry of the Word

After each reading:
This is the word of the Lord.
Thanks be to God.

Before the Gospel:
Glory to Christ our Saviour.

and at the end:
Praise to Christ our Lord.

There are two or three **Readings, Psalms** or **songs** and a **Sermon**.

Affirmation of Faith_____

We say together in faith:

Holy, holy, holy
is the Lord God almighty,
who was, and is, and is to come.

We believe in God the Father,
who created all things:
for by his will they were created
and have their being.

We believe in God the Son,
who was slain:
for with his blood,
he purchased us for God,
from every tribe and language,
from every people and nation.

We believe in God the Holy Spirit –
the Spirit and the Bride say, 'Come!'
Even so, come Lord Jesus! Amen.

Prayers_____

In joyful expectation of his coming
we pray to Jesus, saying,
*   Maranatha.
Come, Lord Jesus.

Come to your church as Lord and Judge.
We pray for. . .
Help us to live in the light of your coming
and give us a longing for your rule.
Maranatha.
Come, Lord Jesus.

Come to your world as King of the nations.
We pray for. . .
Before you rulers will stand in silence.
Maranatha.
Come, Lord Jesus.

Come to your people with a message of victory and peace.
We pray for. . .

* This Aramaic word means 'Our Lord, come.'

Give us the victory over death, temptation and evil.
Maranatha.
Come, Lord Jesus.

Come to us as Saviour and Comforter.
We pray for. . .
Break into our failure and distress,
and set us free to serve you for ever.
Maranatha.
Come, Lord Jesus.

Come to us from heaven with power and great glory,
to lift us up to meet you,
with all your saints and angels,
and to live with you for ever.
Maranatha.
Come, Lord Jesus.

We stand for the Peace.

The God of peace makes us holy in all things
that we may be ready at the coming of our Lord Jesus Christ.
The peace of the Lord be always with you.
And also with you.

After the gifts have been prepared, the president says:

The Eucharistic Prayer

The Lord be with you.   or   The Lord is here.
And also with you.   **His Spirit is with us.**

Lift up your hearts.
We lift them to the Lord.

Let us give thanks to the Lord our God.
It is right to give him thanks and praise.

The president leads the Thanksgiving, ending
. . . for ever praising you and saying,
Holy, holy, holy Lord,
God of power and might,
heaven and earth are full of your glory.
Hosanna in the highest.

This Anthem may also be used:
Blessed is he who comes in the name of the Lord.
Hosanna in the highest.

The words of Christ at the supper end:
. . . in remembrance of me.
Christ has died:
Christ is risen:
Christ will come again.

The Eucharistic Prayer ends with:
Amen.

or

Blessing and honour and glory and power
be yours for ever and ever. Amen.

Breaking bread and sharing in communion __

Let us pray for the coming of God's kingdom in the words our Saviour
taught us:
Our Father in heaven,
hallowed be your name,
your kingdom come,
your will be done,
on earth as in heaven.
Give us today our daily bread.
Forgive us our sins
as we forgive those who sin against us.
Lead us not into temptation
but deliver us from evil.
For the kingdom, the power, and the glory are yours
now and for ever. Amen.

The president breaks the consecrated bread.
We break this bread
to share in the body of Christ.
Though we are many, we are one body,
because we all share in one bread.

The president invites the people to receive communion.
The gifts of God for the people of God.
Jesus Christ is holy,
Jesus Christ is Lord,
to the glory of God the Father.

Each communicant replies **Amen** to the words of distribution.

After communion

Generous God,
you have fed us at your heavenly table.
Kindle us with the fire of your Spirit
that when Christ comes again
we may shine like lights before his face;
who with you and the Spirit lives for ever. Amen.

or

Almighty God,
we thank you for feeding us
with the body and blood of your Son Jesus Christ.
Through him we offer you our souls and bodies
to be a living sacrifice.
Send us out in the power of your Spirit
to live and work
to your praise and glory. Amen.

A blessing may be said, and the service ends.

Go in peace to love and serve the Lord.
In the name of Christ. Amen.

Peace to His People on Earth
HOLY COMMUNION AT CHRISTMAS

Preparation

Singing, Scripture sentence, Greeting, Introduction or **Prayer,**
which may include:
We meet to celebrate the coming of Christ into the world.
The Word was made flesh and dwelt among us:
and we beheld his glory.

Confession

Christ the light of the world has come to dispel the darkness of our
hearts. In his light let us examine ourselves and confess our sins.

Silence is kept

Lord of grace and truth,
we confess our unworthiness
to stand in your presence as your children.
We have sinned:
forgive and heal us.

The Virgin Mary accepted your call
to be the mother of Jesus.
Forgive our disobedience to your will.
We have sinned:
forgive and heal us.

Your Son our Saviour
was born in poverty in a manger.
Forgive our greed and rejection of your ways.
We have sinned:
forgive and heal us.

The shepherds left their flocks
to go to Bethlehem.
Forgive our self-interest and lack of vision.
We have sinned:
forgive and heal us.

The wise men followed the star
to find Jesus the King.
Forgive our reluctance to seek you.

We have sinned:
forgive and heal us.

The president declares God's forgiveness.

We say or sing:

**Glory to God in the highest,
and peace to his people on earth.**

**Lord God, heavenly King,
almighty God and Father,
we worship you, we give you thanks,
we praise you for your glory.
Lord Jesus Christ, only Son of the Father,
Lord God, Lamb of God,
you take away the sin of the world:
have mercy on us;
you are seated at the right hand of the Father:
receive our prayer.**

**For you alone are the Holy One,
you alone are the Lord,
you alone are the Most High,
Jesus Christ,
with the Holy Spirit,
in the glory of God the Father. Amen.**

The president says the prayer of the day, the **Collect**.

The ministry of the Word

Either two or three **Readings**

After each reading:
This is the word of the Lord.
Thanks be to God.

Before the Gospel:
Glory to Christ our Saviour.

and at the end:
Praise to Christ our Lord.

There may be **Psalms** or **songs**

Sermon

Affirmation of Faith
We proclaim the Church's faith in Jesus Christ.

**We believe and declare that our Lord Jesus Christ,
the Son of God, is both divine and human.**

God, of the being of the Father,
the only Son from before time began;
human from the being of his mother, born in the world.

**Fully God and fully human;
human in both mind and body.**

As God he is equal to the Father,
as human he is less than the Father.

**Although he is both divine and human
he is not two beings but one Christ.**

One, not by turning God into flesh,
but by taking humanity into God.

**Truly one, not by mixing humanity with Godhead,
but by being one person.**

For as mind and body form one human being
so the one Christ is both divine and human.

**The Word became flesh and lived among us;
we have seen his glory,
the glory of the only Son from the Father,
full of grace and truth.**

Prayers

The intercessions may include the response:
Lord in your mercy:
hear our prayer.

and end:
God our Saviour:
**you know us and love us
and hear our prayer:
keep us in the eternal fellowship
of Jesus Christ our Saviour. Amen.**

We stand for the Peace.
Glory to God in the highest,
and peace on earth to all on whom his favour rests.
The peace of the Lord be always with you.
And also with you. Alleluia!

After the gifts have been prepared, the president says:

The Eucharistic Prayer

The Lord be with you.   or   The Lord is here.
And also with you.   **His Spirit is with us.**

Lift up your hearts.
We lift them to the Lord.

Let us give thanks to the Lord our God.
It is right to give him thanks and praise.

The president leads the Thanksgiving.

We join in the words:
Holy, holy, holy Lord,
God of power and might,
heaven and earth are full of your glory.
Hosanna in the highest.

This Anthem may also be used:
Blessed is he who comes in the name of the Lord.
Hosanna in the highest.

The words of Christ at the supper end:
. . . in remembrance of me.
Christ has died:
Christ is risen:
Christ will come again.

The Eucharistic Prayer ends with:
Amen.

or

Blessing and honour and glory and power
be yours for ever and ever. Amen.

Breaking bread and sharing in communion __

As our Saviour taught us, so we pray:
Our Father in heaven,
hallowed be your name,
your kingdom come,
your will be done,
on earth as in heaven.
Give us today our daily bread.
Forgive us our sins
as we forgive those who sin against us.
Lead us not into temptation
but deliver us from evil.
For the kingdom, the power, and the glory are yours
now and for ever. Amen.

The president breaks the consecrated bread.
We break this bread
to share in the body of Christ.
Though we are many, we are one body,
because we all share in one bread.

Before the distribution the president says:
Christ is the bread which has come down from heaven.
Lord, give us this bread for ever.

and invites the people to receive communion.
Each communicant replies **Amen** to the words of distribution.

After communion

Almighty God,
we thank you for feeding us
with the body and blood of your Son Jesus Christ.
Through him we offer you our souls and bodies
to be a living sacrifice.
Send us out in the power of your Spirit
to live and work
to your praise and glory. Amen.

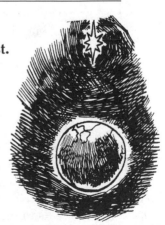

A blessing may be said, and the service ends.

Go in peace to love and serve the Lord.
In the name of Christ. Amen.

In Penitence and Faith
HOLY COMMUNION DURING LENT

Preparation

Singing, Greeting and **Prayer,** which may include:
The Lord our redeemer be with you.
The Lord bless you.

Jesus is the Lamb of God:
who takes away the sins of the world.

Almighty God,
to whom all hearts are open,
all desires known,
and from whom no secrets are hidden:
cleanse the thoughts of our hearts
by the inspiration of your Holy Spirit,
that we may perfectly love you,
and worthily magnify your holy name;
through Christ our Lord. Amen.

We call to mind our sin and God's promise of forgiveness.

Cast your burden upon the Lord:
and he will sustain you.
Create in us clean hearts, O God:
and renew a right spirit within us.
Cast us not away from your presence:
and take not your Holy Spirit from us.
Give us the joy of your saving help again:
and sustain us with your life-giving Spirit.

Lord God,
we have sinned against you;
we have done evil in your sight.
We are sorry and repent.
Have mercy on us according to your love.
Wash away our wrongdoing and cleanse us from our sin.
Renew a right spirit within us
and restore us to the joy of your salvation,
through Jesus Christ our Lord. Amen.

May almighty God have mercy on *us*,
forgive *us our* sins,
and bring *us* to everlasting life,
through Jesus Christ our Lord. **Amen.**

Kyrie eleison may be said.

Lord, have mercy.
Lord, have mercy.

Christ, have mercy.
Christ, have mercy.

Lord, have mercy.
Lord, have mercy.

The president says the prayer of the day, the **Collect**.

The ministry of the Word

Either two or three **Readings**

After each reading:
This is the word of the Lord.
Thanks be to God.

Before the Gospel:
Glory to Christ our Saviour.

and at the end:
Praise to Christ our Lord.

Psalms or **songs**

Sermon

Let us affirm our faith in Jesus Christ the Son of God:

**Though he was divine,
he did not cling to equality with God,
but made himself nothing.
Taking the form of a slave,
he was born in human likeness.
He humbled himself,
and was obedient to death –
even the death of the cross.**

Therefore God has raised him on high,
and given him the name above every name:
that at the name of Jesus
every knee should bow,
and every voice proclaim that Jesus Christ is Lord,
to the glory of God the Father. Amen.

Prayers

These may include the response:
Lord, in your mercy:
hear our prayer.

and end with:
Merciful Father,
accept these prayers
for the sake of your Son,
our Saviour Jesus Christ. Amen.

All may say:
We do not presume
to come to this your table, merciful Lord,
trusting in our own righteousness,
but in your manifold and great mercies.
We are not worthy
so much as to gather up the crumbs under your table.
But you are the same Lord
whose nature is always to have mercy.
Grant us therefore, gracious Lord,
so to eat the flesh of your dear Son Jesus Christ
and to drink his blood,
that we may evermore dwell in him
and he in us. Amen.

We stand for the Peace.
Being justified by faith,
we have peace with God through our Lord Jesus Christ.
The peace of the Lord be always with you.
And also with you.

After the gifts have been prepared, the president says:

The Eucharistic Prayer

The Lord be with you.   or   The Lord is here.
And also with you.   **His Spirit is with us.**

Lift up your hearts.
We lift them to the Lord.

Let us give thanks to the Lord our God.
It is right to give him thanks and praise.

The president leads the Thanksgiving, ending
. . . for ever praising you and saying,
Holy, holy, holy Lord,
God of power and might,
heaven and earth are full of your glory.
Hosanna in the highest.

This Anthem may also be used:
Blessed is he who comes in the name of the Lord.
Hosanna in the highest.

The words of Christ at the supper end:
. . . in remembrance of me.
Christ has died:
Christ is risen:
Christ will come again.

The Eucharistic Prayer ends with:
Amen.

or

Blessing and honour and glory and power
be yours for ever and ever. Amen.

Breaking bread and sharing in communion

Jesus taught us to call God our Father, so we have the courage to say:
Our Father in heaven,
hallowed be your name,
your kingdom come,
your will be done,
on earth as in heaven.
Give us today our daily bread.
Forgive us our sins
as we forgive those who sin against us.

Lead us not into temptation
but deliver us from evil.
For the kingdom, the power, and the glory are yours
now and for ever. Amen.

The president breaks the consecrated bread.
We break this bread
to share in the body of Christ.
**Though we are many, we are one body,
because we all share in one bread.**

Every time we eat this bread
and drink this cup:
**we proclaim the Lord's death
until he comes.**

The president invites the people to receive communion.
Each communicant replies **Amen** to the words of distribution.

After communion

**Merciful God,
you have called us to your table
and fed us with the bread of life.
Draw us and all people to your Son,
our Saviour Jesus Christ. Amen**

or

**Almighty God,
we thank you for feeding us
with the body and blood of your Son Jesus Christ.
Through him we offer you our souls and bodies
to be a living sacrifice.
Send us out in the power of your Spirit
to live and work
to your praise and glory. Amen.**

A blessing may be said, and the service ends.

Go in the peace of Christ.
Thanks be to God.

Alleluia! Christ is Risen
HOLY COMMUNION AT EASTER

Preparation

Singing, Greeting and **Prayer,** which may include:
Alleluia! Christ is risen.
He is risen indeed. Alleluia!

Jesus is the resurrection and the life. Alleluia!
Those who believe in him shall never die. Alleluia!

Almighty God,
to whom all hearts are open,
all desires known,
and from whom no secrets are hidden:
cleanse the thoughts of our hearts
by the inspiration of your Holy Spirit,
that we may perfectly love you,
and worthily magnify your holy name;
through Christ our Lord. Amen.

We confess our sins.

Almighty God, our heavenly Father,
we have sinned against you and against our neighbour,
in thought and word and deed,
through negligence, through weakness,
through our own deliberate fault.
We are truly sorry,
and repent of all our sins.
For the sake of your Son Jesus Christ, who died for us,
forgive us all that is past;
and grant that we may serve you in newness of life
to the glory of your name. Amen.

The president declares God's forgiveness.

This song may be said or sung:
Glory to God in the highest,
and peace to his people on earth.

Lord God, heavenly King,
almighty God and Father,
we worship you, we give you thanks,
we praise you for your glory.
Lord Jesus Christ, only Son of the Father,
Lord God, Lamb of God,
you take away the sin of the world:
have mercy on us;
you are seated at the right hand of the Father:
receive our prayer.

For you alone are the Holy One,
you alone are the Lord,
you alone are the Most High,
Jesus Christ,
with the Holy Spirit,
in the glory of God the Father. Amen.

The president says the prayer of the day, the **Collect**.

The ministry of the Word

Either two or three **Readings**

After each reading:
This is the word of the Lord.
Thanks be to God.

Before the Gospel:
Glory to Christ our Saviour.

and at the end:
Praise to Christ our Lord.

or

Alleluia! Christ is risen:
He is risen indeed. Alleluia!

Praise the God and Father of our Lord Jesus Christ:
he has given us new life and hope!
He has raised Jesus from the dead!
God has claimed us as his own:
he has brought us out of darkness!
He has made us lights to the world!
Alleluia! Christ is risen:
he is risen indeed. Alleluia!

Psalms or **songs**

Sermon

The Nicene Creed

We believe in one God,
the Father, the almighty,
maker of heaven and earth,
of all that is,
seen and unseen.

We believe in one Lord, Jesus Christ,
the only Son of God,
eternally begotten of the Father,
God from God, Light from Light,
true God from true God,
begotten, not made,
of one Being with the Father.
Through him all things were made.
For us men and for our salvation
he came down from heaven;
by the power of the Holy Spirit
he became incarnate of the Virgin Mary, and was made man.
For our sake he was crucified under Pontius Pilate;
he suffered death and was buried.
On the third day he rose again,
in accordance with the Scriptures;

he ascended into heaven
and is seated at the right hand of the Father.
He will come again in glory
to judge the living and the dead,
and his kingdom will have no end.

We believe in the Holy Spirit,
the Lord, the giver of life,
who proceeds from the Father and the Son.
With the Father and the Son he is worshipped and glorified.
He has spoken through the Prophets.

We believe in one holy catholic and apostolic Church.
We acknowledge one baptism for the forgiveness of sins.
We look for the resurrection of the dead,
and the life of the world to come. Amen.

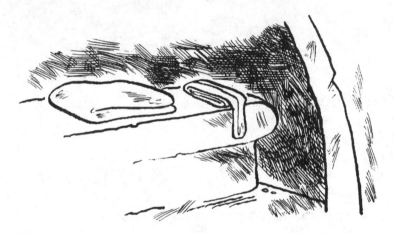

Prayers

These may include the response:
Lord, hear us.
Lord, graciously hear us.

or

Lord, in your mercy:
hear our prayer.

and end with:
Merciful Father,
**accept these prayers
for the sake of your Son,
our Saviour Jesus Christ. Amen.**

All may say:
We do not presume
to come to this your table, merciful Lord,
trusting in our own righteousness,
but in your manifold and great mercies.
We are not worthy
so much as to gather up the crumbs under your table.
But you are the same Lord
whose nature is always to have mercy.
Grant us therefore, gracious Lord,
so to eat the flesh of your dear Son Jesus Christ
and to drink his blood,
that we may evermore dwell in him
and he in us. Amen.

We stand for the Peace.

The introductory words end:
Alleluia! The peace of the risen Christ be always with you.
And also with you. Alleluia!

After the gifts have been prepared, the president says:

The Eucharistic Prayer

The Lord be with you.   or   The Lord is here.
And also with you.   **His Spirit is with us.**

Lift up your hearts.
We lift them to the Lord.

Let us give thanks to the Lord our God.
It is right to give him thanks and praise.

The president leads the Thanksgiving for the work of Christ, ending:
. . . for ever praising you and saying,
Holy, holy, holy Lord,
God of power and might,
heaven and earth are full of your glory.
Hosanna in the highest.

This Anthem may also be used:
Blessed is he who comes in the name of the Lord.
Hosanna in the highest.

The words of Christ at the supper end:
. . . in remembrance of me.
Christ has died:
Christ is risen:
Christ will come again.

The Eucharistic Prayer ends with:
Amen.

or

Blessing and honour and glory and power
be yours for ever and ever. Amen.

Breaking bread and sharing in communion __

As our Saviour taught us, so we pray:
Our Father in heaven,
hallowed be your name,
your kingdom come,
your will be done,
on earth as in heaven.
Give us today our daily bread.
Forgive us our sins
as we forgive those who sin against us.
Lead us not into temptation
but deliver us from evil.
For the kingdom, the power, and the glory are yours
now and for ever. Amen.

The president breaks the consecrated bread.
We break this bread
to share in the body of Christ.
Though we are many, we are one body,
because we all share in one bread.

The president invites the people to receive communion, ending with
these words:
Alleluia! Christ our passover is sacrificed for us.
Let us keep the feast. Alleluia!

Each communicant replies **Amen** to the words of distribution.

After communion

God of truth,
we have seen with our eyes
and touched with our hands
the bread of life.
Strengthen our faith
that we may grow in love for you
and for each other;
through Jesus Christ our risen Lord. Amen.

Alleluia! Christ is risen.
He is risen indeed. Alleluia!

A blessing may be said, and the service ends.

Go in peace to love and serve the Lord. Alleluia! Alleluia!
In the name of Christ. Alleluia! Alleluia!

The Day the Spirit Came
HOLY COMMUNION AT PENTECOST

Preparation

Singing, Greeting and **Prayer,** which may include:
This is the day which the Lord has made.
Let us rejoice and be glad in it.

God has given us his Spirit.
He has poured out his love.

Almighty God,
to whom all hearts are open,
all desires known,
and from whom no secrets are hidden:
cleanse the thoughts of our hearts
by the inspiration of your Holy Spirit,
that we may perfectly love you,
and worthily magnify your holy name;
through Christ our Lord. Amen.

We confess our sins.

You raise the dead to life in the Spirit:
Lord, have mercy.
Lord, have mercy.

You bring pardon and peace to the broken in heart:
Christ, have mercy:
Christ, have mercy.

You make one by your Spirit the torn and divided:
Lord, have mercy.
Lord, have mercy.

The president declares God's forgiveness.

This song may be said or sung:
Glory to God in the highest,
and peace to his people on earth.

Lord God, heavenly King,
almighty God and Father,
we worship you, we give you thanks,
we praise you for your glory
Lord Jesus Christ, only Son of the Father,
Lord God, Lamb of God,
you take away the sin of the world:
have mercy on us;
you are seated at the right hand of the Father:
receive our prayer.

For you alone are the Holy One,
you alone are the Lord,
you alone are the Most High,
Jesus Christ,
with the Holy Spirit,
in the glory of God the Father. Amen.

The president says the prayer of the day, the **Collect**.

The ministry of the Word

Either two or three **Readings**

After each reading:
This is the word of the Lord.
Thanks be to God.

Before the Gospel:
Glory to Christ our Saviour.

and at the end:
Praise to Christ our Lord.

Psalms or **songs**

Sermon

The Nicene Creed
We believe in one God,
the Father, the almighty:
**maker of heaven and earth,
of all that is, seen and unseen.**

We believe in one Lord, Jesus Christ,
the only Son of God,
eternally begotten of the Father:
God from God, Light from Light,
true God from true God,
begotten, not made,
of one Being with the Father:
through him all things were made.
For us men and for our salvation
he came down from heaven;
by the power of the Holy Spirit
he became incarnate of the Virgin Mary,
and was made man.
For our sake he was crucified under Pontius Pilate;
he suffered death and was buried.
On the third day he rose again
in accordance with the Scriptures:
he ascended into heaven
and is seated at the right hand of the Father.
He will come again in glory
to judge the living and the dead,
and his kingdom will have no end.

We believe in the Holy Spirit:
the Lord, the giver of life,
who proceeds from the Father and the Son:
with the Father and the Son he is worshipped and glorified.
He has spoken through the Prophets.

We believe in one holy, catholic and apostolic Church.
We acknowledge one baptism for the forgiveness of sins:
we look for the resurrection of the dead,
and the life of the world to come. Amen.

Prayers

These may include the response:
Lord, in your mercy:
hear our prayer.

and end with:
Lord of the church:
hear our prayer,
and make us one in heart and mind
to serve you with joy for ever. Amen.

All may say:
**We do not presume
to come to this your table, merciful Lord,
trusting in our own righteousness,
but in your manifold and great mercies.
We are not worthy
so much as to gather up the crumbs under your table.
But you are the same Lord
whose nature is always to have mercy.
Grant us therefore, gracious Lord,
so to eat the flesh of your dear Son Jesus Christ
and to drink his blood,
that we may evermore dwell in him
and he in us. Amen.**

We stand for the Peace.

The fruit of the Spirit is love, joy, peace.
If we live in the Spirit, let us walk in the Spirit.
The peace of the Lord be always with you.
And also with you. Alleluia!

After the gifts have been prepared, the president says:

The Eucharistic Prayer _____

The Lord be with you.   or   The Lord is here.
And also with you.   **His Spirit is with us.**

Lift up your hearts.
We lift them to the Lord.

Let us give thanks to the Lord our God.
It is right to give him thanks and praise.

The president leads the Thanksgiving, ending:
. . . for ever praising you and saying,
**Holy, holy, holy Lord,
God of power and might,
heaven and earth are full of your glory.
Hosanna in the highest.**

This Anthem may also be used:
**Blessed is he who comes in the name of the Lord.
Hosanna in the highest.**

The words of Christ at the supper end:
. . . in remembrance of me.
Christ has died:
Christ is risen:
Christ will come again.

The Eucharistic Prayer ends with:
Amen.

or

Blessing and honour and glory and power
be yours for ever and ever. Amen.

Breaking bread and sharing in communion

As our Saviour taught us, so we pray:
Our Father in heaven,
hallowed be your name,
your kingdom come,
your will be done,
on earth as in heaven.
Give us today our daily bread.
Forgive us our sins
as we forgive those who sin against us.
Lead us not into temptation
but deliver us from evil.
For the kingdom, the power, and the glory are yours
now and for ever. Amen.

The president breaks the consecrated bread.
We break this bread
to share in the body of Christ.
Though we are many, we are one body,
because we all share in one bread.

The president invites the people to receive communion.
Each communicant replies **Amen** to the words of distribution.

After communion

God of power,
may the boldness of your Spirit transform us,
may the gentleness of your Spirit lead us,

may the gifts of your Spirit
equip us to serve and worship you
now and always. Amen.

or

Almighty God,
we thank you for feeding us
with the body and blood of your Son Jesus Christ.
Through him we offer you our souls and bodies
to be a living sacrifice.
Send us out in the power of your Spirit
to live and work
to your praise and glory. Amen.

A blessing may be said, and the service ends.

Jesus said, 'Receive the Spirit:
as the Father sent me, so I send you.'

Go in peace to love and serve the Lord. Alleluia! Alleluia!
In the name of Christ. Alleluia! Alleluia!

All Creation Worships
HOLY COMMUNION

Preparation

The minister welcomes the people with a greeting which may
include:
The Lord of all creation be with you.
And also with you.

Great is the Lord and worthy of all praise:
Amen! Praise and glory and wisdom,
thanksgiving and honour, power and might,
be to our God for ever and ever! Amen. (Alleluia!)

Almighty God,
to whom all hearts are open,
all desires known,
and from whom no secrets are hidden:
cleanse the thoughts of our hearts
by the inspiration of your Holy Spirit,
that we may perfectly love you,
and worthily magnify your holy name;
through Christ our Lord. Amen.

We confess our sins, and the sins of our society,
in the misuse of God's creation:

After each section
Hear our prayer, and in your mercy:
forgive us and help us.

The president declares God's forgiveness.

Glory to God in the highest,
and peace to his people on earth.

Lord God, heavenly King,
almighty God and Father,
we worship you, we give you thanks,
we praise you for your glory.

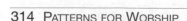

Lord Jesus Christ, only Son of the Father,
Lord God, Lamb of God,
you take away the sin of the world:
have mercy on us;
you are seated at the right hand of the Father:
receive our prayer.

For you alone are the Holy One,
you alone are the Lord,
you alone are the Most High,
Jesus Christ,
with the Holy Spirit,
in the glory of God the Father. Amen.

The ministry of the Word

Either two or three **Readings**

After each reading:
This is the word of the Lord.
Thanks be to God.

Before the Gospel:
Glory to Christ our Saviour.

and at the end:
Praise to Christ our Lord.

Psalms or **songs**

Sermon

Creed

Do you believe and trust in God the Father,
who made all things?
**I believe in God, the Father almighty,
creator of heaven and earth.**

Do you believe and trust in his Son Jesus Christ,
who redeemed the world?
**I believe in Jesus Christ, his only Son, our Lord.
He was conceived by the power of the Holy Spirit
and born of the Virgin Mary.
He suffered under Pontius Pilate,
was crucified, died and was buried.**

He descended to the dead.
On the third day he rose again.
He ascended into heaven,
and is seated at the right hand of the Father.
He will come again to judge the living and the dead.

Do you believe and trust in the Holy Spirit,
who gives life to the people of God?
I believe in the Holy Spirit,
the holy catholic Church,
the communion of saints,
the forgiveness of sins,
the resurrection of the body,
and the life everlasting.

This is the faith of the Church.
This is our faith.
We believe in one God,
Father, Son and Holy Spirit.

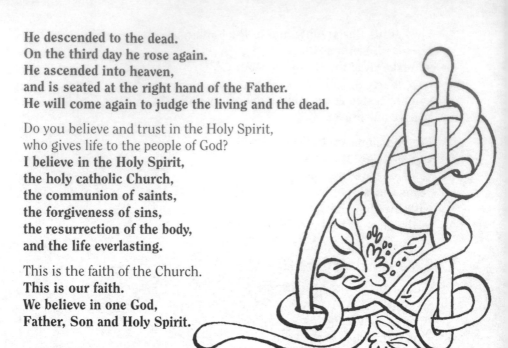

Prayers

These may include the response:
Lord, in your mercy:
hear our prayer.

and end with:
Lord of creation, God our Saviour:
you know us and love us
and hear our prayer:
keep us in the eternal fellowship
of Jesus Christ our Saviour. Amen.

The president says the prayer of the day, the **Collect**.

The service may conclude with the **Lord's Prayer** and the **Peace**,
or continue with the **Peace** and the **Eucharist**.

We stand for the Peace.
Peacemakers who sow in peace raise a harvest of righteousness.
The peace of the Lord be always with you.

And also with you.
After the gifts have been prepared, the president says:

The Eucharistic Prayer

The Lord be with you.   or   The Lord is here.
And also with you.   **His Spirit is with us.**

Lift up your hearts.
We lift them to the Lord.

Let us give thanks to the Lord our God.
It is right to give him thanks and praise.

The president leads the Thanksgiving, ending:
. . . for ever praising you and saying,
Holy, holy, holy Lord,
God of power and might,
heaven and earth are full of your glory.
Hosanna in the highest.

This Anthem may also be used:
Blessed is he who comes in the name of the Lord.
Hosanna in the highest.

The words of Christ at the supper end:
. . . in remembrance of me.
Christ has died:
Christ is risen:
Christ will come again.

The Eucharistic Prayer ends with:
Amen.

or

Blessing and honour and glory and power
be yours for ever and ever. Amen.

Breaking bread and sharing in communion

As our Saviour taught us, so we pray:
Our Father in heaven,
hallowed be your name,
your kingdom come,
your will be done,
on earth as in heaven.
Give us today our daily bread.
Forgive us our sins
as we forgive those who sin against us.

Lead us not into temptation
but deliver us from evil.
For the kingdom, the power, and the glory are yours
now and for ever. Amen.

The president breaks the consecrated bread.
We break this bread
to share in the body of Christ.
Though we are many, we are one body,
because we all share in one bread.

God our Creator,
as many grains are gathered into one bread:
gather your Church from the ends of the earth
into the life of your kingdom.

The president invites the people to receive communion.
Each communicant replies **Amen** to the words of distribution.

After communion

Creator God,
you give seed for us to sow,
and bread for us to eat;
make us thankful for what we have received;
make us able to do those generous things
which supply your people's needs;
so all the world may give you thanks and glory. **Amen.**

Almighty God,
we thank you for feeding us
with the body and blood of your Son Jesus Christ.
Through him we offer you our souls and bodies
to be a living sacrifice.
Send us out in the power of your Spirit
to live and work
to your praise and glory. Amen.

A blessing may be said, and the service ends.

Go in the peace of Christ.
Thanks be to God.

A service from *Patterns for Worship*. Text copyright © The Central Board of Finance of the
Church of England 1989, 1995. Illustrated by Taffy © The Central Board of Finance 1995.
Reproduced with permission for use in

Believe and Trust
CELEBRATING BAPTISM AT HOLY COMMUNION

The preparation

Singing, Scripture sentence, Greeting, Introduction or **Prayer,**
which may include:
The grace of our Lord Jesus Christ, the love of God,
and the fellowship of the Holy Spirit be with you all.
And also with you.

There is one body and one Spirit:
one Lord, one faith, one baptism.

We confess our sins.

God our Father,
long-suffering, full of grace and truth.
You create us from nothing and give us life.
You redeem us and make us your children in the water of baptism.
You do not turn your face from us,
nor cast us aside.
We confess that we have sinned
against you and our neighbour.
We have wounded your love and marred your image in us.
Restore us for the sake of your Son,
and bring us to heavenly joy,
in Jesus Christ our Lord. Amen.

The president declares God's forgiveness.

The president says the prayer of the day, the **Collect**.

The ministry of the Word

Either two or three **Readings**

After each reading:
This is the word of the Lord.
Thanks be to God.

Before the Gospel:
Glory to Christ our Saviour.

and at the end:
Praise to Christ our Lord.

Psalms or **songs**

Sermon

If children are to be baptized, the minister reads the duties of
parents and godparents, who answer:
I am willing.

We thank God for our baptism to life in Christ, and we pray for *these
children (names)* and say together:

Heavenly Father, in your love
you have called us to know you,
led us to trust you,
and bound our life with yours.
Surround *these children* with your love;
protect *them* from evil;
fill *them* with your Holy Spirit;
and receive *them* into the family of your church;
that *they* may walk with us in the way of Christ
and grow in the knowledge of your love.   Amen.

The decision

The minister asks:
Do you turn to Christ?
I turn to Christ.

Do you repent of your sins?
I repent of my sins.

Do you renounce evil?
I renounce evil.

After the minister has made the sign of the cross on the forehead of
those to be baptized:
Do not be ashamed to confess the faith of Christ crucified.
Fight valiantly under the banner of Christ
against sin, the world, and the devil,

**and continue his faithful *soldiers* and *servants*
to the end of your *lives*.**

The baptism

Praise God who made heaven and earth:
who keeps his promise for ever.

After the prayer over the water of baptism the minister addresses
the parents and godparents.

Do you believe and trust in God the Father,
who made all things?
I believe and trust in him.

Do you believe and trust in his Son Jesus Christ,
who redeemed the world?
I believe and trust in him.

Do you believe and trust in his Holy Spirit,
who gives life to the people of God?
I believe and trust in him.

This is the faith of the Church.
This is our faith.
We believe and trust in one God,
Father, Son, and Holy Spirit.

The minister baptizes each one:
N, I baptize you in the name of the Father,
and of the Son, and of the Holy Spirit. **Amen.**

A lighted candle may be presented for each person.
Receive this light.
This is to show that you have passed
from darkness to light.
Shine as a light in the world
to the glory of God the Father.

We stand for the Welcome and the Peace.

The president says:
God has received you by baptism into his Church.
We welcome you into the Lord's family.
We are members together of the body of Christ;
we are children of the same heavenly Father;
we are inheritors together of the kingdom of God.
We welcome you.

The peace of the Lord be always with you.
And also with you.

After the gifts have been prepared, the president says:

The Eucharistic Prayer

The Lord be with you.   or   The Lord is here.
And also with you.   **His Spirit is with us**

Lift up your hearts.
We lift them to the Lord.

Let us give thanks to the Lord our God.
It is right to give him thanks and praise.

The president leads the Thanksgiving, ending
. . . for ever praising you and saying,
Holy, holy, holy Lord,
God of power and might,
heaven and earth are full of your glory.
Hosanna in the highest.

This Anthem may also be used:
Blessed is he who comes in the name of the Lord.
Hosanna in the highest.

The words of Christ at the supper end:
. . in remembrance of me.
Christ has died:
Christ is risen:
Christ will come again.

The Eucharistic Prayer ends with:
Amen.

or

Blessing and honour and glory and power
be yours for ever and ever. Amen.

Breaking bread and sharing in communion

Jesus taught us to call God our Father, so we have the courage to say:
Our Father in heaven,
hallowed be your name,
your kingdom come,
your will be done,
on earth as in heaven.
Give us today our daily bread.
Forgive us our sins
as we forgive those who sin against us.
Lead us not into temptation
but deliver us from evil.
For the kingdom, the power, and the glory are yours
now and for ever. Amen.

The president breaks the consecrated bread.
We break this bread
to share in the body of Christ.
Though we are many, we are one body,
because we all share in one bread.

The president invites the people to receive communion.
Each communicant replies **Amen** to the words of distribution.

After communion

Father, in baptism we die to sin,
rise again to new life
and find our true place in your living body.
Send us out sealed in Christ's blood of the new covenant,
to bring healing and reconciliation to this wounded world.
through Jesus Christ our Lord. Amen.

or

God of our pilgrimage,
you have led us to the living water.
Refresh and sustain us
as we go forward on our journey,
in the name of Jesus Christ our Lord. Amen.

The Lord God almighty is our Father:
he loves us and tenderly cares for us.
The Lord Jesus Christ is our Saviour:
he has redeemed us and will defend us to the end.
The Lord, the Holy Spirit, is among us:
he will lead us in God's holy way.
To God almighty, Father, Son and Holy Spirit,
be praise and glory today and for ever. Amen.

Go in the peace of Christ:
Thanks be to God.

A Service of Healing

We say together the lines in **bold type**.

The preparation

The minister welcomes the people with a greeting.

The Lord be with you.
And also with you.

Prayers of penitence

The minister introduces the confession in suitable words.

Kyrie eleison may be said, with these or other suitable sentences
before each petition:
Friend of sinners, you bring hope in our despair.
Lord, have mercy.
Lord, have mercy.

Healer of the sick, you give strength in our weakness.
Christ, have mercy.
Christ, have mercy.

Destroyer of evil, you bring life in our dying.
Lord, have mercy.
Lord, have mercy.

The minister declares God's forgiveness.

The ministry of the Word

Readings (or a Reading) from Holy Scripture

After each reading:
This is the word of the Lord.
Thanks be to God.

A Psalm, or **Scriptural song**

Sermon

This **Affirmation of Faith**, or an authorized **Creed**

Let us declare our faith in God:

We believe in God the Father,
from whom every family
in heaven and on earth is named.

We believe in God the Son,
who lives in our hearts through faith,
and fills us with his love.

We believe in God the Holy Spirit,
who strengthens us
with power from on high.

We believe in one God;
Father, Son and Holy Spirit. Amen.

Prayer for healing

The time of prayer for individuals may include one or more of these prayers:

Be with us, Holy Spirit;
nothing can separate us from your love.

Breathe on us, breath of God;
fill us with your saving power.

Speak in us, Spirit of God;
bring strength, healing and peace.

The Lord is here.
God's Spirit is with us.

In the name of God most high
we lay our hands upon you.
Receive Christ's healing touch to make you whole
in body, mind and spirit.
The power of God strengthen you,
the love of God dwell in you
and give you peace. **Amen.**

At the end of the time of prayer brief biddings may introduce prayer for the world and the Church. The prayers may end with:

Merciful Father,
accept these prayers
for the sake of your Son,
our Saviour Jesus Christ. Amen.

Our Father in heaven,
hallowed be your name,
your kingdom come,
your will be done,
on earth as in heaven.
Give us today our daily bread.
Forgive us our sins
as we forgive those who sin against us.
Lead us not into temptation
but deliver us from evil.
For the kingdom, the power, and the glory are yours
now and for ever. Amen.

The **Collect** and this or another suitable prayer:

Bless the Lord, O my soul;
forget not all his benefits.
God forgives all our iniquities
and heals all our diseases.
God redeems our lives from the pit
and crowns us with steadfast love and mercy.

The conclusion

The service ends with the **Peace**.

Peace to you from God our Father who hears our cry.
Peace from his Son Jesus Christ whose death brings healing.
Peace from the Holy Spirit who gives us life and strength.

The peace of the Lord be always with you.
And also with you.

Genesis 1.26-28	10H15	Matthew 4.17	16B17
Genesis 2.24	14N25	Matthew 5.3-12	0Q25
Genesis 3.18	10B12	Matthew 5.9	0R23
Exodus 15.1,2,11,13,17	6Q10	Matthew 5.14	13K15
Numbers 6.24,25	9T25	Matthew 5.24	14B15
Deuteronomy 8.7,8	10H15	Matthew 9.37,38	10H15
Deuteronomy 32.3	0A18	Mark 10.45	2K3
1 Samuel 2.1-4,7,8	16Q20	Luke 1.78,79	1R1
1 Samuel 12.20	0R24	Luke 2.14	2R3
1 Chronicles 29.11	7T19	Luke 2.29	0R29
Job 38	10M9	Luke 13.29	0G12
Psalm 40	0M11	Luke 15	16C8
Psalm 46	0M12	Luke 19.41	13B14
Psalm 48.2	13T34	Luke 24.29	0L24
Psalm 51	4C2	John 1.1-14	2P2
Psalm 51	4T12	John 1.5	0L24
Psalm 51.15	0A18	John 1.14	2K2
Psalm 51.15; 70.1	0A13	John 1.29	4K6
Psalm 51.17	4B4	John 1.29	6L9
Psalm 66.4-8	6M7	John 1.29	2N4
Psalm 85.8	0R24	John 2.1-11	3T11
Psalm 102.1,2,12,13	4M4	John 4.35	10H15
Psalm 118.24	0A6	John 6.33	0G14
Psalm 119.105	11K12	John 6.35	6L9
Psalm 119	11H16	John 8.12	3K5
Psalm 130	1M1	John 8.12	0L24
Psalm 141.1,2	0A14	John 11.25	6K8
Psalm 145.3,4,10,11,12	15L20	John 11.25	6L9
Ecclesiastes 12.1-8	6M8	John 12.32	5N10
Isaiah 2.2-5	17Q22	John 14.27	0R22
Isaiah 6.5,7	9B11	John 15.1-10	10N21
Isaiah 9.6	2H3	John 15.12	17R18
Isaiah 9.6	2R4	John 16.8	8B9
Isaiah 9.2-7 adapted	2Q3	John 16.13	10H15
Isaiah 11.1-4,6	2Q4	John 17.11-18	0H29
Isaiah 12.2-6	16Q21	John 20.21,22	8K10
Isaiah 35.1-6,10	1Q1	John 20.21,22	8N16
Isaiah 40.9-11	12Q17	John 20.28,29	6L9
Isaiah 49.1,8-10,13	3Q6	John 21.15-17	6L9
Isaiah 53	5P6	Acts 2.1-4	8T20
Isaiah 53	4T12	Acts 3.15,13	12M10
Isaiah 53.3-6	5Q8	Acts 4.24	12M10
Isaiah 53.5	5L5	Acts 4.30,31	12M10
Isaiah 55.6-11	11Q16	Acts 17.25,26	16P20
Isaiah 60.1-3,11,14,18-19	3Q5	Acts 17.26	16T41
Isaiah 61.1-3	16H22	Romans 5.1-9	5P7
Isaiah 61.1-3,10,11	8Q13	Romans 5.1	5R6
Isaiah 61.10,11; 62.1-3	1Q2	Romans 5.1,2	8L16
Isaiah 64.8,9	10L18	Romans 5.6,8	5L6
Isaiah 66.10-14a,18b	17Q23	Romans 5.8	5B6
Ezekiel 47.1,9	8L15	Romans 6.4,8,9	5L7
Hosea 6	17C9	Romans 6.5	8K11
Hosea 6.1-6	4Q7	Romans 8.2,14-25	8P12
Malachi 4.2	3B3	Romans 8.6	8R9
Wisdom 10.15-19,20b,21	15Q19	Romans 8.15	8N15
Wisdom 16.20,21,26	10Q14	Romans 8.17,22	14N25
Ecclesiasticus 51.13-18a,20b-22	0Q28	Romans 8.22	10B12
Matthew 1.21	2B2	Romans 8.23-39	13P17
Matthew 1.21,23	2P1	Romans 9.21	10L18

Romans 12.1	0S4	1 Thessalonians 5.23	1R2
Romans 12.9,17,18	17R20	1 Thessalonians 5.23	1T3
Romans 14.17	0R25	2 Thessalonians 3.16	0T46
Romans 15.5,6	12T33	1 Timothy 1.2	0A3
Romans 15.13	8T23	1 Timothy 1.17	0T50
1 Corinthians 1.26-29	12M10	2 Timothy 2.11-13	6L10
1 Corinthians 4.4	3T9	Titus 2.11	8B10
1 Corinthians 5.7,8	6B7	Hebrews 1.3	7P11
1 Corinthians 5.7	5N9	Hebrews 1.3	4P5
1 Corinthians 7.17	0R26	Hebrews 3.12,15	13A11
1 Corinthians 12.4-6	8L12	Hebrews 4.12	11B13
1 Corinthians 12.4-13	0S4	Hebrews 4.14,16	7K9
1 Corinthians 12.13	12R12	Hebrews 4.15,16	7B8
1 Corinthians 15.3-7	6F7	Hebrews 4.15,16	4P5
1 Corinthians 15	6P9	Hebrews 9.12	4P5
1 Corinthians 15.23	10H15	Hebrews 10.19-22	4P5
2 Corinthians 4.4	3T9	Hebrews 11.10	13N23
2 Corinthians 4.6	3N6	Hebrews 12.1	15B16
2 Corinthians 4.8-10	5A9	Hebrews 12.22-24	0G11
2 Corinthians 5.14,20	12K14	Hebrews 12.22-24,28	6A10
2 Corinthians 5.15	5T13	Hebrews 13.12	13N24
2 Corinthians 5.18	16R17	Hebrews 13.12,15	13A11
2 Corinthians 12.9	12M10	Hebrews 13.14	13N23
2 Corinthians 13.11	0R27	James 1.17	13J37
Galatians 2.20	5T13	James 3.18	10R11
Galatians 3.28	12R13	1 Peter 1.3,4,18-21	6Q11
Galatians 5.22	10H15	1 Peter 1.3,4; 2.9,10	6P8
Galatians 5.22,23	8H12	1 Peter 2.9	0A7
Galatians 6.14	5K7	1 Peter 2.9	3K4
Ephesians 1.3-6	0L26	1 Peter 2.21-25	5Q9
Ephesians 1.3-7	0Q26	1 Peter 2.24	4B5
Ephesians 1.3-10	7Q12	1 Peter 5.14	17R19
Ephesians 1.9-13	16P20	1 John 1.5,7	0L25
Ephesians 1.17,18	15T37	1 John 4.7,8,16,18-21	17Q24
Ephesians 2.13	5R7	1 John 4.12	17L23
Ephesians 2.13-17	16P20	Jude 1,2	0T47
Ephesians 2.14	15T37	Jude 24,25	6J20
Ephesians 2.14,15	16R15	Revelation 1.14-18	7P11
Ephesians 3	0F9	Revelation 4.8,11	0F8
Ephesians 3.15-19	14T36	Revelation 4.11	9L17
Ephesians 3.20,21	12T32	Revelation 5.9	16T41
Ephesians 4.4,5	12K13	Revelation 5.9	0F8
Ephesians 4.4-13	8L13	Revelation 5.9	5L5
Philippians 2.8	5L5	Revelation 5.9,10,13	9L17
Philippians 2.8,9	7N14	Revelation 5.13	0A17
Philippians 2.9-11	2F6	Revelation 7.9	15A12
Philippians 2.9-11	2P1	Revelation 14.15	10H15
Philippians 4.4	0K16	Revelation 15.3	15L21
Colossians 1.12	15T37	Revelation 19.5	0A15
Colossians 1.13	3T9	Revelation 19.6	0A19
Colossians 1.15-18	10P15	Revelation 19.6,9	0A16
Colossians 1.15-18	10P16	Revelation 19.9	10H15
Colossians 1.15-20	7P11	Revelation 21.1-5a	13Q18
Colossians 1.27	1K1	Revelation 21.5	1N1
Colossians 3.14	17R21	Revelation 22.1-3	8L15
Colossians 3.15	0R28	Revelation 22.5	15L22
Colossians 3.16,17	0L27	Revelation 22.17	0F8
1 Thessalonians 5.13-22	13T35		

Reproduction for local use_____

The copyright owners and administrators of texts included in *Patterns for Worship* have consented to the use of their material in local reproductions on a non-commercial basis which must conform to the terms laid down in the CBF's booklet of guidance, *Liturgical Texts for Local Use*. This is available from the Copyright Administrator, Central Board of Finance (for address see page 236), or from Church House Bookshop, 31 Great Smith Street, London SW1P 3BN, price (1995) 50p, by post 75p. A reproduction which meets the conditions stated in the booklet can be made without application or fee.

The sample services on pages 243-327 may be photocopied for local use. In case of local reproduction please include below the copyright acknowledgement the words:

> Reproduced with permission for use in. . .
> [add name of parish, team or group ministry,
> cathedral or institution].

The illustrations by Taffy may be reproduced as part of the sample service which they illustrate, but not otherwise. Six of the sample services are also published as two-colour illustrated cards which may not be photocopied without written permission.

*Permission must be obtained in advance from the appropriate copyright owner or administrator for any reproduction not covered by **Liturgical Texts for Local Use**.*

The copyright owner or administrator of each text is identified in the right-hand column of the list of Sources which follows the Acknowledgements (see also Abbreviations, page 341). The Copyright Administrator of the CBF is able to help with addresses of the copyright owners or administrators of this material.

Acknowledgements _____

Thanks are due to the churches, societies, publishers and individuals whose texts have been made available for inclusion in *Patterns for Worship*, either in original or in adapted form. The relevant section numbers in *Patterns for Worship* are shown against each acknowledgement and the source of every item included in the Resource Sections is shown in the list of Sources which follows the Acknowledgements.
* indicates adapted
** indicates substantially adapted

It has not been possible to establish the original source of every text included, and the Central Board of Finance apologizes in advance to any whose copyright may have been overlooked.

Published sources include the following:

Anglican Church of Canada: *The Book of Alternative Services* (1985) 0A14, 6H7, 8H11, 0H23, 1J4, 2J7, 3J10, 4J11, 4J12, 4J13, 4J14, 4J15, 6J18, 8J22, 8J23, 12J32, 1L1, 2L2, 4L4, 5L5, 8L14, 10L19, 15L20, 1M1, 4M4, 6M7, 0M11, 0M12, 5P6, 5Q8, 10Q14, 12Q17, 13Q18, 15Q19, 0Q25

Anglican Church in Aotearoa, New Zealand and Polynesia: *A New Zealand Prayer Book - He Karakia Mihinare o Aotearoa (1989)* OA5, 0A17, 0A18, 0A19, 0H28, 2J8, 2J9, 5J16, 6J17, 8J24, 8J25, 10J27, 12J30, 12J33, 0J48, 2Q4, 3Q6, 6Q10, 8Q13, 16Q20, 17Q24, 12R12, 16R15, 16R16, 6T16, 15T39

Anglican Church of Australia: *An Australian Prayer Book* (1978) 7T17

Episcopal Church of the USA: *The Book of Common Prayer* according to the use of the Episcopal Church of the USA (1979) (The ECUSA Prayer Book is not subject to copyright.) 0F10, 0H26, 12J32

Scottish Episcopal Church: *Scottish Liturgy 1982* 6D5

Extracts from *The Book of Common Prayer* (1662), the rights in which are vested in the Crown in the United Kingdom, are reproduced by permission of the Crown's Patentee, Cambridge University Press. Adapted versions of certain passages have been made and reproduced by permission of the Crown's Patentee, Cambridge University Press. 0A13, 0B18, 0H27, 0J46

Augsburg Fortress Publishers: *Contemporary Worship 5: Services of the Word*, copyright ©1975 6L8

  Manual on the Liturgy: Lutheran Book of Worship 2P4

Cassell PLC: *In Penitence and Faith: Texts for Use with the Alternative Services*, compiled by David Silk (Mowbray) 1B1, 3B3, 4B5, 5B6, 6B7, 15B16, 16B17, 0C16, 10D7

  Prayers for Use at the Alternative Services, compiled by David Silk (1980, revised 1986) (Mowbray) 1J1, 1J6, 15J39, 10T27

  After the Third Collect, Eric Milner-White, © 1959 (Mowbray) 17J40

  After Communion, C L MacDonnell (Mowbray) 1J5, 7J21

G I A Publications Inc., Chicago, USA: *Praise God in Song*, © G I A Publications Inc. 6H7 (part), 10L19

Methodist Publishing House, Peterborough, UK: *The Methodist Service Book* (1973) 0J44

National Christian Education Council: *When You Pray with 7-10s*, by Richard Hughes 6M6

Oxford University Press, New York: *Praise in All Our Days*, © 1977 OUP New York 4M4

Saint Andrew Press: *Worship Now* Book 1 2P3

SPCK: *My God My Glory*, by Eric Milner-White, definitive edition 1967, as adapted for *In Penitence and Faith* 0C15

United Methodist Publishing House, Nashville, USA: *At the Lord's Table* (Supplemental Worship Resource 9), copyright © 1982 The United Methodist Publishing House 6P8

Westminster John Knox Press, Louisville, USA: *Daily Prayer: The Worship of God* (Supplemental Liturgical Resource 5) prepared by the Office of Worship for the Presbyterian Church (USA) and the Cumberland Presbyterian Church, © 1987 Westminster Press 12J34, 0J47, 0J50, 0J51, 9L18, 15L22

International Commission on English in the Liturgy: *The English Translation of the Roman Missal 1970*, © 1973 International Committee on English in the Liturgy Inc. (ICEL) 3N7, 5N11, 10N19, 16N28, 17N29, 0R22, 2T4, 8T20

International Consultation on English Texts: *Prayers We Have in Common*, © 1970, 1971, 1975 International Consultation on English Texts (ICET) 0F1, 1R1

Sources

Ref	Source	Page / Section No.	Whether Adapted	Copyright Owner or Administrator
A	**Introductions**			
6A1	PG	97		CBF
0A2	LC			Freely available
0A3	LC			Freely available
0A4	PG	283		Freely available
0A5	NZPB	404		ACANZP
0A6	RSV			NCCC
0A7	PG	155		Freely available
0A8	Source not identified			
5A9	Scripture version by LC			Freely available
6A10	GNB		*	BS
13A11	Scripture version by LC			CBF
15A12	Scripture version by LC			Freely available
0A13	BCP			Cambridge UP
0A14	BAS		*	ACCan
0A15	Scripture version by LC			Freely available
0A16	GNB			BS
0A17	NZPB	35		ACANZP
0A18	NZPB	69		ACANZP
0A19	NZPB	82	*	ACANZP
0A20	Based on a prayer in *For the Family* (Diocese of Chelmsford)			CBF
0A21	*For the Family:* Report of the Bishop's Working Party on non-statutory worship			Diocese of Chelmsford Council for Education and Training
B	**Invitations to Confession**			
1B1	© David Silk, IPF	No. 1	*	Mowbray
2B2	Scripture version by LC			Freely available
3B3	© David Silk, IPF	No. 2	*	Mowbray
4B4	Scripture version by LC			Freely available
4B5	© David Silk, IPF	No. 11	*	Mowbray
5B6	© David Silk, IPF	No. 4	*	Mowbray
6B7	© David Silk, IPF	No. 5		Mowbray
7B8	Scripture version by LC			CBF
7B9	Scripture version by LC			Freely available
8B10	Scripture version by LC			Freely available
9B11	LC			CBF
10B12	LC			CBF
11B13	Scripture version by LC			Freely available
13B14	Scripture, LC			Freely available
14B15	Scripture, LC			Freely available
15B16	© David Silk, IPF	No. 8	**	Mowbray
16B17	© David Silk, IPF	No. 13		Mowbray
0B18	BCP			Cambridge UP
C	**Confessions**			
2C1	© Kenneth Stevenson 1989			Kenneth Stevenson
4C2	© Stuart Thomas 1989			Stuart Thomas
5C3	CFW	No. 220	**	Jubilate
6C4	Michael Perry, CFW	No. 244	*	Jubilate
9C5	CFW	No. 330	*	Jubilate

Ref	Source	Page/Section No.	Whether Adapted	Copyright owner or Administrator
10C6	Michael Perry, CFW	No. 511	*	Jubilate
13C7	Michael Perry, CFW	No. 51	*	Jubilate
16C8	© Stuart Thomas 1989			Stuart Thomas
17C9	© Stuart Thomas 1989			Stuart Thomas
0C10	Michael Perry, CFW	No. 135	*	Jubilate
0C11	© Bryan D Spinks 1989			Bryan D Spinks
0C12	BCP modernised by LC			CBF
0C13	BCP modernised by LC			CBF
0C14	Concept from BAS	576		CBF
0C15	Eric Milner-White, *My God My Glory*, definitive edn 1967, as adapted for IPF			SPCK
0C16	© David Silk, IPF	No. 81		Mowbray
8C17	Portsmouth Cathedral, IPF	34		Portsmouth Cathedral
11C18	Portsmouth Cathedral, IPF	35		Portsmouth Cathedral
11C19	Source not identified			
13C20	© PCC Holy Trinity, Wealdstone			Holy Trinity, Wealdstone

D	**Absolutions**			
2D1	© Kenneth Stevenson 1989			Kenneth Stevenson
2D2	PG	185		CBF
5D3	CFW	No. 220	**	Jubilate
6D4	Scottish Liturgy 1982			Scottish Episcopal Church
9D5	LC			CBF
10D6	© David Silk, IPF	No. 31		Mowbray
13D7	LC			CBF
16D8	© Stuart Thomas 1989			Stuart Thomas
17D9	© Stuart Thomas 1989			Stuart Thomas
0D10	PB 1928 as adapted for PG			CBF
0D11	© Bryan D Spinks 1989			Bryan D Spinks
0D12	Common form			Freely available
0D13	PG	118		CBF

F	**Affirmations of Faith**			
0F1	Nicene Creed, ASB			ICET
0F2	Baptism Service, ASB	232	*	CBF
0F3	Apostles' Creed and Baptism Service, ASB			CBF
2F4	Athanasian Creed modernised by LC			CBF
0F5	Timothy Dudley-Smith, *A Voice of Singing* (1993)	40		Timothy Dudley-Smith
2F6	CFW	No. 212	*	Jubilate
6F7	CFW	No. 256		Jubilate
0F8	CFW	No. 591		Jubilate
0F9	CFW	No. 192		Jubilate
0F10	ECUSA Book of Common Prayer	304	*	Freely available

G	**Responses, Endings, Introductions to the Lord's Prayer**			
0G1-8	Common forms			Freely available
0G9	LC			Freely available

Ref	Source	Page/ Section No.	Whether Adapted	Copyright owner or Administrator
0G10	LC			Freely available
0G11-	*Intercessions in the Eucharist,*			Michael Vasey
14	Michael Vasey, Grove Booklet 77, 1982			
0G15-	LC			Freely available
20				

H	**Responsive Intercessions and Litanies**			
1H1	LC			CBF
2H2	CFW (based on a prayer by Simon Baynes)	No. 107	**	Freely available
2H3	LC			CBF
2H4	© Michael Perham, PG	178		Michael Perham
4H5	© Trevor Lloyd, ECY	1C2		Trevor Lloyd
5H6	© Trevor Lloyd, ECY	3C2		Trevor Lloyd
6H7	BAS	122		ACCan
	(two lines from *Praise God in Song,* GIA Publications Inc., Chicago, IL)	277		
6H8	LC			CBF
6H9	Portsmouth Cathedral			Portsmouth Cathedral
7H10	© Michael Perham, ECY	5C1	*	Michael Perham
8H11	BAS	133		ACCan
8H12	CFW	No. 324		Jubilate
8H13	© PCC Holy Trinity, Guildford			Holy Trinity, Guildford
9H14	Source not identified			
10H15	© PCC St George's, Oakdale, ECY	14C1	*	St George's, Oakdale
11H16	LC			CBF
12H17	LC			CBF
13H18	Origin uncertain			
14H19	LC			CBF
14H20	Origin uncertain			
15H21	PG	53		CBF
16H22	LC			CBF
0H23	BAS	118		ACCan
0H24	CFW	No. 150	*	Jubilate
0H25	Michael Perry, CFW	No. 126	**	Jubilate
0H26	ECUSA Book of Common Prayer		*	Freely available
0H27	BCP with PB 1928 adaptation			Cambridge UP
0H28	NZPB	50	*	ACANZP
0H29	Source not identified			

J	**Prayers after communion and Endings for a Service of the Word**			
1J1	© David Silk, PAS	No. 323		Mowbray
1J2	Westcott House			Westcott House
1J3	Westcott House			Westcott House
1J4	BAS	389		ACCan
1J5	C L MacDonnell, *After Communion*			Mowbray
1J6	© David Silk, PAS	No. 58		Mowbray
2J7	BAS	276		ACCan
2J8	NZPB	526	**	ACANZP
2J9	NZPB	527	**	ACANZP
3J10	BAS	350		ACCan
4J11	BAS	286		ACCan
4J12	BAS	295		ACCan
4J13	BAS	399		ACCan

Ref	Source	Page/Section No.	Whether Adapted	Copyright owner or Administrator
4J14	BAS	302		ACCan
4J15	BAS	290		ACCan
5J16	NZPB	535	**	ACANZP
6J17	NZPB	535	**	ACANZP
6J18	BAS	414		ACCan
6J19	LC			CBF
6J20	Scripture version by LC			Freely available
7J21	C L MacDonnell, *After Communion*			Mowbray
8J22	BAS	363		ACCan
8J23	BAS with ECY			ACCan
8J24	NZPB	537	**	ACANZP
8J25	NZPB	541	**	ACANZP
9J26	*All Desires Known,* © Janet Morley 1988			Janet Morley
10J27	NZPB	141	*	ACANZP
11J28	ASB 1980			CBF
11J29	Westcott House			Westcott House
12J30	NZPB	540		ACANZP
12J31	Westcott House			Westcott House
12J32	BAS, adapted from ECUSA Prayer Book	400		Freely available
12J33	NZPB	141	*	ACANZP
12J34	*Daily Prayer: The Worship of God,* © 1987 Westminster Press			Westminster John Knox Press
12J35	LC			CBF
12J36	LC			CBF
13J37	LC, based on Aus PB			CBF
14J38	LC			CBF
15J39	© David Silk, PAS	No. 331	*	Mowbray
17J40	*After the Third Collect* Eric Milner-White			Mowbray
0J41	Aus PB and BCP (part)		*	CBF
0J42	LC, based on prayer by Geoffrey Rowell			CBF
0J43	© Kenneth Stevenson 1989 Translated from Danish Lutheran Rite			Kenneth Stevenson
0J44	*The Methodist Service Book* (1973)			Methodist Publishing House
0J45	*All Desires Known,* © Janet Morley 1988			Janet Morley
0J46	BCP			Cambridge UP
0J47	*Daily Prayer: The Worship of God,* © 1987 Westminster Press			Westminster John Knox Press
0J48	NZPB	51	*	ACANZP
0J49	*The Daily Office,* © Joint Liturgical Group 1968	96	*	Joint Liturgical Group
0J50	*Daily Prayer: The Worship of God,* © 1987 Westminster Press		*	Westminster John Knox Press
0J51	*Daily Prayer: The Worship of God,* © 1987 Westminster Press		*	Westminster John Knox Press

K   Short Acclamations and Responses

Ref	Source	Page/Section No.	Whether Adapted	Copyright owner or Administrator
1K1-3K4	Scripture version by Colin Buchanan		*	1K1- 0K16 all freely available
3K5	LC, PG			
4K6	Scripture version by Colin Buchanan			
13K15	LC			
0K16	Scripture version by Colin Buchanan			

Ref	Source	Page/ Section No.	Whether Adapted	Copyright owner or Administrator
L	**Acclamations and Responses**			
1L1	BAS	96	*	ACCan
2L2	BAS	96	*	ACCan
3L3	LC (Adapted from PG p. 16 and *Patterns* Report)			CBF
4L4	BAS	97	*	ACCan
5L5	BAS	98		ACCan
5L6	LC			CBF
5L7	Joint Liturgical Group			Joint Liturgical Group
6L8	*Contemporary Worship 5, Services of the Word*, 1975, by permission of Augsburg Fortress			Augsburg Fortress, Minneapolis MN, USA
6L9	Scripture versions by Colin Buchanan			Freely available
6L10	Scripture version by LC			CBF
7L11	© Michael Perham, ECY	5D1		Michael Perham
8L12	Scripture version by LC			CBF
8L13	Scripture version by LC			CBF
8L14	BAS	98	*	ACCan
8L15	Scripture version by LC			CBF
8L16	Scripture version by LC			CBF
9L17	Scripture version by LC			CBF
10L18	*Daily Prayer: The Worship of God*, © 1987 Westminster Press	79	*	Westminster John Knox Press
10L19	*Praise God in Song*, GIA Publications Inc.			GIA Publications Inc., Chicago, IL, USA
15L20	BAS	99		ACCan
15L21	LC (cf PG p. 13 and *Patterns* Report)			CBF
15L22	*Daily Prayer: The Worship of God*, © 1987 Westminster Press	68	*	Westminster John Knox Press
17L23	Scripture version by LC			CBF
0L24	Scripture versions by LC			CBF
0L25	Scripture versions by LC			CBF
0L26	Scripture version by LC			CBF
0L27	Scripture version by LC			CBF
M	**Longer Acclamations and Responsive Scriptures**			
1M1	BAS	105		ACCan
2M2	PG	297		CBF
3M3	LC (Te Deum: ICET)			CBF
4M4	BAS	105		ACCan
5M5	CFW	No. 236	**	Jubilate
6M6	*When you pray with 7-10s*	No. 74	*	National Christian Education Council
6M7	BAS	108	*	ACCan
6M8	Scripture (Jerusalem Bible)			DLT
10M9	Scripture (Jerusalem Bible)			DLT
12M10	Scripture versions by LC			CBF
0M11	BAS	103		ACCan
0M12	BAS	103		ACCan
0M13	Michael Perry, CFW	No. 364	*	Jubilate
0M14	Emmanuel Church, Northwood, CFW	No. 478	*	Jubilate

Ref	Source	Page/Section No.	Whether Adapted	Copyright owner or Administrator
N	**Proper Prefaces**			
1N1-3N6	LC			CBF
3N7	Roman Missal 1970			ICEL
4N8-5N10	LC			CBF
5N11	Roman Missal 1970			ICEL
6N12-8N16	LC			CBF
8N17	ECY attributed there to PG	16H2		CBF
8N18	LC			CBF
10N19	Roman Missal 1970		*	ICEL
10N20-16N27	LC			CBF
16N28	Roman Missal 1970			ICEL
17N29	Roman Missal 1970			ICEL
0N30	LC			CBF
P	**Thanksgivings**			
2P1	© PCC Holy Trinity, Wealdstone			Holy Trinity, Wealdstone
2P2	LC			CBF
2P3	*Worship Now* Book 1			Saint Andrew Press
2P4	Manual on the Liturgy: Lutheran Book of Worship			Augsburg Fortress Minneapolis MN, USA
4P5	LC			CBF
5P6	BAS	107	*	ACCan
5P7	LC			CBF
6P8	*At the Lord's Table* (Supplementary Worship Resource 9) Copyright © 1982 The United Methodist Publishing House			United Methodist Publishing House, Nashville TN, USA
6P9-8P13	LC			CBF
9P14	© Michael Vasey 1990			Michael Vasey
10P15-0P21	LC			CBF
Q	**Scriptural Songs**			
1Q1	LC			CBF
1Q2	Daily Office SSF (1981)			SSF
2Q3	Daily Office SSF (1981)			SSF
2Q4	RSV via NZPB	97	*	NCCC
3Q5	Daily Office SSF (1981)			SSF
3Q6	NZPB	97	*	ACANZP
4Q7	Daily Office SSF (1981)			SSF
5Q8	BAS	77	*	ACCan
5Q9	RSV via Daily Office SSF (1981)		*	NCCC
6Q10	NZPB	100	*	ACANZP
6Q11	Daily Office SSF (1981)			SSF
7Q12	Daily Office SSF (1981)			SSF
8Q13	NZPB	58		ACANZP
10Q14	BAS	81	**	ACCan

Ref	Source	Page/ Section No.	Whether Adapted	Copyright owner or Administrator
10Q15	Daily Office SSF (1981)			SSF
11Q16	Daily Office SSF (1981)			SSF
12Q17	BAS	76	*	ACCan
13Q18	BAS	76	*	ACCan
15Q19	BAS	81	*	ACCan
16Q20	NZPB	82	*	ACANZP
16Q21	RSV via Daily Office SSF (1981)		*	NCCC
17Q22	RSV			NCCC
17Q23	NEB			Cambridge UP
17Q24	NZPB	78	*	ACANZP
0Q25	BAS	85		ACCan
0Q26	BAS No. 21 and NZPB p. 59 combined and further revised		**	CBF
0Q27	© Michael Vasey 1987			Michael Vasey
0Q28	Source not identified			

R	**Introductory Words to the Peace**			
1R1	Benedictus: ICET			ICET
1R2	Scripture version by LC			Freely available
2R3	Scripture version by LC			Freely available
2R4	Scripture version by LC			Freely available
3R5	PG	244		CBF
5R6	Scripture version by LC			Freely available
5R7	LHWE			CBF
8R8	Scripture version by LC			Freely available
8R9	Scripture version by LC			Freely available
9R10	LC			CBF
10R11	Scripture version by LC			Freely available
12R12	NZPB	419	*	ACANZP
12R13	Scripture version by LC			Freely available
14R14	LC			CBF
16R15	NZPB	466	**	ACANZP
16R16	NZPB	485	*	ACANZP
16R17	Scripture version by LC			Freely available
17R18	Scripture version by LC			Freely available
17R19	LC			CBF
17R20	Scripture version by LC			Freely available
17R21	Scripture version by LC			Freely available
0R22	Roman Missal 1970			ICEL
0R23	LC			CBF
0R24- 0R29	Scripture version by LC			Freely available

S	**Words for Dedication**			
0S1	LC			CBF
0S2	LC			CBF
0S3	LC			CBF
0S4	LC			CBF

T	**Blessings and Endings**			
1T1	LC			CBF
1T2	LC			CBF
1T3	Scripture version by LC			Freely available
2T4	Roman Missal 1970		**	ICEL
2T5	PG	183		CBF
2T6	PG	189		CBF
2T7	LC			CBF
2T8	LC			CBF

Ref	Source	Page/ Section No.	Whether Adapted	Copyright owner or Administrator
3T9	PG	227	*	CBF
3T10	LC			CBF
3T11	LC			CBF
4T12	© PCC St George's, Oakdale, ECY	1F1		St George's, Oakdale
5T13	LC			CBF
6T14	LC			CBF
6T15	© PCC St George's, Oakdale, ECY	4F1		St George's, Oakdale
6T16	NZPB	538	*	ACANZP
7T17	Australian Prayer Book 1978	152		GSACA
7T18	© Michael Perham, ECY	5F1		Michael Perham
7T19	Scripture version by LC			Freely available
8T20	Roman Missal 1970		**	ICEL
8T21	© PCC St George's, Oakdale, ECY	6F1	*	St George's, Oakdale
8T22	LC			CBF
8T23	Scripture version by LC			Freely available
8T24	© Michael Perham, ECY	17Q1		Michael Perham
9T25	LC			CBF
9T26	Thomas Ken 1637-1711		*	Freely available
10T27	© David Silk, PAS (Sarum Missal)	No. 210		Mowbray
10T28	© Trevor Lloyd, ECY	14Q1		Trevor Lloyd
10T29	© Michael Perham			Michael Perham
11T30	LC			CBF
11T31	LC			CBF
12T32	Scripture version by LC			CBF
12T33	Scripture version by LC			CBF
13T34	LC			CBF
13T35	PB 1928 (Confirmation)		*	CBF
14T36	Scripture version by LC			CBF
15T37	LC			CBF
15T38	PG	58	*	CBF
15T39	NZPB	544		ACANZP
15T40	LC			CBF
16T41	LC			CBF
16T42	LC			CBF
17T43	© Kenneth Stevenson 1995			Kenneth Stevenson
0T44	*Liturgy and Death,* Trevor Lloyd, Grove Booklet 28, 1974			Trevor Lloyd
0T45	LC			CBF
0T46	Scripture version by LC			Freely available
0T47	Scripture version by LC			Freely available
0T48	LC			CBF
0T49	Source not identified			
0T50	The Bible, Authorized Version			Cambridge UP

Abbreviations used in the list of sources _____

ACANZP	Anglican Church in Aotearoa, New Zealand and Polynesia
ACCan	Anglican Church of Canada
ASB	*Alternative Service Book 1980*
Aus PB	*Australian Prayer Book 1978*
BAS	*Book of Alternative Services* (Anglican Church of Canada)
BCP	*Book of Common Prayer*
BS	Bible Society
CBF	Central Board of Finance of the Church of England
CFW	*Church Family Worship*
ECUSA	Episcopal Church of the USA
DLT	Darton, Longman & Todd
ECY	*Enriching the Christian Year,* compiled by Michael Perham, SPCK/Alcuin Club 1993
GNB	*Good News Bible*
GSACA	General Synod of the Anglican Church of Australia
ICEL	International Commission on English in the Liturgy
ICET	International Consultation on English Texts
IPF	*In Penitence and Faith*
LC	Liturgical Commission
LHWE	*Lent, Holy Week, Easter*
MOW	Movement for the Ordination of Women
NCCC	National Council of the Churches of Christ in the USA
NEB	*New English Bible*
NZPB	*New Zealand Prayer Book 1989*
PAS	*Prayers at the Alternative Services*
PB 1928	*The Book of Common Prayer as Proposed in 1928*
PG	*The Promise of His Glory,* Church House Publishing/Mowbray 1991
RSV	*Revised Standard Version of the Bible*
SEC	Scottish Episcopal Church
SSF	Society of St Francis